LEADERSHIP

To Susan
thank you,

Ay Banbinh
11/21/14

LEADER SHIP

POWER
AND
CONSEQUENCES

SY OGULNICK

New York

LEADERSHIP
POWER AND CONSEQUENCES

© 2015 SY OGULNICK.

Published in New York, New York, by Morgan James Publishing. Morgan James and The Entrepreneurial Publisher are trademarks of Morgan James, LLC. www.MorganJamesPublishing.com

The Morgan James Speakers Group can bring authors to your live event. For more information or to book an event visit The Morgan James Speakers Group at www.TheMorganJamesSpeakersGroup.com.

A FREE eBook edition is available
with the purchase of this print book

CLEARLY PRINT YOUR NAME IN THE BOX ABOVE

Instructions to claim your free eBook edition:
1. Download the BitLit app for Android or iOS
2. Write your name in UPPER CASE in the box
3. Use the BitLit app to submit a photo
4. Download your eBook to any device

ISBN 978-1-63047-310-5 paperback
ISBN 978-1-63047-311-2 eBook
ISBN 978-1-63047-312-9 hardcover
Library of Congress Control Number:
2014942291

Cover Design by:
Chris Treccani
www.3dogdesign.net

Interior Design by:
Bonnie Bushman
bonnie@caboodlegraphics.com

In an effort to support local communities, raise awareness and funds, Morgan James Publishing donates a percentage of all book sales for the life of each book to Habitat for Humanity Peninsula and Greater Williamsburg.

Get involved today, visit
www.MorganJamesBuilds.com

Habitat
for Humanity
Peninsula and
Greater Williamsburg
Building Partner

DEDICATION

To my wife, Lenette, without whom I do not
exist, and if I do, only as half or less a person.

TABLE OF CONTENTS

FOREWORD

The following three brief stories are particularly important in that they shed light on a philosophy of leadership from its beginning in the late 1940s to today and continuing its progression. Each of these stories was written by a professional with whom I worked to turn an atmosphere of leadership problems into an environment of genuine dialogue, a feeling of community and a deep awareness of personal responsibility to one's self and the people with whom they live and work. The first is written based on experiences from 1950s and 1960s. The second is based on events that took place in the 1980s and 1990s. The third and final story occurred between 2000 and 2014.

EXPERIENCES FROM THE 1950s AND 1960s

I had the great fortune to have intertwined my early teen years with Sy Ogulnick's exploration into the nature of leadership. First as a twelve-year-old camper and later as a junior counselor, naturalist, counselor and finally as a director, I had the unique experience of not only experiencing the system, but seeing how it worked and finally imprinting a small amount of myself on the system.

What I came away with was a clear picture of essentially two interlocked systems. First was the public face of "summer camp." This was the image Sy presented in living rooms all over the Los Angeles area, and the experience the campers had during their stay at "camp." The camper experience was a sense of unbounded freedom. Everything was possible as long as it was done as a group (of course, there was private time as well). Even the living environment was under their control. Cabins could be decorated, modified, expanded and re-imagined as a Japanese temple. There was only one rule, and it often was unnecessary to even state that the rule existed: Everyone had a say in the daily life of the group. Even the oddest, most individual of desires had to be accommodated in some manner. Groups became small, independently functioning societies. The campers felt empowered, and they were. It was truly a magical experience for them. There was freedom to realize activities, ideas and events that were simply impossible to achieve in their regular home and school world.

The other system was the staff and infrastructure of the camp. We didn't know it at the time, but we were really producing a large piece of collective theatre. We created a stage—our eighty acres in the Northern California woods and provided the props (lumber, paint, balls, arrows, tools, pots, pans, etc.) and the usually invisible direction that kept the system running. It was the means of implementing "direction" that I believe really made the whole production possible. First, of course, the system was decentralized with the focus being on the camper; everything, even the staff, was there for the campers. The counselor was the nucleus, but not the focus of the camper group. Other functions, food service, wranglers, art specialists, water ski instructors were there for the campers as well. Thus, every single decision was made with the camper experience in mind. Even something as mundane as a decision to install path lighting was discussed in terms of the need for safety vs. the need to experience the world in as natural a state as possible.

The counselor, the leader of the small group, is where it all came together. It was the counselor's job to create the magic the campers were to experience. There was not *one* way to make this happen. Instead, there were infinite ways to achieve this goal. At times, for example when there was real physical danger, the counselor became the authority and took on an almost dictatorial role. But most other times the counselor was just another member of the group, but ever aware of his or her responsibilities to the campers. Counselors promoted growth and adventure ideas and created space for the least popular of ideas that came from individual campers.

It was leadership, but yet it did not conform to any of the classic ideas of leadership. It was fluid, dynamic and responsive to the physical and personal situation either in anticipation or during an event. Thus, as the campers passed through the theater we called camp, they were totally unaware of what made this all work; they never saw behind the scenes.

For those who decided to continue on and become junior counselors and move into staff positions, the system slowly opened itself to their view. It was not a hidden system; in fact, considerable time was spent in discussion on how it worked. We shared our ongoing experiences, sought deeper understanding and innovation and creativity in a way that would allow others to recreate the magic in their own groups. In other words, camp was not ruled by a hierarchy but through face-to-face dialogue and ultimately what was best for the camper.

Of course, like Puff, "A dragon lives forever but not so little boys and girls." Campers move on, grow up and enter the adult world. That is the beauty of what I have described above that Sy has nurtured and brought to organizations throughout our country and is found in this powerful and thought-provoking book. It is this ability to create magic that is not limited to children. Magic can be created on a factory floor, in a sales room, an office, a farm field, a classroom full of students and our own homes; but it all depends on leadership and the appropriate and magical use of power.

Understanding and experiencing what trust, safety and respect do for people who come to exercise their own potentials is not only rewarding for the leader and those they are responsible to but also for their relationships, whether personal or business-related. I learned early on how doable this all is, and also how rare it has been to rediscover once again in our living and work relationships.

—**Rick Perlman**

EVENTS THAT TOOK PLACE IN THE 1980s AND 1990s

It was as close to utopia as I could ever imagine. We called it the "Safe Environment." It was the pediatric dental office I owned and operated as a solo practitioner for nearly a quarter of a century.

Imagine an office where everybody looked forward to spending the day. There were no "elephants in the room." The workplace was the healthy, functional environment each of us wished we had experienced growing up and one which most of us wanted in our own homes. It was a remarkably stress-free environment.

This was no accident, but rather the end result of hours upon hours of team-building workshops. The initial focus of these seminars was communication and personal growth beginning with me as the leader. Learning to be vulnerable with the people I worked with was not easy to do. My growing up under a traditional hierarchy as a child, attending The Virginia Military Institute for my college experience and then four years as a military officer did not make it any easier. But, in time, all of us in the office began to experience a sense of family with the end result being that we knew we were "there" for each other. This feeling spread to the children who we cared for and was felt and appreciated by their parents. Needless to say, our practice grew.

Our office was one of the many organizations that Sy Ogulnick worked with throughout the country. As the teacher of his philosophy of leadership and interpersonal relationships he also served as our facilitator and mentor. Over the years of working together he nurtured each of us on our individual and collective journeys to grow as selves and as partners. We became better listeners, confirmed each other, and as a result experienced genuine dialogue among us.

When I started my private practice and hired my first employee, life was simple. As my practice grew, so did my staff. I soon discovered that "two's company, but three's a crowd." Tensions arose in the office when the twosome became a triangle. Petty, non-verbal arguments ensued as the two employees vied for the doctor's attention. The stage was set for the classic "front/back" divisions that are inherent in most professional offices between the clinical staff and the business staff. I knew, at that point, that I needed help. I learned about Sy from a colleague who had heard him speak at a national dental seminar. He came into our office with an extensive background in interpersonal communication.

Sy established the ground rules early on. He made it clear that every single member of the team has something valuable to offer. There are no stupid questions. If something he, I, or others say is not understood, interruptions are invited—even necessary. If a message is not understood it is the speaker's failure to communicate the point. It is not the responsibility of the listener to understand or accept what is being said, but it is the listener's responsibility to verbalize any lack of understanding. Input from anyone and everyone is encouraged at staff meetings. Nobody, especially those in positions of authority, is allowed to put down any member of the team. With this frame work in place, it did not take long for the level of dialogue between all of us to rise to levels most of us had never experienced. Problems were exposed, openly discussed, resolved, and we in the office flourished as did the practice.

We did considerably more than just talk. All members of the team were taught how to express their feelings in ways that facilitated our getting to know and understand each other. Sharing feelings did not come easily. Many of the staff had learned from painful experience that it is often wiser to stay silent or lie. It does not take long to learn how to protect one's self. In our office, slowly, but with assurance of safety, the team began to open up to me as the ultimate authority and then to others. People listened to each other, began to understand the other's view point and affirmed them with responses like, "I understand how you feel, I am sorry for being insensitive," and "Thank you for sharing this with me."

Our office became a "holding environment," that is, a warm, safe, nurturing and happy place for doctor, staff, patients and parents who would often comment on "how good it feels in this office." As this became more common, team members began to bring personal issues to our meetings. Many yearned for similar openness in their personal lives. Because our office seminars led to individual growth and transparency, many of us began to seek personal and family counseling. Sy was careful to suggest this whenever someone's problems began to affect their work. The office is not the best place to deal with personal issues where other family members are not part of and sharing the office experience.

In this remarkable book, *Leadership, Power & Consequences,* Sy shares many stories he has participated in or been a close witness to its unfolding. The people he met, as well as the event itself, as told in each story, helped shape and continue to shape his philosophy on leadership. He has worked and studied close human relationships and the role power plays beginning as a young adult to this very day and, as a result, wrote what I believe is an essential work for all leaders and for those who hope to be leaders one day.

—**Bruce H. Weiner, DDS**

THE PERIOD FROM 2000 TO 2014

When Sy Ogulnick asked me to write a foreword for his book I thought, what a great opportunity to tell others how obvious his philosophy is and yet, for me at least, how it remained hidden in plain sight. I come from the world of the Silicon

Valley startup with all its late-night engineering and circuit boards from the kitchen sink. It was the kind of opportunity that has to be experienced to be understood. Fortunately, our little startup was comprised of several truly enlightened leaders. None of us were self-aware of our power, only the job that needed to be done; but maybe that's why none of us abused it, either, or at the least never considered our positions and power.

My dad, a Depression-era kid who never finished the eighth grade, always said, "Son, git yerself an education and you won't have ta work for a livin'." Well, he was sorta right. And even though I never worked a day in my life because they paid me to do what I loved, after fifteen years of thirty-two-hour days and eight days a week I was ready for a change. Upon leaving the semiconductor hamster wheel, my wife and I acquired a mom-and-pop sheet metal shop that existed in a totally different state of mind. Silicon Valley was replete with truths you couldn't ignore. There was a certain comfort factor knowing Mother Nature ruled over the politics of personal power. But that little sheet metal company—now that beast was wallowing in the problems of power.

As the new owner of a job shop, I was totally unprepared for the crisis of confidence employees found within themselves. I'd walk on the shop floor, and the climate abruptly changed. For the life of me I couldn't figure out why everybody was so afraid of me. Then one day, one brave soul worked up the courage and told me it was because their future was subject to my whims. I was flabbergasted. I had never given that a thought. I never felt that way about my past bosses, and so I didn't even consider that point—until that day.

Shortly afterwards I had a happenstance encounter with Sy Ogulnick, and I thought, "Here's a guy singing the lyrics to my song. I had the music, but never the words!" Sy educated me on the topic of Genuine Dialogue and how communication is the problem to the answer. With our little Silicon Valley company I had experienced Genuine Dialogue, but by accident—not by intent! We listened to the tunes, but nobody was singing the words! I wasn't even conscious of it, so I didn't recognize how our great personal chemistry was nothing more than Genuine Dialogue accidentally working its magic between us.

Most people are afraid of power because they've only experienced the harm it can cause. In response they've learned how to hide, refusing to deal honestly and openly with issues. They conceal and twist reality to the point it's barely recognizable and all the while thinking they've gotten away with something when all they've really done is cheat others of their unique life experiences.

Sy suggested we start Inner Circle meetings with the employees to show them how the truth can set you free. When asked for his thoughts during a meeting, one brave soul responded with, "I think yer trying to figure out whose fer ya and whose agin' ya." Another chimed in with, "A boss's job is to find a reason to fire you!" I knew right then and there that I was the source of the problem. I had not expressed my benevolent viewpoint clearly enough to overcome their lifelong experiences of being beaten up by power. I expected everybody to understand that nobody works *for* me, we all work together to achieve our common goals. That day I got schooled on the meaning of the word naive!

Sy's approach to interpersonal relationships has helped me and dozens of people in our little company grow beyond their self- and experience-imposed boundaries. I can only hope that I and they play it forward and help enlighten others that cross our paths in the future. Life is too short for us to hide from each other while all the time playing a game of manipulation from the shadows. Ahhh, if only everybody thought and expressed themselves as authentically as we learned to do with each other, the world would be a much nicer place, eh?

I hope you get the message reading what we all instinctively know but suppress for one reason or twelve others.

—**Chet Mallory, Ph.D.**

PREFACE

This book is about leadership, the power leaders possess because of their position and the immense influence they have on those closest to them. It is this influence on others that is too little understood by those who have it; but, it is understood or at least felt by those they lead. Because of this separation and unequal power that invariably goes downhill, the people who live and work with the leader know the leader more fully than he or she is probably aware of. What people dependent on the leader know is valuable information which, if shared with the leader, assuming the leader is receptive to knowing how their key people view him or her, might actually nurture a leader's growth. The main barrier to this happening is that unless the leader is perceived as open and receptive and that safety in the sharing is guaranteed, it will never take place. The guarantee is not one of words, but of perception.

The author wrote this book about leadership and power based on what he learned from his experiences during the span of twenty-five years of work with children and employees, and the last thirty and continuing years mentoring powerful leaders and their key people. He would often ask his clients: "Why pick me to deal with your interpersonal communication issues when you have many professionals to select from in your local area?" And their answers were surprisingly similar: "You do what others have not been able to do and that is to make me responsible for most of the interpersonal problems that exist in my firm. I see changes in attitudes and behavior that did not exist before, and we are growing as a family." The answer is hidden in leadership and not the employee or those who are dependent on the leader.

It was a circle of constant return that led the author to question why so much "stuff" had to be reviewed each time he returned to do a workshop. "What was the real problem?" he constantly asked of himself until he had the epiphany: "Is the leader the problem to the answer?" And it was and is. This is what the book is about: *Leadership, Power & Consequences.* Instead of presenting cut-and-dried answers and methodology, the author recounts his lessons on leadership and power in the form of stories based on his experiences for the reader to examine and consider.

The author has written this book about his personally lived experiences and what he has extracted from them. His life experiences came first from his family, elementary school, teenage years, and time in the U.S. Army and as a student, entrepreneur, leader and mentor to other leaders and their associates. Success and failures run throughout the author's life, and he draws lessons from most of them. He learned somewhere along his journey that experiences are vital to growth if only we take the time to reflect on and to learn from those experiences. From this he grew to understand that what counts most profoundly is this moment and our relationships with others.

As the fifth child of six, he and his siblings lived with their parents in two- and three-bedroom tenements on the west side of Chicago, moving frequently to other apartments apparently as one way to avoid paying monthly rent the family couldn't afford. The author remembers the embarrassment of his parents when the welfare box of food was delivered on the street and "Ogulnick!" was shouted for someone to come down stairs and pick up the box. He didn't have his own bed until his next older brother went into the army during the World War II (four boys in the family served) and wore "hand-me-down" clothes. It all influenced the author to be aware of the group(s) he was part of but at the same time, the vital importance of maintaining some sense of self. It is where he first began to develop a philosophy towards life as a person and how we need to be with others. The rest of the story is found in the book.

ACKNOWLEDGMENTS

First and foremost, I will never be able to say enough about my wife, Lenette, and her influence on my becoming and being. She has done more to contribute to what *Leadership, Power & Consequences* is about than any other person. Yes, I am the author, and many of the experiences/stories I share are mine alone; but many she participated in. In fact, we often disagree on salient points of what took place as do two people who witnessed the same accident. Nevertheless, Lenette has been and is so much a part of my life and work that her presence is intertwined and was felt by me when I traveled alone to my workshops around the country. Of course, her presence was felt as the words you read flowed from my mind to the key board.

When I first interviewed and employed her in 1952, and this is a story itself, she quickly became my "go-to person" to share thoughts with. We married in 1956 after the day camp ended for that summer. We were inseparable until twenty years later when I began to mentor firms and professional offices around the country. She was not with me on most of my work trips but was my sounding board when I returned home from the many profound experiences and the often remarkable people I got to know.

I also owe much to the gracious time and wisdom others have given me and my attempts at getting a philosophy of leadership and power on paper. They have all given unselfishly when I reached out to each of them. I thank them all for their time, their minds, hearts and candor. They each know that I love and have used dialogue as my primary vehicle to teach, train and work with literally the hundreds upon hundreds of people I have worked with over the years. Their willingness to assist me in this journey of writing made an important difference as I entered into, relatively, unfamiliar territory. And if you, the reader, come away with value from *Leadership, Power & Consequences*, you, like I, owe them a debt of gratitude.

In no particular order I want to thank: Bruce Weiner, Will McCarthy, Brian Biro, Paul O'day, Brady Keresey, Bill Mahoney, Steve Mahoney, Steve Zuckerman, Lou Sportelli, Vic Demitrios and Mark Shaff. They each voluntarily read my words as they came out in type, and each offered their unique perspective on what they read and where they believed changes were necessary. I also need to acknowledge the hundreds of employees and the, literally, thousands of children over the earlier years who contributed to the testing and feedback as our philosophy grew and changed. In time it all came together while working with organizations as a mentor and for this I am in debt to the leaders who invited me to work with them and their key people. Because of these courageous leaders, the epiphany came to me one day that those who lead are the core problem to the answers they each sought to resolve.

Finally, I am grateful to Jean Stoess, my editor, who came to understand me and the philosophy of leadership and power. Her contribution made *Leadership, Power & Consequences* so much more readable for those who do not know me.

INTRODUCTION

Leadership, Power & Consequences is written to leaders and those who aspire to be leaders. The glossary defines whom I refer to when the word "leader" appears throughout the book.

If you are a leader in any capacity, you need to read this book. *Leadership, Power & Consequences* at its minimum will provide you with a better understanding of your power and influence over those you lead.

If you, as a leader, see yourself as part of the problem, you will want to read this book.

If you, as a leader, see yourself as "key" to the problem, this book is a "must" read.

If you, as a leader, see others as the problem, you'd better read the book not once, but keep it as a well used reference book. Also, learn more about yourself through safe dialogue, if courageous enough, from those closest to you. Note: It won't add up to much unless there is trust between you and the other.

Leadership, Power & Consequences stresses the importance of the leader "knowing thyself." It cannot be done but through the eyes of those who know the leader best and they are one's "Inner Circle."

This book tells pointed true experiences the author went through as both an entrepreneur, a leader (entrepreneurs and leaders are significantly different from each other) and a mentor to other leaders before an epiphany that those who are the true leaders are the primary problem and the barrier to the answers they seek.

This book makes clear the differences between quality leaders and inadequate leaders.

This book takes the positive position that most of what any of us are and become is learned, and what is learned can be unlearned, if we choose. It is equally true that if we are seriously receptive and allow ourselves to be vulnerable to others close to us, we can learn new ways to be. We can grow; and, in the process, as leaders we can influence others to grow.

Nothing is meant to be theoretical in *Leadership, Power & Consequences*. Nor is it a book about tools to use in order to be more effective. It is not about "acting" in ways to better manipulate and win over others. It is, as stated, a courageous commitment to growing into one's potential as a person. It is the acceptance that as a leader we get back that which we sow.

Each chapter may appear to be its own book, complete unto itself. But, in fact, my intentions were to build it to what it became—and that is an interconnected teachable and successful pragmatic philosophy of leadership. Chew on it carefully, and enjoy the thoughts and feeling it may provoke.

CHAPTER 1

POWER

Nothing until used
Without limits in man's hand
So good or evil.

I
n the mid-1950s, publicly traded corporations began to enter Las Vegas, Nevada, as owners and operators of casino resorts. These corporations were well financed and employed many traditionally trained and educated people who certainly understood the complexities of profit and loss, but not the culture they were moving into. One example is the many departments that had operated as "loss leaders" were now required to justify any losses and to become "profit centers." Prior to the corporate invasion, most casino resorts gave many things away or charged very little in order to bring people to the gaming tables. Many people considered this period between the late 1950s to the early 1970s the "golden period" in Las Vegas.

From 1968 to 1972 I was involved in one of the newest and, perhaps, most unique casino resort operations. I was with the resort from its initial construction

1

until its sale in the early 1970s to a major public corporation. Soon after the purchase was announced, I was asked to join in a meeting between the purchasing corporate head and the original and continuing operations leader of the resort. I had no idea why I was invited but was very aware that I would be a witness to two immensely powerful people. One was the chairman of a major publicly traded corporation that included hotels located throughout the world. The other person was the chief operating officer of the successful casino resort recently purchased by the public corporation and in which our "Youth Hotel" operated. Surprisingly, there were only the three of us in the suite: the chairman of the hotel chain and the resort operations leader. I sat off to the side, thrilled to be there as a silent and intense observer.

Why I was there is a question that probably needs to be dealt with. To this day I believe it had something to do with the unique children's program that my wife and I created for children of hotel guests visiting this particular resort. The program most certainly played a part in establishing the resort as special and attractive to its affluent U.S. and international guests traveling with their children. I felt, and was told frequently, how important the program was to the casino. The corporate chairman may have wanted to be sure I would continue the program in their first entry into the world of Las Vegas. I also have a sense that I was invited because of a special and trusting relationship with the operations leader that had grown significantly as we developed the program for children. What was most important to me, at that moment, was that I had the rare opportunity of observing, listening and learning from two powerful, influential and controlling people.

The issue the chairman and the CEO discussed, initially, was about financial compensation; but it soon turned out to be about power and control. At any level, in any case, I had absolutely nothing to contribute; but as an observer I could, and later did, offer my read to the resort leader on what I witnessed, heard and felt. What I took away from that meeting are many important lessons of power and communication found throughout this book.

The power of the hotel leader was absolute as far as I had many times observed. Representing a major corporation, he had been given the job to build and operate the most expensive and unique concept of its time in the modern hotel industry. Wisely, as I came to understand, he did not represent the corporation as a figurehead or mouthpiece but was given full power and resources to do all that needed to be done. This included exerting influence over the architect, builders, hiring management and just about every other aspect of making a unique concept in the resort industry come to be. This was a lesson of power that in my long-term view continues to be rare in that this man was fully empowered by people more powerful than him to drive the whole job. He had been resourced and supported to do what others above him could not do. He was fully empowered and with no strings, that I ever discovered, attached. As I came to know him, I sensed that such power in his hands was the correct and only action the corporate heads could take because he would not have played the "puppet" in any case.

At the beginning of the meeting I felt confident that the two men understood that the public corporation needed the current operations leader in order to flawlessly continue the successful operation and growth of the casino resort. During the discussion, the chairman expressed his thoughts and concerns for the continued success of the resort, including positive comments about the resort's operation and its impact on the public's view of the corporation's move to Las Vegas. Thus, I felt the resort leader had every reason to feel secure in his job.=

Their discussion took on its true purpose when the chairman asked under what circumstances the resort leader would continue as leader of the complex. There was no discussion of authority and where it would have to come from. The corporate leader obviously knew and valued his power, and he was looking at power in the face and reputation of the operations leader. Profits and losses were never discussed because it became obvious to both of them that power and control were the deciding issues, not money. The present leader would accept nothing less than full authority to do what he deemed necessary to operate and grow the resort. The public corporate head would never give that power to any of his subordinates. His desire or need to control those under him was considerable, and it was his corporation that now owned the casino resort. Until that moment I believed success is rewarded, but what did I know about power and influence? Not much! All that took place between them was far beyond my knowledge and experience.

When the operations leader finished his presentation of the goals, plans and compensation he had developed for the resort, the corporation summarily turned the compensation offer down. The general reason given was that if the growth of the program continued as it appeared likely to do, the operations leader would make more money than the chairman of the corporation. This was unacceptable, the corporate chairman made clear, regardless of the considerable increase in profit being assured to the purchasing public corporation. It was not long after the meeting between them that the hotel leader was relieved of his position.

The best possible talent had built and operated this unique casino resort, and in a few short years it had created a new standard for other major resorts to live up to. But after the resort was purchased and management changed, in only a few years the resort became just another hotel of many to choose from. Clearly, a well-run organization and its continuing growth were subordinate to control and power. I discovered the true intentions of the corporate head soon enough and realized that the decisions had been made well in advance of the meeting between the two leaders. That decision was to replace top management with corporate people. Both the corporate head and the operating president were performing as the script, which they both understood, dictated to them.

Money is a strong attraction, to be sure, but it pales next to having controlling power. In fact, many believe that money will give them the power they truly seek. The chairman of the public corporation knew that controlling the behavior of the leader of the casino resort was impossible, but the chairman wanted that control. Money was never the issue. The leader of the resort probably knew this, but he also knew that he could not be the puppet to anyone, regardless of the money. This is why I observed that they both may have "read" from a "dictated" script. The die was cast before the meeting. Although both *may* have been aware of their power, I have reason to question whether this is common because later on I discovered that the great majority of leaders I've worked with have little or no sense of their influence over the behavior of others and, generally, are not in touch with their power.

WHAT IS POWER?

The power I specifically want to isolate and deal with is the power that exists between humans and is made evident in the stories and text throughout this book. In this context, two or more people must be involved; and power, expressed in one form or another, exists between them. When it comes to humans simply living their lives in relationships with others, power exists between them as a potential. It is invisible; but it is there as love, nurturing and sharing or conditional, restrictive or worse. Parents with babies and young children are people with power, as are teachers at school, bosses at work. Power is a potential that may arise at any moment in every relationship.

We recognize the power of the sun, water, fire, wind, money, weapons and armies and so much more, and add the power of words written and spoken. Perhaps the most powerful is belief in God. In fact, to prove how powerful to do good and/or evil that belief in God is, more people have been destroyed over their belief than any other cause; and this in the supposed name of love, giving and brotherhood.

The powers I chose to examine throughout this book are invisible and yet exist between humans. This power is felt, feared, valued, hated and envied. In fact, what emotion is not in one way or another connected to the power that exists between us? And whether it is used for good or evil, power in the hands of people, like air, finds its way into every nook and cranny of our relationships.

I also need to emphasize that power itself is not our problem. Power is neither good nor bad. Power becomes good or bad only when and how it is used by people who hold it. Regardless of how power exists in the hands of people, if it is not used wisely and appropriately, it is likely to harm the relationship. The wise use of power first requires that we be conscious that it exists. Even if it is not seen, the wise know it is there and make use of it as thoughtfully and carefully as possible. Trust and respect between parties in a relationship happen because power, when activated for any reason, does not abuse but nurtures, teaches and empowers. This is necessary to any relationship and is what grows trust and respect. A warning: trust and respect are not "fished" for, expected or demanded but must come from the one who has the power.

Because power influences each of us to the extent that it does, it is critical that it be understood by those who use it. Those at its effect know power too well. This is because both parties are going to be impacted regardless of who wields it. Power does not move in one controlled direction, or as intended. Once ignited, power spreads in all directions like a wildfire, not only for the purpose intended, as in a controlled burn, but even toward nearby people, including those who set the fire. Power, as with fire, needs be handled with care when let loose. Without clear understanding and appreciation of one's power and how it is best used for mutual benefit, difficulty between people is almost guaranteed.

When power is not needed and not used, it may still be an issue in relationships simply due to past experiences. For example, leaders who used power to dominate those dependent on them usually got what they wanted; but a lesson was taught: "Protect thy self!" Present leaders have to deal with the ghosts of the past when they exercise power. If a present leader sincerely wants to receive the best from others, the leader must be perceived as vulnerable, safe and respecting of the other. This takes time and consistency, and is dealt with throughout the book.

Think of human power as a huge wave the surfer rides with dexterity and joy, or the same wave that engulfs a village and destroys the people and their homes. The wave has immense power both to provide exhilarating recreation as well as to destroy humans and their communities. So it is with people who possess power. They have the potential to do good or the potential to abuse and destroy others and, as I will show, themselves.

The human ability to reason raises expectations of both our self and others, and the use of power may be embodied in those expectations. The burden of having to be conscious and aware of one's power falls squarely on those who are themselves in power. Ideally, our best leaders have an acute awareness of their power, their responsibilities to others when exerting power and the consequences power can cause when misused. The good leaders know this, but inadequate leaders too often claim ignorance of their power or instead blame others for problems and negative results. This is one of the more important distinctions between good and inadequate leaders. It is a simple truth: power in the hands of people we live and work with influences our relationship in positive or negative ways, and ignorance of power is no excuse.

People who are ignorant of their power or in self-denial of their culpability in the problems around them may be helped to understand their power and to use it in a more productive manner. Humans are not born to remain in darkness but to seek light and knowledge. No one need remain in the cave. Our problems begin when we are conditioned to be what others are or choose for us to be. Here is our first example of power not understood and used in potentially harmful ways.

The point that needs to be made is that, whether out of ignorance or deliberately, much of our behavior, subtle or not, is learned; and what is learned can be unlearned. This requires not a great teacher or drugs to alter one's perception of the world, but personal courage to allow growth and change to happen from inside out. And one very important caveat is: *Growth does not happen without the help of others.* The people we need in order for us to change from within are those who know us best. And, they will not be honest and candid with us unless they witness, proof positive, our being vulnerable and fully open to them. In other words, people who know us best must be empowered to be as much themselves as is possible and as we must be to them.

WHENEVER POWER IS USED BETWEEN PEOPLE, CONSEQUENCES FOLLOW

The stories shared throughout this book are true real-life accounts that demonstrate the widest possible variations in the uses of power and leadership (good or bad) and their consequences. I was a participant in most stories, indirectly played a part in some stories, or, as in the preceding story, I was a witness to interactions between powerful people. None of the stories in this book are hearsay or retold from a secondary source.

My growth, appreciation and knowledge of power came by way of many different hands-on experiences beginning with my earliest memories of leaders I interacted with, years of teaching, counseling children, being an entrepreneur and actually being a leader and then consultant to a variety of powerful people and their Inner Circles of trusted associates.

As a student of human behavior, it is no great "aha" to appreciate the rarity of excellent leadership and the disproportionate role that inadequate leadership has played in history. There were only a few relatively enlightened leaders and even fewer who left the best lessons of power and leadership in the hands of those who followed them. It took my becoming a consultant to professionals and business leaders before I began to appreciate the power of leaders. Prior to this awakening I have to accept that although I knew I had power to affect people who worked for me, I had no idea or sense of how powerful that power was and is.

What each story, and the many untold, has taught me is that: when people who hold power over others seek to grow, their growth contributes to the growth of those close to them. To put it more precisely, growth is more likely to be reciprocal and mutual for the leaders and those over whom they exercise power. In contrast, when leaders who choose not to grow use power they hold for self-aggrandizement or other selfish and exclusive purposes, the people over whom they exercise power experience a diminution of who they are. What comes from this is an anger that is both inner against themselves for not being and outer against the power who will not let them be. In such cases, no one grows; but those dependent on the leader do learn to protect themselves as best they are able and will find ways to get even with those in power over them.

THE USE OF STORIES IN THIS BOOK

I have been told that I am a pretty fair-to-middling story teller. All I needed as a setting was a campfire, the campers, staff and a moonless night. The written format is a challenge: no feedback and faces off of which to bounce stuff. How could I not miss that? In any case, the stories I share in this book are true and written without embellishments. The purpose of each is that the reader derives some value from each story and that each stimulates the reader's thoughts. My intentions are to present as many applicable stories as I am able to sift out of my bag of experiences. To this extent, I now realize how blessed I have been to have had a variety of experiences and from the worst to the best of them find lessons to grow from.

How else could I have come to as clear an understanding of power and what it means to be a leader? Most of this has little to do with hearsay or books I read, although I suggest that being a student throughout our lives is essential; and I strongly recommend every source as worth checking out. But the truth, for me, is that personal experiences are the most worthwhile and valuable source of all. Understanding and possible growth may actually take place if the reader has reasonably similar life experiences and is able to relate to the stories I share. Those who have not known power and leadership but have been in subordinate roles and dependent on power and leaders above them will find food for thought and probably much to agree with. Those who do know power and are themselves holders of power over others need to read carefully what they find in this book, and even between the lines. It is to them the book is written. Leaders and people with power need to know of the "influence" they hold in their hands and that when power is wielded it needs to be used for mutual good. Also, I may or may not point out the lessons sometimes hidden in each story, often preferring to let the story speak for itself. I know this: The lessons and the people within each story are what influenced me to build a pragmatic philosophy I know to be true, and more importantly, that works and is inclusive.

In the preceding story (an immediate example of my pointing out a few special lessons), I identified four major aspects of the use of power. These invisible dynamics of power appear in the opening paragraph of the Introduction and are found in many of the stories you will encounter in the book.

POWER IS BEST IDENTIFIED IN ONE'S OWN INNER CIRCLE

It is easy to read leaders by witnessing the way they and their Inner Circle (IC) function together. In a healthy IC, power is distributed and shared, and people are themselves, at ease and have learned to trust that power is shared with each. None are puppets to play to the whim of the leader. Also, quality Inner Circles are not accidents but made up of people of merit and experience. Most are not turned into leaders but come into the circle ready, willing and able to lead. (Chapter 5 is devoted to a discussion of Inner Circles, or IC.)

A dysfunctional IC is easily witnessed since members are pawns to the power that is rarely shared. They show their reluctance to be open and a full participant in numerous and apparent ways. An example: The original leader of the casino resort had his IC made up of strong, talented professionals who were in control of their own departments and responsibilities; and each knew Las Vegas well. But even here there were problems of communication perpetrated by the leader. Over time I learned that the leader of operations, as good a leader as I thought he was, was also a barrier and problem to certain others not enabled to do their professional best. I describe this more fully in this chapter.

As for the corporate CEO, I was able to observe in the meeting with the president of the casino resort that he placed his hand-picked puppets—people with hotel experience but not of the casino business or the culture of Las Vegas—to manage the resort, a glaring demonstration of power badly misused and understood. The individual participants of an Inner Circle provide an x-ray look into the mind of the one in power to determine whether the power leader seeks the best by surrounding himself or herself with the best.

GENUINE DIALOGUE ENABLES LEADERS TO USE POWER CORRECTLY

Genuine Dialogue is powerfully important in enabling leaders to exercise power effectively and to attain goals. It requires people of merit and experience who are able and willing to take leadership responsibilities. Genuine Dialogue, much before it is deliberately experienced, needs the following conditions to exist: *Respect* of each person as a unique being, being *Present* in this moment, *Confirmation* through listening to and understanding the other, and *Candor,* which is saying what one feels and needs to say. (See Chapter 6 for a complete discussion of Genuine Dialogue.)

In order for people to be and do their best, they must be acknowledged as the unique being each is. On the one hand, to deny any person the simple act of respect as the person they are is to lose something in the relationship. On the other hand, nurturing people's uniqueness, the self they present to us, will result in a more mutually enriching relationship, one that either "grows or goes." There is no better way to be with another than to create the "safe enough" environment for them to be and express themselves authentically. The alternative approach, when power does not create a "safe enough" environment, which then forces people to hide and, at best, be pawns. What is lost is considerable. In this case, ignorance is not bliss for anyone.

WHEN LEADERSHIP CHANGES, SO DOES THE ENVIRONMENT

Change leadership—and everything dependent on and below the leader must change. In the story of the two leaders I was witness to, no other consideration but change in current leadership was the plan. The changes wrought by this action altered the direction of the casino resort. Its class and quality disappeared, and in a few years a very ordinary hotel existed and was eventually taken over by the banks. The dynamics, problems and positive possibilities inherent in a change of leadership are, apparently, a very difficult lesson to learn. We see and read of it taking place but rarely understand that this is the very mechanism that sets events (good and bad) in motion. Whether the changes wrought by a new leader are positive or negative, as in the story above, depends on the quality, awareness and philosophy of the new leader.

This is worth another story: I worked with a professional and his office staff for many years. During this time, he and I became and remain very close friends. I established many friendships with the people I worked with, but this particular relationship turned into a deep friendship far beyond the office. It did not continue for long as a "one-way" relationship, and as true friends we share our joys and tribulations with each other. In fact, he has been our house guest a number of times.

During the time we worked together, his office became recognized as one of the finest examples of pediatric dental care in the profession. Due to this, he lectures at dental schools and conferences throughout the country on establishing the quality practice. In time, he began to consider turning his practice over to other very capable dentists. The professionals he worked with, through their own efforts and his continuing mentoring, had become excellent dentists. Recently he began to turn his leadership role over to the dentist who would hold a major share of the practice. Prior to the turnover, the leader and I had discussed that the new leader, who was very familiar with and had been part of the work we had done over the years, had to at some point begin to assume the role of leader. Two cannot sit in the same chair.

We discussed in depth the changes the environment might experience once leadership began to shift. It might be an easy continuation of what had been achieved or adopt the philosophy that had been dormant in the dentist who would assume leadership. Only the change of leadership would bring this out, but not as long as my friend remained in the leader's role. As for the staff and existing Inner Circle, they would change with the change in leadership. Some would continue to do their job (albeit, somewhat differently); and others would leave. As the leader, my friend had created and controlled the environment; and it happened to be one that fostered and nurtured personal growth for all. Now the new leader would shape the environment into what it was to become. Whether conscious and intentional or unintentional, a different leader translates into a different environment, which may be better or worse than the previous one. In a brief period of time, the environmental differences are felt by all.

It was not long after the decision to sell was made that the employees, fully aware of the pending changes, began to "feel" that things were not the same. There was a definite change taking place in the environment. New leadership was putting its imprint on the total practice—not by edict, but through nuance and like an invisible gas spreading a subtle change in the environment. New leadership was taking over, and what they brought with them were their belief systems and the power to influence the whole that they now controlled. Although present in a receding way, the former true leader could do nothing to alter the course toward which the practice had begun to shift. All leaders bring their quirks, characteristics and attributes that are easily seen; but they also bring their hidden agendas, whether conscious or not. And changes from top to bottom are impossible to stop.

POWER AND ITS MANY FORMS

It is not surprising that power is cloaked in many costumes and that discovery of power as an issue requires an unmasking of people and the words they speak. Behavior, ultimately, sends the loudest and clearest message. Relative to this, I return once again to the casino resort story.

I did not know then, but soon enough learned, that the corporation that purchased the casino resort held a traditional view of business and the "bottom line." Seeking "uniqueness" and "quality" evaporated, and maximizing profit took over. Yet, the corporation purchased the class, quality and reputation of the facility created by the original builders and operators—but not the existing operating philosophy. The name changed and the structure remained the same, but not its heart, spirit and soul.

The new leadership and management who took immediate control proved seriously inadequate and even dysfunctional for the task at hand. They acted as if they had "all the answers" when they had too few relative to the culture in which they now found themselves. What I began to learn is that whenever power is misused or abused, and this takes many forms, it does not build—it negates. This may happen quickly or it may take time, but "top-down" inappropriate use of power assures eventual dysfunction throughout the whole of an organization.

The purchasing corporation placed a member of the corporate chairman's Inner Circle as the resort's operations leader. He had considerable traditional hotel experience, but nothing in his background prepared him for the unique culture in which he was placed. Instead of surrounding himself with talented, experienced people knowledgeable and experienced in the ways of Las Vegas's unique culture, the new head of operations brought in his own management team to take over. Ego, not experience and talent, was now leading an army of workers who more clearly understood the environment they all lived and worked in than those who led them. What does this do to people being led by leaders woefully inadequate to the task and, worse, who come across as "all-knowing"?

Following the change of leadership, the new operational leader established his authority over each of the remaining department heads. His power was such that it had to be personally established between him and each department head. He believed, and so stated, that his knowledge and experience was such that he knew what needed to be done and how to do it. The department heads who decided to remain did so at considerable cost to their own professionalism and spirit. The philosophy of the culture as well as work methods were changed on a daily basis because the new resort leader wanted to establish his authority as quickly as possible. He, just as quickly, began to undo the quality that was built into the original intentions of the resort and the work of the original leader and his management.

Numerous errors and omissions are to be expected when replacing a former leader with corporate people who carry the same title but not experience or power. Those who possess the power may be thousands of miles distant from any connection to operations, yet they still pull the strings that dictate operations. The puppeteer is the true power, not the puppets that the public sees. The stage is where the story is presented but not where the story is produced or directed.

It is not uncommon for take-over organizations to believe that by temporarily keeping the same leadership personnel but declawing them is a solution to any dramatic changes in the environment. Whenever a business changes the power structure and the original leader becomes a figurehead, negative consequences are soon to follow. Turning a true leader into a mouth-piece is, at best, deception and can be easily seen for its manipulation. At its worst it is a cancer in the continuing organization.

Back to the public corporation taking over the casino resort: a private meeting with the new operating leader gave me direct experience and knowledge about what department heads were going through. Instead of asking me about the youth program my wife and I created and operated, or what he could do to further its success, he proceeded to tell me that he was an expert when it came to educating and providing a recreation program for a wide age-range of children because he had children of his own. And armed with this superior knowledge and experience, he would decide what the new direction of our program would be. Furthermore, he said he believed that much of what we did was unnecessary and exposed the corporation to possible litigation. Yet when our program was in its planning stages and during its operational period, the original leader of the resort had given me complete freedom and the resources I requested to create the finest example of a program for children of a broad age-range. If there were restrictions to certain activities, they were placed by us and not the administration of the resort. What a remarkable difference in the use of power, leadership styles and philosophy. It was not long after our meeting that my wife and I parted from the corporation. The eminently successful youth program disappeared soon after. Leadership and how power is used make all the difference.

WHAT IS TRUE POWER, AND HOW DO WE ACQUIRE IT?

Identifying true power—where the "buck" can go no farther—is paramount if meaningful change and growth are to take place in an organization, whether of two or thousands. This is easy to identify in a relationship of two. It is also easy to find in a family with young children where either the mother or father is the power source or that power shifts from one to the other depending on issues. It is found in the hands of the owner/operator of a business. It is found in an elementary school teacher, whether excellent or inadequate. It is found in the principal who hovers over the teacher and the school administration at the top of their hierarchy that hovers over the principal. There are situations everywhere that talented and creative people take control of what they are responsible for despite the power that exists above them, and they are allowed to exist only because they are successful in what they do and bring benefits to the larger organization.

The hands-on owners and operators of a small business hire, fire and make decisions that directly influence their employees and, indirectly, employees' families and beyond. They, who hold true power over the lives of so many, as are parents of new-born and young children who literally hold life and death power over their children. Add to this the rare teachers and leaders we are bound to meet who influence us to be what we are and will become. In all phases of our lives we meet people who do influence us even as they themselves are held responsible to someone above them in a hierarchy.

It is relatively easy to identify who holds power in families and small organizations. If those in power use their power as an inclusive and common good we find why growth happens to individuals and the group. Also, people who have power are acknowledged by the people they lead, whether or not this power is well used. Therefore, if power people seek their own growth others are sure to benefit and grow to their own uniqueness. How rare and difficult is this for anyone, particularly if the persons in power do not acknowledge their degree of influence over others and accept that they are the ones who most need to grow?

It should be clear that power, as described throughout the book, is found with parents, teachers, private and professional business owners and leaders of any organization and involves hands-on participation even if indirectly through other voices. In one way or another, these people are the true power and major influence within their environments. However, not one of these leaders possesses more natural power than any other beyond the uniqueness of one's self. It is not an inner power we speak of, but a power that is worn as a suit or dress—but considerably more complex. This is not unlike the king who believed he was dressed in elegant finery when, in fact, he was naked; as are all leaders to those closest to them.

LIKE EACH GRAIN OF SAND, PEOPLE AND LEADERS ARE UNIQUE

What separates leaders is the manner in which they use power over others. Leadership, for many, is not about the leader's responsibility to others but that others are responsible to the leader. So leaders generally resist any education having to do with themselves and what power means to their life and the lives of others. They want others to be more compliant to them. Also, they seek tools to help them be more effective leaders. They will attend workshops and conferences having to do with leadership techniques and come away convinced that they are fine and it is those they lead who are the problem. In such leaders' minds, a problem is always the creation and doing of others. Too many people in leadership positions are blind to accepting themselves as the primary cause of problems in their organization and the barrier to a more mutual and productive relationship and achievements of goals.

People are capable of acquiring knowledge and growing as the unique self each person is, but to do this they must seek to learn from their experiences as well as from those who know them best. This is easier said than done. The evidence suggests that most people do not learn from experience but repeat, time and again, the same omissions and errors they have made in the past.

It is also true that no person is capable of forcing growth on others but, due to power, can change the behavior of others. Altering behavior is not to be equated with growth. Behavior is our face and what we show, and growth happens volitionally and from deep within us. In fact, what results from unwise and forced use of power is an "acting out" of what power wants but also anger at one's self for giving in as well as anger at the one in power.

If leaders hope to grow those with whom they live and work, it is the leaders' own quest to grow and growth itself that must be apparent to those close to

effort and resources to the growth of others without the leaders
he prime example as the willing and able student, all efforts and
will likely fail. It is the leaders who must be the role models through
each and every action because power is what true leaders hold. It is all expressed
through words and behavior. Leaders bring their philosophy of power in the same
way they wear clothes. What their significant others experience sets the tone of the
environment in which they operate. The leaders' power to influence reaches well
beyond their small Inner Circle as each in the circle becomes a carrier to his or her
own Inner Circles. In this way, the leader's power and philosophy reaches to every
corner of the organization. Not generally accepted, but leaders are a contagion for
good or bad.

Power comes in many guises beyond that of a business owner/operator and
parents of the very young and dependent. Becoming a professional and possessing
knowledge as in engineering, hi tech, medicine and law, etc., gives a person
more individual freedom and power in relationships with people more powerful
than they. Add to this list the naturally talented and those who have had unique
life experiences that separate them from the more powerful because they know
themselves and their capabilities. True merit is not given but a power of the person's
own making.

Our better leaders learn about power by personally experiencing power's
outcomes and consequences, both negative and positive, and then reflecting
on lessons captured in the process. One example of this is being thrust into a
responsible position over others due to an unexpected turn of events. For example,
the leader gets sick or dies—someone needs to lead, an individual responds to the
call and people follow. Even if this leader is temporary, he or she has an opportunity
to learn something about power. But most people do not look back and learn from
experience. To a few, value is extracted from each experience; they learn and are
not the same as they were. They are the "true students" to whom I will often refer.

So the power we need to be concerned with is temporary. It can be earned,
given, taken, won or lost and bought. Therefore, whether brief or long-term, few
experiences are without some meaningful and potentially valuable lessons having
to do with power. Those who are our best leaders are students who learn from
experiences. The most valuable lessons are about one's self and following that is
to learn about others. Although rare, experiences may be of such significance that

people may be changed at their core and, essentially, transformed. This is what I intend when I use the word *grow*—and in this case the word has nothing to do with aging. I intend it to mean allowing one's self to see and be touched deeply to our core by the world around us. As a result we are not what we were, having left that being behind; but we are now different and in the process of becoming.

How power is used in human relationships is our greatest concern because lives are affected. Not only the subordinate or dependent, but the one in power is also affected by how power is used. It is an important lesson that needs to be understood. Powerful people influence events and others, and are influenced in return. People do not become powerful and rain their power over others without also getting wet in the process. Our best leaders quickly learn and know that exercising power is like the proverbial double-edged sword—it cuts both ways.

In the following story, I learned that being one's self, doing what one does, is powerful, and although without intent to do harm it may play a significant part in contributing to harm. I also learned that *wanting to be what one is not* is a sickness that is ultimately destructive. It does damage to not only the person who wills it but also to people involved. Because of this, as you will see, jealousy and betrayal took root and destroyed a long and successful relationship. Power and the attraction of respect and influence had much to do with what followed.

My business partner and I owned and operated a co-ed summer day camp for children located in Malibu Canyon, California. I began the camp in the summer of 1949 simply as way to earn a few extra bucks while seeking a professional degree from UCLA. But, the camp grew beyond my expectations and in a few years had close to four-hundred children and a staff of one-hundred coming together five days a week during the summer for fun, recreation and learning. It grew not because of any formal marketing, but, apparently, due to meeting the needs of parents and children. I have to attribute this to a talented staff ranging from college students to credentialed teachers and a philosophy designed to nurture the growth of each child.

As our business grew, the roles of my partner and I became more specific and were largely determined by our talents and interests. My partner, although much less in the public eye, organized and oversaw the big and small details essential to any organization having to do with young adults and children. He dealt with the complexity of scheduling buses and pick-up of children at their homes to dealing with supplies and equipment needs. And the larger enrollment grew, the more important were the mechanical and procedural aspects of the operations, which he handled masterfully. In fact, he made my job easy to do.

I visited parents and prospective campers at their homes, interviewed and hired and trained staff relative to our philosophical picture of what a children's co-ed day camp should be like and how it should function. I was also the main story-teller, folk-singer and hands-on leader of the daily show we put on for the entire camp. I guess at that time, I was the "front man."

Due to the success of our camp, I began to discuss with my partner the seeking, purchasing and developing our own land for a permanent co-ed children's resident camp. I did not learn until my partner's actions were well underway, and during our seeking property, that he had been working behind my back to take over sole ownership and operation of our existing summer camp. He was negotiating for a new lease with our landlord—but with only his name on the contract. At the same time he was doing this, he was also encouraging me to find land that would meet our needs. He was aware of my desire to be independent and saw this as an opportunity to achieve separation from our partnership. During that time we also talked constantly about our plans for the future. I thought we were on the same page; I believed we understood each other and that any problems between us could be resolved. Initially, we moved forward towards what appeared to me to be our mutual goal until I found out his true intentions.

As his acting one way but planning differently became obvious, I asked him why he was doing what he was doing. He openly expressed that he felt unimportant in his role operating the day camp behind the scenes and envied my job on center stage. He wanted the power, influence and prestige he believed I had and that it was only due to position. He said he felt he could do my job and wanted to be acknowledged and respected by the staff and the campers as he believed I was. When I challenged his comments he admitted he had power—but only through me and not directly with staff. This probably was true, not because of the lack of importance of the work he did but rather due to the way he exercised his authority with the staff. He was blind to the environment he built around his behavior. Apparently, he wanted respect from them; and as I was later to learn (and probably knew intuitively), it does not happen that way. The leader must always respect those they lead first, and it must be authentic.

He saw his leasing the land and my desire to own my own land as an opportunity for him to take over the existing day camp and my role. He knew that with this change he would be the camp leader to staff, children and parents. None of this had to do with money, but with power and prestige. Fortuitously, I was eager to move on with my life and create a co-ed camp on land my wife and I would own. In time I came to realize that had we known how to communicate our inner thoughts and feelings to each other, the whole issue could have and would have been easily resolved and possibly a friendship of long standing somehow maintained. I had no intention of remaining a renter, and he had no intention or desire to leave the facility we leased. Both our needs could have been met had we only known how to communicate.

The point of this story is that power in the form of envy played a significant part in what took place. Envy over position, recognition and influence are powerful factors in close relationships. Whether in personal or business affairs they are difficult problems to resolve, but they must be made known and dealt with through Genuine Dialogue if relationships are to work or if those involved are to peacefully go their own ways. When dialogue does not take place people involved suffer negative consequences, and this must be true of both parties. Significant issues between people do not simply fade away, but grow into more complex problems.

Many years later I stumbled on a statement made by an unknown author long forgotten but with continuing impact on me and those I worked with: "If only we knew how to genuinely communicate to each other we would have more good solutions to our human-made problems than the number of problems."

In the story above, my partner and I did not recognize our problems at that time and did not have the understanding and tools necessary to our being able to discuss, and perhaps resolve, our problems. Money was never an issue, but position and power were. I came to understand that he did not want to be *who* I was, but *what* I did and represented to others.

WHY THE MOST QUALIFIED CANDIDATE A BUSINESS CAN AFFORD SHOULD BE HIRED

When those in power select someone to take on an important task, that person needs to be the best available. If money is an issue, it's still worth seeking and talking to top candidates with the attributes needed to fill the position. Money may not necessarily be a barrier. The next, irrefutable, step is to empower the task doer to the degree that the decisions to be made, with few limitations, are as close as possible to what the true power controls. To repeat: when power is given to others, the delivery and acceptance of that power needs to be understood by them to be the kind of power that will enable them to accomplish what they are capable of doing. I label this *actual* power. Actual power is shared power in that decisions are made by the ones given the responsibility, not by another pulling their strings. Here, there are no strings. The opposite is the *pretense* of power, which unfortunately is much more commonplace. This dynamic will be illustrated in a story later in this chapter.

When selecting people to do unusual and important jobs, it is essential to empower them in order reach their potential and to discover whether a leader exists within them. Also, without freedom to act spontaneously, creatively and as events dictate, people given only the pretense of power will do less than what they are capable of doing. Stated in its simplest terms, giving full power to talented people to do what they do best frees them to employ their talents to the benefit of all including themselves. This way of sharing power seems so reasonable an action to take but, at best, is rarely done. Why? Because too many people covet power as if it is all that counts in their life, and in the process of acquiring and holding tightly to their love of power they make bad use of talented people. This wrongheaded use means that capable people work under the handicap of the weight, scrutiny and expectations of those above them. How is this going to allow the most able to contribute to the benefit of the leader, the organization and themselves?

This brings to mind the selection of people to do a specific job, and the wise and best use of power. To explain this further, I return to the story of the casino resort and our children's program there.

My wife was assigned the task of designing the interior space of the youth recreation facility at the casino resort in Las Vegas. The ages of youths who would use the facility ranged from preschool to high school. The interior space to be used was well over 10,000 sq. ft. and had immense income value if it were, instead, used as retail space. Still, the president of the casino resort believed in the value of such a facility to the affluent hotel guests and their families; and he fully supported this facility and program over numerous other money-making uses.

My wife's selection as the designer of the facility was based on her considerable experience designing children's facilities and working with architects and builders.

She had an excellent track record relative to hard-space needs and uses of environments for educational and recreational purposes. During the design and early construction period, the internationally known architect responsible for the whole resort project and my wife crossed swords over the look and design within the youth facility. The hotel president suggested that we visit the architect at his office and work out our issues.

During the visit, the architect continued to be adamant over what he envisioned the youth facility should look like. My wife's position was that the architect's use of columns and angles may have been esthetically attractive but would be useless and potentially dangerous in an environment for active children. She wanted open space and the flexibility for staff and children to be as creative as possible, while the architect wanted rooms that were rigid and "aesthetically pleasing to an adult eye."

I suggested that the architect call the president of the resort while we were there in his office and lay out the disagreement to him. The architect called the president and explained the issues, which we were able to hear on speakerphone.

"Do you like the job of designing the resort?" the president asked the architect.

"Of course," said the architect.

"In this case," the president said firmly, "do whatever she wants done." And he hung up.

So what can we learn from this brief story? To begin, when a major corporation made its decision to come to Las Vegas to build and operate a casino resort, they selected a person with outstanding Las Vegas credentials to oversee every possible aspect of the program. This included overseeing construction to employing executives to marketing and sales. In other words, the corporate people from Los Angeles gave the job to an experienced Las Vegas leader. He knew and understood the unique culture of Las Vegas as did few other people at that time.

Based on what I came to learn, he was selected based on his proven experience and reputation. He had built and operated well-functioning casino resorts for others, and he knew the ins and outs of the town's culture. He was also a person, as I was to learn, who would not accept any responsibility unless given to him with full power to act according to his standards. What I was almost immediately to learn is that when he gave responsibility to another, he fully expected that person to do the best job possible as soon as possible and to deal with problems as if he or she were fully in charge. My personal experience with him while building the youth facility, hiring and training staff, and other related tasks was that I was empowered to oversee every aspect of the project. I was the professional and he simply a resource, only if needed, and that is the way he operated. With all of this he offered very little room for omissions and errors on the part of his executives. In other words, "You know what needs to be done, so do it."

As it relates to the serious issue between my wife and the architect, he knew the architect was an artist and had been given reasonably free reign to design the most unique hotel for its time. He also knew that my wife was the more experienced with what it was that we needed and wanted. It was an easy decision for him to make. He sided with the professional with experience, the only decision he could have made if he wanted the best results. To his credit, I thought he always did.

Quality leaders establish direct lines of communication between themselves and their key people so when problems occur they can be dealt with ASAP. The person selected has the experience called for because knowing what to do is part of the selection package. This experience of control, decision-making and problem-solving is part of the whole that comes with employing legitimate, proven talent. And since the recognized professionals know more about what they are hired to do than the leader who hires them, they are unafraid to stand up to a more powerful force in order to maintain their control over the project. This behavior is common to the more enlightened power leader who seeks this from every important member of the organization.

Direct, unfiltered communication with the resort leader was one of the most useful resources provided as it enabled the designer of the youth facility to resolve the impasse in the architect's office with one phone call. When the architect telephoned the president of the resort, the architect must have assumed that he had the resort leader's full support. However, the conversation between the president and the architect took less than two minutes and was absolute. There was no equivocation. "Do what she wants done." We all witnessed and learned a valuable lesson having to do with what I learned to be the wise use of power.

How direct, simple and important is this lesson for punctuating how power needs to be used when necessary, and only when necessary? The resort leader knew both parties. He knew what motivated them and believed he understood both of them. One was highly emotional, artistic, and supremely confident of his position of importance; the other was a practical, "what you see is what you get," highly focused, disciplined professional educator. The leader clearly knew these key people and how to best use their respective talents. In this case, excellent leadership was demonstrated by the leader of the resort. But, he too made mistakes, and I was student enough to learn from his mistakes.

HOW DOES POWER INFLUENCE PERSONAL RELATIONSHIPS?

The birth of a baby brings substantial responsibility to the parents. This is especially important because parental power over their children is the strongest form of power between humans. How aware or prepared are parents for this vitally important role? Whether ignorant or fully conscious, the influence parents have on their children may have impact that lasts a lifetime. How does anyone argue that power and therefore influence do not exist between us?

Similarly, are entrepreneurs (see Chapter 2) aware that much of their success will have to do with their exercise of power and how it is used when expended towards others? What is a leader to those they lead, if not influential? Finally, what are great teachers to their students, if not influential? There is no question that those who hold power, regardless of reason, influence those they hold power over. Ought not the influence (the exercise of power) be used for mutual good rather than for mutual harm? And, ultimately, how does anyone benefit when power is used against another rather than for the other?

Change Is Never Easy When It Comes to the Human

Although change in the world of technology moves quickly, human behavior relative to personal relationships seemingly changes at a snail's pace. Too often reason fights a losing battle to emotions and our past. Reason is connected to being conscious; and although we are constantly reminded to stay in the moment, it is where we spend too little time. If not in the present, where? In the past or future? Both are ruled by the unconscious and where emotions are the dominant force.

For many, an important belief is that we are slowly evolving towards being and becoming more completely conscious. Is how we use power between us one of the more important indicators that some humans, in fact, are evolving more rapidly than others, that a select few understand their power to do good or evil and choose to do good for self and others? Our problems come not from the few but the many who remain blind and unconscious of their power and its consequences. So how is change possible for those that cut themselves off from the present? The complexity of this problem is compounded when we realize that people who are out of touch with their use of power do not believe they lose or are even aware of the harm that is returned to them.

Another fact to consider: when power is experienced as good but is accidentally or unconsciously played out, the beneficial result may lead to expectations of more to come. As a happening, it may or may not be repeated; and this leads to other problems. Not being sure of when and how power will be exercised in any relationship places the relationship on insecure ground. What good is done in one moment may be undone in the next. Insecurity is generated through guessing intentions and inconsistent behavior coming from power that places recipients on edge. How can this be defended as desirable or beneficial?

Power is an Invisible Thread that Links Us

e also HePower is an invisible thread that exists between us and links us together. When consciously used for the common good, it is felt and received as love that nurtures, supports and allows those who are affected to grow. We may not think of this as power, and yet it is. When power is good we rarely think or feel any sense of it any more than we feel or think of the air between us. In fact, when power in our interactions facilitates events and issues that protect and nurture us to move forward, feel understood, respected and accepted, what is our response in a hierarchical relationship? Do we become positive and feel like a true participant in the event? Do we become more receptive to the other? When this happens and we are awake to what is taking place between us, is there a sense, a feeling, a knowing that the ground we are on is secure? What is the likelihood that creativity and cooperation flow between the one in power and the other? All of the above are the positive consequences that result from wise and proper use of power.

In contrast, it is difficult to comprehend that when power is used to control people to one's own end, it will more often than not accomplish the results those in power seek, but at what level of quality, efficiency and other residue? Leaders who use power without consideration for mutual benefit to those they have power over do achieve goals, but at what costs? Does any human respond to abuse and indifference with love, cooperation, creativity, productivity? Creativity is given over to escape, withdrawal, getting even, destruction and survival. What form does denial of others and their sense of being more than a tool to be used and then set aside take when it returns to the person who wielded the power? In what way is this good for anyone?

Why do so many people allow themselves to be used and even abused by those who lead them? Many, certainly not everyone, come to believe they have no way out or have been so mistreated and hurt that playing the "pawn" is their accepted lot. It is difficult to understand this sense of helplessness and despair unless one has gone through constant abuse and defeat that forces them to comply, to give in. They lose, but so do those who do this to them.

Numerous experiments have shown that when people are given power to discipline or deny something to innocent volunteers, most of the empowered people in the experiment use this temporary power in negative ways. Instead of caring for the volunteers in the study, they chose to make things tougher for them. The question, then, is why do people given momentary power over others appear to use it more to punish innocent participants than to care for and assist them? And what does this tell us about the attraction of power or one's own experiences with having been at the receiving end of power? Power is at the core of what influences almost every aspect of relationships. Yet, this power is nothing until used between humans.

The problem is complex because the people who seek and love power and the influence it has are not necessarily aware that power when used tends to move in all directions. When power is used badly against another there is going to be, at least, a "get even" effect. When power is used to the benefit of others involved, the good that comes from this is complementary to both. We might ask, "If this is true, why be abusive in one's use of power, particularly if power harms the user as well as the abused?" Ignorance and blindness to consequences appears to be the answer.

People, who are fully aware of their power and use it to do "good" for others, are the ones who know what they do and why. They are motivated to the "common good" and understand and appreciate that the manner in which they exercise their power is what will likely result in positive ends both as related to material and people goals. They, surprisingly, have few and perhaps no expectations. It is who and what they are and do.

Power Is a Potential until Used

Since power is dormant until used by anyone in a relationship, the ideal is that power needs to be a dynamic in the sense that it constantly shifts from one person to the other, depending on the event and experiences each has. In personal, family relationships or organizations, if power remains frozen in the hands of only one person, serious and dysfunctional issues exist in the respective environments. The place we expect to find fixed power is where we have leaders who cannot be voted out of power, such as true entrepreneurs and small-business owners. They not only accept their power to influence and lead but expect those they lead to follow them. Our better leaders, however, understand the values inherent in and the immense good that results from sharing power and empowerment of others—which in turn empowers the leader even more.

People who are unaware of what powers they possess are playing with volatile explosives. After all, what do most people know of power's immense capacity to do "good" or to destroy? People know what is done to them by those who have power because this is what they experience. The point here is that leaders may not know that their use of power does harm to others and, therefore, to themselves. The conditioning that results is exemplified in the study above that gave temporary power to people to use or not use with innocent participants and paints a bleak picture.

Personally experiencing the good and bad use of power has value if one reflects on the experience, as I luckily did from the Las Vegas casino resort-hotel experience. Most personal stories, whether at home, work or school, offer vital opportunities to learn something about power and relationships. Power is either hidden, or is blatantly obvious; either way, a learning opportunity exists having to do with power and its influence. People do not suffer experiences without some scar tissue being left behind. The wise amongst us learn from their life experiences the lessons of good and bad relationships and of power, and these are the students I will often refer to.

HOW MENTORS CAN HELP YOU MAKE THE BEST USE OF POWER

Clearly, power is ubiquitous and found everywhere human relations exist. Let us consider an example of "climbing the corporate ladder." It is a highly competitive environment in which many seek power and few share the prize. To begin, climbing the ladder is never easy; the higher one ascends the more challenging and perhaps dangerous the climb gets. Second, a wise way to facilitate getting power is through affiliation with an established power person, or mentor. However, in most cases the relationship has little to do with excellence and quality leadership because in this context it is about how to use others to one's own end.

Why do many of our brightest and most capable youth become so transfixed by what they witness as the fruits of power? Is it the good that can be done with power, or is it the material benefits and control over others that are so attractive? Perhaps it could be a "will to power" that has to do with one's own self, being and independence. Does holding power over others come without a cost to one's self? These questions are not easy to answer because it takes relationships with others to tell the true story. And, events have a way of forcing unexpected changes in whom and what we are to be and become.

If becoming powerful is what aspiring people want to achieve, what will be the cost to them for taking on an existing hierarchy, whether public or private? Is it worth the emotional, intellectual and personhood cost? On the one hand, for some people any cost is worth paying because being powerful or independent is more important than being at the affect of others in power over them. Being in power is a popular choice among bright and talented people because they see material and personal rewards, or that power is a reward unto itself. And, there are those who desire only to be the best in their chosen field. For them it is all about merit and quality, and power is a non-issue except as it relates to their own freedom to learn and grow. By becoming experts in their chosen field, they also gain power that helps them stay more in control of their own destiny. Obvious talent is rarely taken for granted. Relative to this, is finding the appropriate mentor helpful in achieving one's ends? I argue in the affirmative because having an experienced hand that knows the way must be helpful, that is, if one is a student.

When an aspiring student of power seeks a mentor to advance their personal growth, this journey is more difficult than when seeking a mentor to help one scale the corporate ladder. This is because personal growth is a struggle from deep within one's self. Whereas, climbing the corporate ladder have external rules and protocols. He who plays by the rules will probably win. The personal journey, on the other hand, is an unknown and full of conditioned barriers to overcome. The mentors sought for the personal journey need to be what they teach, and this is so much more than merely possessing tools. Mentors to assist climbing an organization's ladder are more about the tools they have acquired on their own personal journey. This is intellectual and experiential through successes and failures as part of their credentials. Mentors who teach personal growth must know the difficulty of this journey into one's deepest recesses, and they themselves must have been there. These mentors are selective and open to only those students who demonstrate passion to learn about their self and have the courage to be vulnerable. Personal growth without also being vulnerable is a journey that goes nowhere.

It is why I write that the ideal leader is on this journey of personal growth which never ends. This leader must also be a mentor who brings their awareness of self to their relationships. The mentor/leader is able to create an appropriate environment in which personal growth takes place without interference from any power above them that fears the growth of those they control. Quality mentor/leaders and quality students seek each other out because they have a strong need for each other. It is the courage to persevere that assures growth.

The story that follows is about the seeking of power for what the person believes is a common good, but events dictate otherwise and become his mentor. He eventually does become a leader and a mentor to others, but in a totally different way from what he first envisioned.

He was a bright boy just entering his teens, and he came across as unique for his age in that he demonstrated an unusual interest in fairness and justice. He often came to the aid of his friends while also voicing concern for broader social issues. He activated this propensity when issues arose from authority that appeared to him as heavy-handed. I observed that he liked being responsible for his friends, and he agreed. I asked him why and he told me, "I want to help them be more concerned for themselves and others."

I talked to him about his thoughts on our summer camp and the friends he lived with. He saw himself as a leader in his group, not through any formal selection process but, it seemed, through his quick mind and verbal abilities. The others in the group were also verbal and bright, but he was quick to speak for them and on their behalf. It was important to him that "What was good for the goose was also good for the gander," and he did not back off in making his case and expressing his opinions.

This was in the mid-1960s; and he was, for his age, well informed about social and political issues. The Vietnam War was taking place at that time and was a cause about which he expressed concerns. During our broad-ranging conversation, I asked him to share his views on the Vietnam War. Even at his age he had strong opinions that he backed up with facts as he understood them. I asked him if he wanted to, perhaps, go into politics, to be a leader in the future; and he eagerly agreed that he felt he could and wanted to do this. I felt good about him and his leadership desires. He was sincere in what he believed and in his concern for the "common good." Nothing in his behavior indicated a need for power over others but, rather, a desire to assist and empower others.

We continued our conversation in some depth, and I eventually asked him more about his desire to lead. At one point he broke down and began to emotionally express that he thought he had answers that others did not have or see. It was obvious that in his mind and heart he believed in doing "good" for others and society and he was unafraid to take a responsible role. He apparently saw that leadership was a necessary condition of group dynamics and that he had leadership qualities.

After college he became a Peace Corps volunteer, and during his experience in North Africa he found himself living virtually alone for extended periods of time. He read and thought much about the problems of the world, and after much reflection he actually believed he had discovered many of the answers to the world's social ills. Years later he told me, "When I came out of my hut after days upon days of torrential rain, I attempted to confirm my thoughts about what I was convinced would solve the problems of the world. But within minutes of being with people, I was shattered to realize that I really knew nothing and had no answers."

When he finished his Peace Corps stint, his journey took a totally different path. He neither became the political leader he first aspired to be nor did he build on the science degree he had completed at college. Instead, he became and remains a top professional guitar player and teacher of guitar. He continues to be socially and politically concerned, and is very much aware of the social ills of the day. He lets his love of music do his talking for him. I know him today as the same perceptive, caring person that I remember as a child and young adult whom I admired then, as I do today.

Did our young wannabe leader in the story above check with the group he lived with and determine whether or not they needed or wanted him to represent them? Did they even concern themselves with one of their own being their leader? The individuals within the group were each strong personalities, and they lived and recreated closely without friction. They were each unique and had an exceptional counselor to guide them. It was unlikely that any one specific leader would come out of the pack. What did result were memorable experiences for each of them and closeness to each other to this day.

It is likely that many people defer to more assertive or verbal people not chosen formally but whose thoughts and feelings are expressed forthrightly. With fixed-in-place leadership, problems remain hidden and unresolved, not because they are too difficult or too hot to handle but due to not being openly discussed. It is only through wise and shared use of power from any leader that environments become a haven for dialogue, ideas and solutions. How fine and exciting it is for people when any person of power is perceived as safe, mutual and invites honest participation and shares his or her power.

DO WE KNOW OURSELVES?

Knowing one's self is difficult, if not impossible, because no one can be fully objective about one's self. Even those who are somewhat objective are still unable to see and know themselves in the same way significant others see and know them. Thus, if we are to know ourselves as leaders and to create and shape healthier environments, we need to listen to those who know us best. They witness our behavior; we do not. It is their perception of us that influences them. How is it possible for people to stand apart from themselves in order to be witness to whom and what they are? In the ideal world we are students to those closest to us, and they are students of ours. This is the result of empowerment and the gift of mutuality.

In the real world, we as leaders are the *cause* and they, those we lead, are the *effect*. If feedback is less than forthright, honest, genuine, and spontaneous or there is no feedback at all, how do leaders know the quality of their leadership? We will not know who and what we are, as experienced by those significant to us, without safety and trust existing between us. This is not a promise made or based on expectation but a result of the confirmed trust we have in each other.

The following story is about a strong, focused, goal-driven, want-to-be leader. I find it intriguing that he was in the same summer camp group at the same time as the young man who wanted to lead in order to bring fairness and equality to the members of the group he was part of.

This young man, however, literally stood outside his group but somehow thrived. He never spoke for or represented anyone but himself and appeared, at least to me, to be a trouble-free camper. Later, as a teenage helper at camp, he did an outstanding job on any task he was given. Apparently he had his own agenda even as a young boy, and his attitude of independence did much to alienate him from his peers. He was an outsider without apparent desire to become an insider. Had any of this become a problem for him or the group, it would have been dealt with at that time.

Although he was not nurtured by his own group, he felt nurtured by his relationship to the camp in general. He wanted responsibility and, as time would show, power over others. He thoroughly believed in his ability to do any job, loved challenges, and one way or the other he was going to get things done.

As he matured, so did his desire for power. I also discovered that as he developed into a young man he began to envision a society much different from the one he grew up in, whether at camp or personal.

When he became an adult he began his entrepreneurial journey. He created a business and employed people who were somewhat similar to each other in that they appeared to be searching for meaning in their life and also were looking for a strong leader to show them "the right way." He would use anyone who might contribute to his goals—but not to mutual ends. Bright and remarkably self-sufficient, he attracted people through his charismatic behavior and what tools he believed necessary to attaining his vision. He became a powerful leader. He believed in what he and others needed to do if his vision was to be given life. Was mutuality or resourcing others to grow to their potential part of his philosophy? Not at all, but this was never his goal. We'll return to this story shortly.

The following story of power and leadership is vastly different from the two preceding stories having to do with power and influence, and it also comes out of our camp experience.

During this particular summer both my wife and I were unable to be directly involved with the operation of our summer camp in Northern California. In the position of director we placed one of our finest and most able counselors. As a counselor he was as good as they come, and we never doubted his ability with children and his understanding and application of our philosophy towards the education of children.

A few words about the camp philosophy because it is at the root of what eventually grew into a philosophy having to do with power and quality leadership that influenced leaders and their organizations throughout our country. Each group of campers was designed to act as its own camp. It began with membership in a group of rarely more than eight children, a junior counselor and a counselor. The group would hold meetings in order to give each person in the group the freedom to pick activities in which to participate. For many of the campers it might have been the first time they had been given this opportunity and power to choose. But, there was an important caveat to this: the choice one made was a choice made for all. This assured that everyone had as many different learning experiences as possible. It also assured that each child had the experience of leading others through the selection of activities plus the responsibility for having to organize time, etc., with the specialists.

An example: if a camper expressed a desire to ride horses, it became his or her responsibility to organize this with the wrangler in order to schedule time for learning and riding. Every member of the group was required to learn about care of horses, equipment and corral maintenance. There may have been a camper or two who feared horses, but such campers were still required to go along with their group even if they never rode a horse. If they chose to not ride, they worked around the corral while the rest of their group rode. The same would happen with all activities. Individual group members picked activities they wanted to do and learn, and they soon realized that each had a responsibility to the other. They lived, played and learned together as a group. They became their own camp, and it was the bigger camp's job to resource a group's creative desires. The role of the counselors was to mentor and facilitate relationships and to seek learning experiences for their group that pushed the envelope of the campers' normal experiences.

The role of the director of camp was to meet the resource needs of a group and to support a group's desire to innovate, but not to dictate or oversee activities. That took place within each group on its own. Interestingly, no group was ever identical to any other group although everyone used the same camp facilities. In this particular case, the outstanding counselor we selected to direct camp functioned brilliantly as a counselor within the camp's philosophy; yet, as we discovered, he had his own twist on the philosophy as a director compared to that when he was counselor to the group in which he and his group so prospered.

His attitude as camp director was laissez-faire, and he did not interfere or take action unless demanded by events. Problems had to fully form before he attended to them, and only then. From the start of his reign as camp director his behavior towards governance was based on a belief in as little interference as possible. Under his unique approach, camp became looser and less restrictive, and each group moved to its own beat. This, on first sight, was exactly the way the camp was supposed to be and for which the staff was trained, except that we intended the campers to experience and learn from as wide a choice of activities as possible for a children's camp. But under his leadership the groups began to spend most of their day at the lake enjoying the sun, water and each other.

Into this temporary vacuum of leadership stepped a member of the staff who had an interest in anarchistic governance. He manipulated people, including the director, as if they were puppets on a string. During this brief period of non-direction, the camp, primarily at the lake, became one big social gathering and each person their own camp.

When my wife returned to camp, the environment immediately returned to its accepted and expected ways. In the brief time this all took place there was no harm, no foul; but much was learned about leadership. The director accepted his responsibility for the philosophy of "do not interfere unless absolutely necessary." He saw power only as a tool to use in an emergency. And since none existed, his leadership was unnecessary. As for the supposed anarchist he wanted to experiment with the idea that individualism does lead to community responsibilities. Does this story tell us how powerful a leader's influence is whether they lead out front, stand behind or simply blend in?

The story I tell below is also about power, but is power of the mind and experiences difficult to explain; nevertheless, important lessons are couched in them. One quiet Sunday morning on a beautiful day in September 1956, I felt compelled to drive to our children's camp in Malibu Canyon and check it out. The camp was closed for the season, and only the caretaker lived on the property. I greeted the caretaker and walked to the corral with nothing on my mind that I can remember. It was that type of pleasant day, bright, warm and very quiet. I guess I could say that I was in the very center of the moment. The picture I saw was the horses in the corral. I heard the sounds of chewing, snorting and could smell the sweetness of hay and alfalfa. It was a peaceful day, and I felt totally present. As I approached, two or three of the horses lifted their heads in acknowledgment of a familiar face and smell, and I decided to go for a ride.

I always rode a big Tennessee Walker that I called 71 because that's what she had branded on her left hind-quarter. As an aside, I am a kid from the West Side of Chicago who grew up during the Great Depression of the 1930s and knew nothing about horses although I always felt very much at ease with them. My relationship with 71 was unusual in that she always preferred me as her rider over anyone else. It was as if we had known each other for a long time. She was not an easy ride for others, including the wrangler; but when I sat astride her it was as if we had become one. Go figure.

But this day the horse that first approached me was the one the campers called Blue. She was small, stocky and a beautiful dapple gray-blue color, a gentle horse the kids loved to ride. It was as if she said, "Hey! I'm the one you're going to ride today." I thought it strange that 71 paid no attention to me.

I grabbed a hackamore, which fits over the head and nose but has no metal bit, and is usually used to lead a horse while walking next to it. I decided not to saddle Blue because she had such a nice round back or to use a bridle because I was just planning a short ride in the big meadow leading north of the corral. We began at a slow, easy walk, the pace perfect for the setting. After a few minutes, Blue began to stand more erect and became tense and alert, her ears forward. We began a lope as she lengthened her stride and speed.

In seconds she was stretching and reaching for ground, it seemed, like a racehorse. We were off galloping at full speed. Holding the hackamore loosely and sitting as if in a form-fitting chair, I flew across the hundreds of acres of open meadow on Blue. Suddenly, I became a warrior riding across the arid land in the steppes of Asia heading in a full-out charge towards the village that lay in front of me. The landscape had changed and, I guess, so had I; but I was aware and fully into what was taking place.

Then Blue hit a gopher hole, and we both tumbled forward. I literally flew off of her and rolled as I hit the ground. Normally, being free of a rider and control,

Blue would assuredly have turned for the corral and headed home at a gallop. But she did the strangest thing—she bent her front leg and extended the other so that her back was low enough for me to simply get on, and then she rose once I was mounted. I held the hackamore loosely, and we slowly turned towards the corral at a gentle walk.

What did I just experience? Clearly, something very "powerful" between us had taken place. I had passed into a different time and place but had no sense that I had become someone else. And I remember clearly it was Blue that I was riding! We were together now, and then. The experience had clearly altered our relationship. Blue was not the same animal I had ridden out of the corral. We had become one, rider and horse, sharing an experience that was so powerful that I went back to examine where we had fallen.

Did that really happen? The marks were all there, including the gopher hole Blue tripped in, the damaged meadow grass, the ground, dirt on my shirt and pants; and yet neither of us had suffered as much as a scratch! Did we cross a line, or was it all just the "power" of a fertile imagination? If so, why did Blue approach me at the corral instead of 71, who always came to me? And, Blue waiting for me after the fall, bending so my mounting her was as simple as stepping over her back? And, what of the village in the closing distance I saw as we charged towards it?

The true occurrences of this story describe power in a totally different way from how I have used the word power and its meanings heretofore. This is about the power of our minds, imagination, relationship between human and animal, the power of beliefs set against reality, and concrete evidence. Riding Blue in preference to 71 was a first, and using only a hackamore and no saddle on an unfamiliar horse was foolish. Also, going from a leisure gait to a full charge across wide-open grassland begged a fall and harm to both horse and rider. If time is a barrier, I believed we broke through and entered a different time and place, or at least in my mind I did, and, apparently, in Blue's, too.

We fell, and *we* recovered without any injury. The tumble of both horse and rider was as real as a cold shower. And what of the behavior of a horse that without rider otherwise would head back to the corral, while Blue waited and kneeled down for me to mount? No fantasy here. I went home and shared the full experience with my wife, and never in the many years between the "happening" and this moment have I doubted that this event took place. The power of the awakened mind is obviously considerable, but so are the powers that are of a different dimension, or unexplainable.

Another story about power, but in this case the power of the environment: an eight-year-old boy considered so hyperactive that he was required to take the behavior-controlling drug Ritalin daily in order to be in a "normal" school setting joined his age group in our summer camp. His parents enrolled him in the camp, hoping he could have as normal an experience as possible. They believed that their son was bright and much more capable than he presented in the formal education setting. After meeting with the parents and the boy, I called the school psychologist and told him that we would accept the boy for the whole summer—a decision that was based on my being given permission to take the child off Ritalin if his behavior warranted it.

My feeling at the time was that if his experience at camp remained under the cover and control of a drug, the camp's impact would be lessened to a considerable degree. I believed that because the camp and group environments were safe, loving, nurturing and creative, the experiences and relationships there could and would alter his perceptions of himself and that this change in his self-image would influence his behavior. I knew that the power of a healthy, stable environment could make striking behavioral changes in children. Might this influence his need for mood-altering drugs? You bet it did!

In a broad-brush sense, I know and have experienced much evidence that the power of an environment is capable of influencing how our mind and behavior work. Environments can and do destroy humans and/or can and do grow humans to discover and use their potential. The boy's behavior in camp proved, without question, the positive powers of the environment.

As he adapted to the immersion into the camp's philosophy, he began to change; and from about the beginning of the third week, the remainder of the summer he was drug-free. His behavior and relationships with his peers and adults grew into his being admired and respected as every bit a normal boy as was possible. In fact, he became a leader within his own group of seven others his age and, more significantly, a contributor outside of his group. His innate intelligence and sense of morality to do "good" came through loud and clear. The environment as promulgated by his counselor and a camp philosophy that emphasized relationship and dialogue were the powers that had to have made this possible.

I learned additional lessons about the power of the environment from my experience with this boy. Was it the setting, the pristine forest, the pure spring waters, our lake, recreational activities and the learning about one's self and those we lived with and shared almost every moment? In other words, was it the house in which we lived and played and the people therein? No question that everything, including relationships, is a factor. But, primarily it was through the relationship between the counselor, junior counselor and the gang of seven kids in his group that made the most meaningful differences. But it all had to begin with a pragmatic philosophy that came from the leaders of camp. It is likely that without the freedom, resources, training and other support available coming from the true holders of power, any personality and growth change would have been accidental. In any case, when the boy returned to his family and school, it was not long before he was placed on a controlled substance once again. Alter an environment, and you affect behavior. Where humans and relationships are concerned, nothing seems fixed beyond birth and death.

What I believed and hammered into each counselor in countless meetings was that their relationships with every child and the relationships between the kids themselves were the most important activity happening at camp. And we emphasized that every activity, whether horses or art and crafts, was a vehicle in which relationships with people happen and the camper either moves forward or backward. Our goals were always dialogue, relationships and personal responsibility to self and others. Going "backward" was not an alternative for us.

Since I was responsible for teaching the philosophy, my relationship to each counselor became the example of what they and the role they played had to be. Suffice to say that they had to transmit my power to influence them to their group. The better counselors were simply being what they were to begin with. Healthy egos and good, caring people thrive in an environment that nurtures them. The less adequate counselors, and there were always a few, worked harder to live and use a philosophy with which they were unfamiliar through their own life experiences. Most counselors grew into the philosophy and prospered in their own relationships and leadership roles. On the one hand, a few seemed unable to escape their past conditioning; and not surprisingly, those were the counselors and individual campers we gave the most time and guidance. On the other hand, it was always possible that seeds of change and growth were planted in them and would, under the right circumstances—*grow*.

I also learned that by changing counselors or working more intensively with the same counselor, the environment they created and controlled relative to their campers changed. It changed because people in positions of power influence those they lead. Change the leader or grow the same leader, and the environment has to change. There is no altering what I believe to be a natural law. I may have been aware of my responsibilities but did not yet fully comprehend the power I had to influence others who, in turn, influenced others. Is this because power is not seen but is deeply felt by those affected? It may be soft, tender and nurturing as in true love or may be as destructive as a bulldozer. One way or the other, and with certainty, power between humans cannot be taken for granted.

Thus far, each story illustrates power between humans, except, that is, the one between me, the horse and the consequences that follow. They also show that through the exercise of power, so are environments created and changed. And, in order to change environments from destructive to constructive, it is those in power who hold the key. Leaders are the ones who must change first; and if perceived as such, others will also change. People in power may demand that others change, but change does not happen that way—and what leaders get is compliance. This is what we learned through the behavior of campers in an environment that nurtured "being a responsible self." And, what happened when the campers returned home to the power and influence of their parents? The story that follows makes this very clear.

A professor of the social sciences from a major university enrolled her son at camp. After a few years of her son's participation, her interest in the working philosophy of camp so intrigued her that she asked if she could come to camp for a week to observe. To have a practiced observer study camp and its pragmatic philosophy was exciting; but how were we to do this without the observer influencing the observed, or at least with minimum impact?

We came up with the perfect prop in a perfect location—the dining room next to the kitchen, where groups gathered for a minimum of three times a day to eat, use the library, do arts and crafts, dance and engage in other creative endeavors. An old upright piano in the mess hall not only needed a complete tune-up but a brand new paint job. Taking on the task of remaking the piano, the professor blended right in to whatever was happening and soon became invisible to one and all. In the process, she witnessed group activities from quiet research to loud, dynamic meetings to exciting creativity and spontaneously occurring song and dance.

About five days into her stay she suggested that we talk about her observations and concerns. I looked forward to this as an opportunity to learn how outsiders view our working philosophy. Generally, I was always pushed or pulled by events; and whether emergency or not, happenings dictated where I went and what I did, whether it might have been personal and individual, group-centered problem-solving or joining in the fun of the activity. What called to me and occupied my attention were things to do, not thoughts and contemplation about our experiment in individual and community growth and development. Who had the time?

Her look told me that these were serious issues that needed a complete airing, but none of what she discussed had to do with physical safety and health of campers. In fact, she lauded what she observed as everyone's caring for themselves, each other, and even the appearance of camp as their own living environment. The level of responsibility campers and staff took was remarkable to her, and this became the actual core of her concern.

She stated that, "What you are doing at camp is impossible to replicate at their homes. Here they are responsible for almost everything in their life from caring for themselves, making their beds, cleaning their cabins to cleaning community toilets—not to exclude caring for the grounds of the camp, working in the kitchen, reconstructing or constructing their own living quarters as a group, if they choose, and finally, creating their own daily program as a group." Most important to us, she saw that every activity, including relationships with each other and the counselor, was a possible growth experience.

What this professional social scientist witnessed was the power of an environment that contributed to every participant's view of themselves and others. Further, she said they grew in beneficial ways for themselves and for the culture in which they lived. Her questions and concerns were about, "What do they do when they return home to relationships that are generally blind hierarchies or cast in concrete? Parents will see their kids as more independent and responsible, and this is a wonderful shift in expectations. But, will their children stay that way?"

In general, at too many homes communication is rarely more than monologue and, worse, the unilateral exercise of "power downward." When compared to the respect for the individual demonstrated through dialogue and mutuality emphasized at camp, monologue, at least temporarily at camp, is non-existent. She questioned out loud whether these young but definitely more fully mature humans would challenge their being forced into molds at home they did not fit into any longer. "What would be the outcome," she wondered, "of going from an environment that facilitates personal responsibility and growth to one that," in her mind, "impeded growth?" And, is this not exactly what happened to the camper who went from the necessity of Ritalin to no Ritalin to Ritalin once again soon after he returned home?

I had no easy answer at that moment, but our taking note of parent comments over the years provided an answer to what actually does take place in a transition that to all appearances is going backwards in time. What we came to realize is that people live in multiple environments through adaptation. Even here, as in so many instances, it is about power. The young, as with employees, students and any who find themselves in dependent situations, have little power and resources to do anything but comply. Most people take on the roles "expected" of them from those in power. It is not a win-win situation, and how can it be? But if conflict or quitting the relationship is to be avoided, adaptation becomes necessary; and most people do just this. They bend to the winds of power and, as a result, everyone loses when people comply with those who wield unyielding influence over them. And, where dialogue does not exist, what is the possibility for mutual and beneficial growth and change?

This is the core of the power issue that must be understood and, once understood, needs to be used for the common good of those involved. Power cannot be taken for granted or too lightly considered. Ignorance of the role power plays leaves people, both those who have power and those at its effect, gambling with each other and with consequences unpredictable for both.

Consider the typical camper returning home to parents and an unchanged environment that expects the children are the same as they were before the camp experience. There is an interesting comparison here with soldiers returning home from war and expectations laid on them by their loved ones that they are the same persons who left for war. This scenario carries with it interesting complexities and problems. Parents did acknowledge that changes had taken place in their child and often made laudatory comments about what "miracles" were achieved at camp as observed through their child's behavior at home. But—and this is very important—

in weeks to at most a few months camper behavior returned to what existed before summer camp. We had to learn why this happened.

What we discovered is that a camper's behavior reverted to their "BC" (Before Camp) behavior (albeit somewhat changed) because those in power (in this case, parents) did not change or grow their own understanding of the power they wield over those dependent on them. In other words, power, when used to influence behavior and attitude, when used to force compliance, even if unconsciously exercised, wins; but it also loses. As I have taught and written time and time again, if power is used unconsciously, the outcome depends on the "roll of the dice"; and results are accidently good or bad. As illustrated in several of the stories in this book, inconsistencies in relationships do not make for secure feelings and safety, and do not create a nurturing environment.

In spite of an unchanging power structure and environment at home, campers did continue to grow their sense of self. And the relationships and experiences that occurred at camp continued to percolate in the mind and spirit of the camper. The campers old enough to drive developed ongoing relationships with their friends from camp and continued seeing each other during the school year. For many, friendships continue to this day (sixty-plus years and counting). In fact, a few have married the person they met at camp as campers, and several staff members also married. It is why I write that people do live in multiple environments and that they adapt to differences and particularly to the way power is used. This is true regardless of whether power is used to force compliance or to nurture and empower. The difference in this case is obvious: negative use of power in relationships between people is *destructive* and positive use of power is *constructive*.

If power is perceived as good, nurturing, accepting and comes to us, invites us, we go to it, become part of it, receive from it. We prosper and give back to it in kind. If we perceive little respect for who we are and/or want to become, most humans still comply, in particular when dependent but in the process of compliance do not give back any more than what it takes to protect themselves. So, which is the more desirable relationship to have with those important to a leader? Is it to be resistance and "protection of one's self" or "full and creative participation?" The answer is obvious, but rare; and where does the fault lay?

The power that surrounds us is never the problem; in fact, it exists and fills the space between us. But when power is activated, it is as real to the recipient as an act of love or a hard punch in the stomach. This is true whether we refer to parents, teachers, bosses, church leaders, political leaders, gang leaders and even camp directors. In other words, power as used here is not simply a thing of nature but is also what people possess because of their position relative to others. People who have influence on the behavior and attitude of others, as do parents over their young and bosses over their employees, need to be conscious of their power at all times. The consequences of being unaware and ignorant of one's power are potentially devastating to relationships and relative to business, the "bottom line."

WHERE IS POWER NOT AN ISSUE?

Everything human ultimately has to do with our basic need for relationships with others, and because of these needs we have responsibilities towards each other. How is it possible to have a need for another without also tending to and caring for that need? And, are we not the other to the other? When one's power is understood and used wisely, the consequences are most likely to be good for the relationship and the individuals involved. But if power is used blindly or only to the advantage of the more powerful, how is this perceived and translated by those at the receiving end?

People used as pawns, or worse, pay back in kind but often in indirect ways. The wiser are subtle and protect themselves in the process, but all pay back the power abuser in one way or another. But, this tit for tat does not stop the powerful from doing what they do or getting their way. Those who have power usually win over those who do not. Some might believe that considerations of possible consequences are taken into account by most leaders and that they are aware of payback. This would require that leaders learn from experience the difference between good and bad leadership, and the quality of relationships and response. History, and personal experiences with powerful people, do not support that most leaders use experience as the valuable opportunity to learn and grow. "If it works, don't fix it" is the mantra of most people. Ignorance and "hard-headed" positions rule decision-making.

How does any power-down relationship bring solid problem-solving and growth to any endeavor and its people? Leaders who fall into this large population do not understand the damage their way of exercising power contributes to either outright failure or inadequate results. The minimum, at the least, is to accept that if you lead others, you are the role model and teacher. The powerful should not ask the mirror, "Who is the fairest and best leader of all?" Instead, they should ask those who are closest to them. It is the people that leaders depend on to do their bidding who know them best. They are the mirror on the wall, and not only witness but in many ways judge and jury.

Relationships between two or more people too often develop into a fixed hierarchy that resists sharing power and true mutuality. In healthier relationships this rarely occurs, and power and influence shift from one to another depending on the issues at hand. Healthier relationships are dynamic and fluid to the extent that leadership roles are exchanged easily as people come to know and understand each other and their capabilities. Ideally, it is the event that dictates which one leads rather than a single fixed-power person who drives the relationship. When this is the case, the relationship, then, is inclusive and power is easily shared and well used.

When the role of being a leader is fixed in the hand of persons who are either blind to their use of power or are aware of their power and control over others, relationships must be dysfunctional. The ones in power, because they hold their power closely to themselves, lose the value of individuals to participate as the unique being each is. It is said that, "Many hands make light"; but what is not said is that the ways of leadership either facilitate many hands working as one, or working to protect themselves against the leader.

POWER AND HIERARCHY

When any group of people who live and work together increases in number, organization becomes essential or chaos begins to take over. To deal with the problems of which hand does what and when is one good reason why forms of governance evolve. As numbers increase people may select a committee, or a majority of the group picks a leader out of a few who are trusted. Or a strongman takes over the role by brute force or a person with verbal and charismatic attributes wins the position. In self-owned business, it's the owner/operator who holds the power or in larger organizations a small group of people select a leader whose power is limited by the small group called a board of Directors. What matters most is that there is movement towards a hierarchy in one form or another when numbers of people increase, and as this takes place the freedom of each individual is usually diminished in one way or another.

Building a hierarchy of leadership in order to organize a large number of people is problematic, to be sure. The issues of leadership and power are usually about goals and the tasks at hand and rarely a philosophy that also considers the people involved. Is opportunity, growth, participation in the community and individual rights an important part of the working philosophy? Is conformity demanded of the group? Is power shared to any degree, and is the organization inclusive or exclusive of others?

Political power is comparatively weak when compared to the examples above and is not our concern here. The power I am most concerned with has to do with the state of our close and personal relationships, whether at home or work. And, this power is not power found within but is external and fleeting. Consider how the power of parents over their children shifts from the parents as they age and grow less able compared to their (now) adult children. No, the power I refer to throughout the book is not in a person, but external to and temporary.

Because power is external and fleeting, leaders who believe that "they themselves" are the power and that it is not due to position, influence, money, etc., are living a fantasy. More importantly, to the degree they abuse their relationships not only do others suffer but they, the leaders, "reap what is sown." Any diminishment of individuals must also diminish their ability to contribute back to their leader and likely to the common good. However, when quality leaders use their power and resources to contribute to the growth of individuals, everyone benefits. There is wisdom and considerable awareness in quality leaders that the power they possess over others is a gift to be shared with others—and that it is not them and infinite.

I have known and experienced some excellent leaders. But, too often I have experienced leaders who used their power more to affect compliance than growth. What many leaders seek are tools as if the interpersonal problems are mechanical or that others are the cause of problems within the organization. They look elsewhere than to themselves for causes and in the process treat symptoms, never considering that they may be the problem. Leaders, in this case, do not accept that they are at the core of their interpersonal and/or organizational problems. It is so easy to see and fault others and very difficult to see and fault one's self.

Many of the greatest philosophers have made the issue of power and leadership the very essence of their philosophy. And yet, why, over thousands of years and hundreds of thousands of leaders, have so few leaders used their power for the "common good"? Why do so many leaders evidence a considerable reluctance to learn about themselves from those who know them best and also to learn from experience? Why have so many leaders not prepared others to lead when they are gone? Here, I relate to those leaders and events I've personally experienced. They and their styles of leadership are what I know, and in the process I have learned a great deal more about myself as a leader and person. This is what I share.

My life experiences and consultant work with other leaders have mixed enough over the years for me to believe I know "good" leadership when I witness it. And, if "good" leadership is understood so is my confidence in how to bring it about for others. It is relatively easy as long as the leaders I work with, deeply and unequivocally, want to be the best leaders (and persons) they can be. It takes a *courageous* person to be *vulnerable* with those most significant to them. These two words are neither to be taken lightly nor are they idealistic jargon or altruistic—but what and who enlightened parents, teachers and leaders are. *Courage* to be and express one's self is the meaning I refer to. *Vulnerable* as I intend it to mean, is being open to the other, without an agenda and to listen, to understand and to confirm that understanding.

To use one's power well and for the good of others is the easiest pathway to success, to problem-awareness, problem-solving, and creative and innovative work. It is an inclusiveness that not only assures participation but a commitment at an "ownership" level of participation.

The following story is worth telling again, again and again. It demonstrates so well that what we have learned in our lives can be unlearned in environments that are safe enough for us to be vulnerable with others. This story also shows that as we let go of our past we are able to replace what we knew (and believed) with what we now begin to know; and with this, our view of our immediate world changes, and so do we.

On a never-to-be-forgotten morning, the following experience took place. It was during our fourth workshop with a doctors' office over a period of about a year and a half. A staff member, who had three years earlier left her Central American country because of civil war asked to speak before we began one of our continuing workshops.

Looking directly at the two leaders across from her, she took a deep breath and shared the following: "When I was a little girl in my small village in Nicaragua, I would go to church each Sunday, where the priest would teach us about our church and how to be good Catholics. The best part was that he, also, told us stories. One day he told us about Jews, and that they were evil, that they killed our Christ, and that we must be very careful because Jews kidnap, kill and drink the blood of children. I remember this story and others about Jews but had never met any until I came to this country.

"When I began to work here, I realized that the two people I worked for are Jews; and what I was told as a child really disturbed my relationships with them. You have always been good to me; but I never trusted you, always thinking what evil must Jews do, and maybe to me one day?

"And then one day," and she looked at me and said, "this man came to us and taught us how to communicate and to be honest with ourselves and those we live and work with. He taught us things I have never heard or experienced before. It meant so much to me to hear this and actually see it happening. I wanted so much to believe that this is the correct way to be and live. Today I feel love for all of you, and for [looking at the doctors] you. I know that Jews do not do what the priest taught us, and that he was wrong and harmed us, not Jews. I am going back home, and I am so much a better person and understand so much more than when I came. I was a child, and now I am a woman and a person. I will let my people know. Thank you."

Her words were spoken with such emotion and candor that not one word was uttered by anyone in the room. Each person in the room, including myself, realized that this moment was very special. It had to do with her being so vulnerable, courageous, present and clear.

No words were exchanged, but the two leaders/owners of the practice got up, walked across to her, and hugged and kissed her. Even now, as I write, I see and feel the love and power of this women and her story in that room. I am sure that each person in our gathering was similarly affected.

I'd like to be able to write that I was fully conscious of what I needed to do and be as a leader, and the power I had to influence my co-workers. But the truth is that I was much too busy; and events dictated my behavior, not my mind or heart. It is one thing to "accidentally" be a good leader, but what if I am not so the next time I have to lead? It is, qualitatively, different when one is aware and intends to nurture as one knows the others also need to be nurtured. Also, and of considerable importance, is to be present in the moment and to relate to what is, and not to what was and the influence of the past. As the leader I am always a student and a teacher when the event to teach presents itself, and never to be forgotten, a leader is a role model. Being conscious of each of these attributes has nothing to do with intentions, it has only to do with "being" itself.

Questions to reflect on: Do parents think about the power and influence they have over their children and consciously use this awareness to nurture the unique being over whom they hold power? Does the child's inner need "to be" have to fight so that their own "will to power" ever sees the light of day? Need there be conflict over the two primary forms of power: the one which needs "to be" and comes from nature, and the other, to conform to what our parents and others *want us to be* in order to meet their and society's expectations?

Parents are our role models for good and bad as will be, to varying degrees, every other person who has power over us. As infants, our basic needs to simply survive are so obviously provided by parents. In the earliest of stages, the newborn actually communicates what is needed, and caregivers understand and meet the needs. Both baby and parents, temporarily, make it work; and mutuality on the part of both the parents and the baby is a reality. For many, this time period does not last long; and power and the history of the parents, as does the baby's need to be itself, enter into a conflicting relationship.

So initially, parents and baby are connected; and whether conscious, buried in the subconscious or hormonal, power throughout this brief period comes in the form of love. Too soon power begins to manifest itself through the ways parents have been themselves conditioned. If the relationship continues to be expressed through listening, sharing, touching, giving and sensitivity, power is used well and nurtures another self to "be itself." If and when power is used to force compliance to what parents consider acceptable behavior or is given with an expected response in mind, power is misused or even harmful. As a result, conditioning takes place, and the more powerful wins over the less powerful. But this is a lie that has been perpetrated for thousands of years: that one human can actually win over another human and all benefit. It is only forced behavior that is won, but not the inner person.

ALL BENEFIT WHEN POWER IS USED WELL

I have experienced excellent cooperation brought about through quality relationships, healthy Inner Circles, and the ingredients and actuality of Genuine Dialogue. Both the Inner Circle and Genuine Dialogue are so important that each has its own chapter and also is briefly defined in the Glossary. I suggest checking the Glossary once again to be sure that you understand the importance I place on terms such as Genuine Dialogue and Inner Circle. For example, I believe we each have an Inner Circle, but most are accidental and dysfunctional, and little understood for its potential value. How is Genuine Dialogue to be experienced when one's Inner Circle members are themselves less than authentic, unsafe, insecure and dependent?

Because of a healthy and optimally functioning Inner Circle, the experience of Genuine Dialogue, quality communication and interpersonal relationships, moves throughout the whole of a body of people whether personal or that of an organization. When an Inner Circle is inclusive, mutual and nurturing beginning at the top and is shared with those less powerful, it spreads to others. Power, control and influence continue to exist (they always do), but are positive forces growing relationships and organizations.

To compare the above cooperative environment and organization with one where communication takes place through a fixed hierarchy, directives, written, verbal and top-down communication is akin to comparing a verdant jungle to a moonscape. In fact, there is no competition between cooperation that takes place through face-to-face dialogue that is mutual and monologue. The cooperatively led organization maximizes its people power and uses its human and non-human resources efficiently and effectively. Top down organizations with many levels of diminishing power waste both human resources and non-human resources.

People thrive in the nurturing, open and power-sharing environment that makes personal growth possible. This is true even if previous experiences have damaged people's trust of those in power. If something has been learned, it can be unlearned. It is a matter of how safe people feel and the safer they feel the more likely they dare to become vulnerable once again. Outsider influence, such as a mentor, does not make it happen; but it will happen through the conscious efforts of the leader demonstrating through words and behavior the courage to be vulnerable.

Also, there are the few people who will more quickly welcome the opportunity to fully and candidly participate. They make it easier for others who may need more assurance of safety. When one has been deeply hurt and conditioned to not trust those in power, it takes time, patience and proof as only perceived by each individual.

The final story of this chapter about the woman from Central America defines what a safe and cooperative environment may achieve through the efforts of honest, thoughtful good leadership and the empowerment of others. We need to accept that our power as parents, teachers and leaders to influence another's life is not well understood and maybe (for too many) not understood at all. This is true relative to any leader possessing the power to potentially change a person's life. When power is used to empower our significant others as compared to over-powering and abusing them, the result is a more loving home, a more productive organization and growth. The process is the same in a relationship of two or many. All humans need dialogue, a feeling of being understood, mutuality and respect. Are there better ways for this to happen? I think not.

What more is there to say about those in power who are responsible for the crucible that is the environment whether in an organization or in their personal lives? How much better it is to deliberately seek the best possible communication between employers and employees, parents to each other and children, and teachers to students. And, more importantly, how much better it is to understand that to the degree we are with and for each other, so do we all benefit both within and without.

Finally, why is it necessary to have a mentor who is an outsider rather than part of the body of the office or organization? It's because it is necessary to show that the one in power is able and willing to share his or her power with another, even a stranger and yes, to show subordinates that the one in power is a student to a teacher. This cannot be an act or simply a demonstration of, "See, I can listen and learn." The mentor has to be able to take and use power over and against the leader when the leader, unconsciously, attempts to retake the role as the power person in the room. It is a "teachable moment" for the mentor, a learning opportunity for the leader, and is felt by the others in the room that the leader is serious about growth and mutuality with those they live and work with.

Power in the hands of quality mentors, as with any quality leader, is used when it must be used. Equivocation is not for them. And like all leaders, mentors need to create learning and open environments against what exists. Change in perceptions becomes essential. But, to dismantle what exists must fail without the full approval and support from the leader. After all, it is construction of the leader's making that needs to be deconstructed. Obviously, this takes a courageous leader who is unafraid to be vulnerable with one's own subordinates. This dialogue is only temporarily meaningful coming from the mentor and has no staying power. When it begins to come from the leader it is then that we begin to see a change in the behavior of others.

What in our lives is not about power, whether used to benefit our being and becoming or shape us as others in power would have us be? And does this use of power not shape our world and the way we live in it?

CHAPTER 2

TRUE ENTREPRENEURS

They are different
Blinders on, intense focus
No give, win or lose.

n 1949, as described more fully in Chapter 1, I created and operated a summer
day camp for boys and girls in Malibu Canyon, California. It quickly grew
beyond my expectations and intentions into a large and complex operation.
In fact, an operation of this type would be impossible in the Los Angeles that
exists today. The time spent in picking up and transporting children to camp and
returning them safely to their homes Monday through Friday would literally take
up the day and be much too dangerous on the road. Day camps that flourish in Los
Angeles today are neighborhood-based, where the children live and close to parks
and recreation centers.

The camp's success kept prodding me, and I could not escape an inner
voice that spoke to me about owning our own land. The entrepreneur in me,

a word I did not understand at the time, was making itself known. Up to this point, I was what I needed to be: the owner and leader of a going and growing business as well as a student at UCLA heading for a professional career as a child psychologist.

After graduation, I continued as a part-time graduate student, worked for the Los Angeles education system and operated camp. Instead of finding it all too much, I discovered that my heart was clearly in being my own boss, owning and operating my own organization. Although finishing graduate school and working for the Los Angeles Board of Education offered a more secure future, I was more attracted to the idea of freedom to work for myself instead of being part of an organization and the security it offered. With each of the different options pulling at me, I knew I could not follow all the paths and do each well. I felt that I needed to make a choice about which direction to go in and where to place my energies. Do I complete the doctoral program, work for the school system or be my own person dictated by my own philosophy?

The hidden entrepreneur in me spoke loudest and felt right with me as I began to realize how important it was to be independent. This required that I find and purchase land where we would then build and operate a camp for girls and boys. This became my vision, and I confidently chose to be my own leader rather than have others directing my life. I do not remember having any fear or doubts about making so drastic a decision. In fact, I felt excited about taking on the challenge to discover, purchase and build our own facility.

My wife of one year—my most important supporter and confident—and I began setting down the conditions that had to be met before we could consider any piece of land. Wilderness land was our preference. It had to be large enough to contain a community of about 150-plus people, cabins to live in, dining and indoor and (mostly) outdoor recreational facilities as well as plenty of acreage and space to do our own thing. Also, and hopefully, we would have a lake on the land or at least the potential to create one, and space for every type of sport and activity, and finally meadows and forest. We needed access to electricity, plenty of good clean water and accessibility during all seasons and weather conditions. We also envisioned enough space around the property so that the noise sure to be generated would not be an issue for any possible neighbors. Also, we needed to be reasonably close to the Los Angeles area since this was where our *campers* lived and we were well known. Relative to it all, it is said that if you're going to dream, dream big—and we did.

It is important to note that we had little income and no savings, but while creating our vision it seemed not to matter. Maybe visions are supposed to be about a fantasy journey or picture and that only when visions get close to being possible does reality begin to set in. It's not that we did not talk about money and where it would come from; we simply believed that one way or another it would be taken care of. In any case, the money issue did nothing to dampen our determination to seek out the ideal piece of property. All we could do was to take one step at a time, and finding land that met our vision was the step we needed to take. We had no intention of being denied our dream simply because we did not have the cash to make it happen. We had the knowledge of operations and enough energy to make it happen, at least to the degree we believed necessary.

Having placed our dream on paper, we set aside weekends to explore California by beginning as close to home as possible. We made circles around Los Angeles, and traveling every direction led us quickly to greater distances from home. Eventually, with our accumulating knowledge about land prices, our search took us further from Los Angeles. In fact, we ended up one weekend driving about six-hundred miles north to Redding, California. At that time, Redding was a town of 9,000 residents surrounded by lovely rolling hills and near the headwaters of the Sacramento River. It was the fall of the year when we discovered the area, and it looked wonderfully green and inviting as much rain had fallen during the previous weeks. Who knew that in the summertime this same place becomes hot enough to fry eggs on the street?

When we began our search, we never expected to end up far from Los Angeles. L.A. was our market, and we had the following and quality reputation to fill any camp to the brim. To go too far from our source would be a huge risk that we did not expect to have to deal with. Yet, we found ourselves in the hills rising out of the Redding valley and heading towards a little village by the name of Round Mountain, a twelve-hour drive from Los Angeles. In spite of this problem of distance, we continued to believe that when we saw the right piece of land we would know it, own it and children would come to it. In retrospect, if we had allowed the many problems we would have to face interfere with our vision, we would have gone back to our jobs with the school system and graduate school.

By the end of this very eventful day and after an exhausting search of the surrounding countryside, we found nothing that met our needs. Weary and hungry but not disappointed, we needed to begin the long journey back home. We had to keep in mind that we were both still with the Los Angeles Education System, and Monday was a workday. We wondered how much further from Los Angeles to look next (note: not in despair or with thoughts of giving up but simply, "just where we go next?"). I believe it was our taking one step at a time that may have played a big part in keeping us on our journey.

While searching the countryside northeast of Redding for some sign of land that met our needs, we lost our way and could not find any signs to help us get back to Redding and Highway 99 South to Los Angeles. There were no freeways at that time, and 99 South was a two-lane road that went through every little farm community, very slowly, all the way home.

Searching for direction, I spotted a man standing in the rain and darkness on the road across from a small country cafe and bar; and I stopped to ask him the way back to Redding. It was apparent that he had been drinking heavily, and rather than give us directions he demanded to know why we were there in the first place. Out of pure frustration, I gave a quick answer about why we were there and what we were looking for. Almost incoherently, he said, "I know the man you ought to see. He's got all kind of forest and meadowland, and I'm sure he would be happy to sell you some land." He also told us we were near where the landowner lived and we ought to "see him right now." We had turned every other stone during a year and more of searching, so why not one more "knock?"

We found the landowner's home up a country road. By this time it was raining heavily and in nearly complete darkness. Feeling a bit foolish, I knocked on his door. A rough-looking man opened the door, and I blurted out why we were there. Apparently he saw no problem with our looking for land and simply asked, "Do you ride a horse?" I answered, "Yes!" He then told me, "Show up tomorrow about 9:00 in the morning and we'll go see what I think might work for you." Magic, providence, blessings, answered prayers or whatever (?) does happen at the most unexpected moments; but not if you don't make yourself available to it. "Ask and it will be given to you; seek and you will find; knock and the door will be open to you," Matthew 7:7. Life is surely stranger than fiction. Be careful what you ask and work for. It's liable to all come true.

The following morning, in a heavy downpour, sitting on a big brown horse, I saw my dream come to life all around me. It was 80 acres of virgin forest—Sugar Pine, Ponderosa, Blue and White Fir, large Oak, Black Walnut—truly a deciduous and evergreen forest of great beauty. We later learned that at its 3,000-foot elevation it had all of the forest growth that the mid-California country offers up to an elevation of 8,000 feet in the Sierra Nevada.

The land contained a large natural meadow and a beautiful meandering stream. Another smaller meadow looked perfect to construct and fill a three- to five-acre lake. A stream of water came right out of the rocks on a small hill, supplying enough clear and pure water for a village. Also essential to our vision, the land was surrounded by thousands of wilderness acres yet was only one mile to an electricity source, fifteen miles to a small town needed for basic supplies and medical services, and forty miles to the biggest city in the area, Redding.

Sitting on the horse in the heavy downpour, I was ecstatic. The land was my dreams come true. The owner asked, laconically, "Can you afford $5,000?" My immediate thought was that he was asking for a down payment! I gulped and saw the miracle disappear behind the reality of our financial limits. He must have seen something in my body language because he then added, "Can you afford $50 down and $50 each month until the $5,000 is paid off?" When I heard his offer and understood the full price and payments, my hand shot out to his and we made the deal right there in the heavy rain, he and I sitting on our horses. Our vision had become a reality.

We had boldly and fortuitously made our way through steps numbers 1, 2 and 3: search, discover and buy. Now, step 4 became the issue at hand. Where do we get the money to actually build a facility on our land? And this was only the beginning. Even as we set out to find the solutions to what I believed to be the immediate problem, many other serious obstacles appeared. First, we discovered that the spring source was not on our land but was owned by our neighbor to the south, a lumber company that wanted the land we purchased for their own use. Their plan was to deforest the area of valuable virgin timber and to turn the land into a camp for their employees. Worse yet for us, there was no dedicated easement to the land. The one mile of dirt road that was the only possible entry to the land crossed through the lumber company's land. We were land-locked. "No problem!"

Two weeks after the "horseback purchase," I drove the six-hundred miles from Los Angeles to explore the land more thoroughly. When I arrived at the dirt road to our land, the road was closed off by a large spanking brand-new wood and Iron Gate. It was painted bright silver with a big sign attached warning: "No Trespassing!" with the name and address of the lumber company imprinted on the sign. I immediately drove back to the lumber company office in Redding.

After a brief encounter at the information desk I was led to the office of the manager/owner. He knew why I had come and candidly stated that I would have to give up on my plan to purchase "that piece of land." The lumber company felt it was perfect for their needs and planned to begin work immediately. With his company's designs clearly and succinctly stated, he proceeded to place a .45 cal. handgun on his desk. "You really do not belong here," he growled. I leaned over the desk, and with my face about four inches from his, said, "Go f— yourself!" More determined than before, I walked out of the office and immediately drove back to my land, my vision of the ideal children's camp.

I now know that only a true entrepreneur would take the actions I did at that time. Using a chain I attached to my car, I pulled the gate from the ground and dragged it to where our land began and the dirt road ended. With a bit of inspired hard work, I attached the gate solidly to two trees that, as if planned, perfectly closed off the entrance to camp. And, with my own chain and lock securing it, I enjoyed walking and touching our own land. Trust me; I had a long but wonderful drive back home.

The story ends, miraculously, well. A large national lumber company purchased the land belonging to our unfriendly neighbor. I found my way to their main office in Northern California, and we were able to arrange a trade of unneeded forest land for the spring and the full use of the road. We built a wonderful fresh-water lake, and the beautiful virgin forest and meadows became a co-ed resident camp that brought rich experiences, lifelong memories and lessons to many children, teens and adults. Finally, there were numerous young people from our camp in Los Angeles who volunteered to do whatever was asked of them to help this whole adventure come to reality. Nobody, not even the strongest and best entrepreneurs, do what they do and achieve alone. Today, more than sixty years later, the memories continue to bring emotions and lessons to the surface for many people. Like ripples on a pond, the good, nurturing environment and relationships that were camp continue to influence our former campers and staff to this day.

What is said about any journey was certainly true for us: One step at a time, staying present in the moment and learning every minute of the way. Each event to come would dictate our behavior. For us, such issues as driving twelve-hundred-plus miles on a weekend seeking land to purchase, and it had to be the right kind of land; knocking on a strange door in a rainstorm in the darkness; checking out the land on a horse; purchasing without knowing all of what we purchased; being threatened by words and a handgun; removing the sign barricading the road to our property was what we had to do. Events most certainly dictated our behavior. Not one issue proved to be insurmountable, but simply an unanticipated challenge waiting to be tackled as directly and immediately as possible. Were we the "true entrepreneurs" I refer to in this chapter? I never thought about this until I wrote the book, but it feels like we might have been then and again in events and adventures to come.

WHAT DRIVES TRUE ENTREPRENEURS?

True entrepreneurs create something from nothing. They are *initiators*, visionaries and doers who are going to reach their goal or, literally, burn themselves out in the process. True entrepreneurs are repeatedly knocked down but not out—they are never out unless the road dead-ends; and then they may find a way to build a new road.

One step at a time, staying present in the moment and learning from each experience is the way of the true entrepreneur. Each event to come dictates behavior, not preconceived notions. Their problem is hardly one of energy or creativity, and they are like a laser beam. Their focus and determination is what separates them from others who would call themselves entrepreneurs.

So what are the lessons extracted from the preceding story? What comes from an entrepreneur's vision and effort is, more often than not, unexpected; and each turn in the road is new. For true entrepreneurs, setbacks that might stop an ordinary entrepreneur rarely keep them from going forward; and they rise like the Phoenix from the ashes again and again. They travel their own learning curve, alert to what happens; and every meeting is a possibility of connection and perhaps new venues of which they will take advantage. They are open to mentors but never to another's control. They are not about the journey although they learn invaluable lessons from each event, accidental and otherwise. Their concentration become more about ends not means.

TRUE ENTREPRENEURS, IN GENERAL

- They do not rest or seek comfort. Theirs is an all-out 24/7 effort.
- They have a propensity to do what they do without first having a well-thought strategy.
- They are emotional, but also thoughtful. And they grow as they go; they do not remain what they were for long. They learn from personal experience, and it is their most important teacher. Denials and barriers only add fuel to the fire that burns within them.
- They are willing to risk it all, including the resources of family and friends.
- They will not back down but will back out and try another way.
- Failure is not an option.

True entrepreneurs use their "will to be" beyond what other humans are willing to risk. What they desire and seek beyond this inner drive is achievement of goals. And, their extrinsic goals vary from pure social efforts for the common good to the material and power they intend to use over others. True entrepreneurs do not do what they do to put food on the table; their goals are far more complex. No, what these special people envision is something beyond the natural drive to be that all humans are born with. External resources are important to them, but losing or making money are only issues to deal with along the way. Challenges are logs thrown on the existing fire and will be overcome one way or another, and they will be themselves.

All entrepreneurs face emotional, intellectual and physical uncertainties. Many have mountains to climb, dangerous rivers to cross, and dark and dense forests to get through with no trail map to guide them. Each problem must be dealt with mano e mano and with absolute conviction. And since there is no guarantee of success, it has to be the entrepreneurs' belief in their own self, those they trust and the hard work that has the greatest impact on transforming vision into reality.

We find true entrepreneurs in every area of human endeavor. The "social entrepreneurs" seek to aid starving populations and the disenfranchised; and those who build schools, health facilities, water systems and in general give all they have to making the world a better place for those who have little or nothing. They, too, are powerful; and they need to be in order to overcome ignorance, indifference, and political and economic barriers. Name the area and the field, and we find true entrepreneurs.

What distinguishes true entrepreneurs from ordinary entrepreneurs are not words but their use of power, personal and otherwise, that might either propel them to success or destroy them. The possibility of failure increases when true entrepreneurs have too little control over what they feel and think needs to be done. This is because they simply focus on what needs to be done—and not necessarily the consequences that are sure to follow any act.

True entrepreneurs are the people who have, past and present, gone to the extreme for what they believe in and are committed to attain. In the process they use relationships, both close and distant, they believe may help them. They use power, regardless of source, human and otherwise, that they can garner to this end. The need for power is essential to the true entrepreneur and how they use this power makes a considerable difference in whether they succeed or fail.

As stated above, there are true entrepreneurs who seek social change having nothing to do with the building of businesses and the seeking of monetary gains. They are every bit as passionate and focused as any true business entrepreneur. In fact, we find attributes of this type in super athletes, entertainers and professionals of every kind. For them it is less about power, money and winning over others, but achieving their own expectations they place on themselves.

True entrepreneurs are rarely swashbuckling, charismatic extroverts. Most do not do what they do to be recognized, acclaimed and honored. Yet many come across as dynamite salespeople, but this is not how they see themselves. It is not their appearance to others and what the other see, but their inner force that propels them. They are the "different ones" amongst us. They intend to bring change that is significant and enduring. They are found in every time period and every culture and place. True entrepreneurs may be pains and trouble-makers or gifts to society—only time and achievement tells which.

True entrepreneurs are individuals, not a committee. They are self-motivated to push and pull to achieve their goals, and they will enlist others to aid them in every possible way. This is how they create the organization that surrounds them. And this is where, when they achieve their goal that their behavior must change from that of an entrepreneur to a leader.

Once an entrepreneur's goal is attained this brings a whole different set of opportunities and problems. For many it is the need for considerably more capital and different expertise from others. Also, true entrepreneurs must recognize the need to trade some of their power and creation in order to take their vision, now a reality, to places and heights they are incapable of reaching on their own. It is here that the separation between a true entrepreneur and an entrepreneur is made apparent. The story that follows clarifies this.

Some years back I was invited by an investment firm to create a leadership training program. The firm was aggressively investing in small to midsized companies that they believed had the potential to be taken public, and the firm appeared determined to do what was best for each company they had selected. I optimistically thought the leadership training program would be successful with the firm's apparently strong support.

The head of the investment firm informed me that they needed a leadership training program for businesses they selected to invest capital in with the goal of taking them public. The selection process of which companies to invest in was done by a team of experts whose task was to do "due diligence" on the business, the entrepreneur and operating leader. Their plan, I was informed, was to provide the owner/operator with the best possible leadership skills and to aid in every possible way to grow the business. The firm accepted my proposal and recommendations for assisting selected entrepreneurs and operating leaders (most wore both hats) to become effective leaders. Other teachers were employed to hold training programs having to do with every possible business discipline. The investment firm also put in place numerous checks, balances and "numbers" people to oversee the whole operation.

It certainly seemed to me that every possible resource, professional and financial, was going to be made available to grow each firm to its full potential. The investment firm's goal to take the more successful companies to a public stock offering appeared to me to be well thought out. If and when this was achieved, considerable profits were expected to be made by the investment firm and, most likely, to the original entrepreneur/operator of the business.

The education plan as presented by the investment firm appeared to cover what was needed to grow entrepreneurs and their companies. This plan covered intensive leadership education and continuing access to a broad range of resources including, but not limited to, marketing, sales, legal and financial professionals guiding the operation. My responsibility was to mentor each entrepreneur to become a more effective leader. But as I learned later on, being both a successful entrepreneur and an excellent leader is a difficult transition to achieve and most do not make it.

When first approached with the proposal to teach entrepreneurs leadership skills, I believed that to provide leadership tools was all that was needed. It took considerable experience and years of consulting with a variety of organizations before I had the epiphany that teaching merely leadership skills is a dead-end journey that wastes time, money and energy. In this particular situation, I had no opportunity to discover this truth, but it did come at a later time.

Much to my surprise and disappointment, the training programs never took place. Classrooms the firm built were never used, and neither were any of the consultants. Apparently, building for show was all about dough, that is, the classrooms were built in order to attract firms to the investment firm's program. The investment firm staged a remarkably visual and expensive setting knowing exactly what they were doing, and why. And it became clear that we, the consultants, were part of the staging and nothing more.

When a firm passed the due diligence tests and was acquired for its potential to go public, the company had to give up controlling interest to the investment bankers. This meant that power was transferred from the entrepreneurs to outside professional "managers," who, not surprisingly, were strangers to the company's employees and culture. These managers were to operate and market the company the investment firm controlled. In other words, strangers with a strong numbers orientation and the single-mindedness of going public were placed in power positions. They were not leaders, but controllers of a financial investment.

As I disappointedly learned, the vision of support sold to the entrepreneurs and to the educators, of whom I was one, was not going to happen. But it was not a fruitless experience. I harvested a huge amount of new understanding of how certain businesses operate.

What I witnessed was professionals taking power over the entrepreneurs, who were, not so subtly, placed in subordinate roles to new and specific goal-directed leaders. What were once inclusive and open relationships between the original entrepreneur and employees was replaced by people who had no handle on or interest in the existing company's culture. The professional "bean counters" concentrated on bringing "the numbers" in line with the goals now being set by the investment firm. As a result, the company environment began to change and become disconcerting to employees who felt things were not as they were and with this a sense of despair and helplessness. They had been a part of an exciting adventure to suddenly perceiving being used as pawns. This is what resulted from the dramatic change of leadership in the casino-resort story in Chapter 1. Any change of leadership is going to alter an environment, and if quality leaders take over, are open and inclusive, things will still change, but do no harm and likely good in the process. But, if new leaders have an exclusive, preset agenda and impose a more traditional hierarchy, things will change, and not for the better.

The leader of the investment firm was a well-respected leader in his world of finance and investment. He understood the power of money and the methodology of taking small firms public. I had much to learn about his world and what drives the way too many businesses are led and operated. This unique experience added to my own entrepreneurial and financial challenges with power and money people, and I grew in my understanding about his world. But I also learned, not happily, that the minds of business people who hold power are too often closed to my world of human relationships, dialogue and mutuality, all at great loss to them and to what they do and their eventual goals.

During a relatively loose conversation the investment leader told me: "Out of every thirty companies we invest in and work with, only one, on average, is actually taken public. But this one makes us enough of a profit that we can write off the other twenty-nine, smiling all the way to the bank. It's ultimately all about money, return on investment, and the sooner the better. Our goals are short-term, and longevity is unimportant to our strategy." Time and serious work with many organizations has since confirmed for me that the intent to hit the home run is too common a reality. This, rather than playing for the long term, one step at a time, and for the good of all involved in the bigger picture, appears to be endemic to our business culture.

I have often wondered what would have been the outcomes if those thirty obviously reasonably well-functioning firms had been given the complete program and education format that they expected. And if the original entrepreneurs could possibly have been taught to be quality leaders with real power remaining in their hands, what would have resulted? What percentage of the thirty small companies would have prospered and then have been taken public successfully? I will never know, but with the knowledge I've acquired since then I have no doubt that considerably more than one would have been successful. Apparently, if I am only partially correct in my assessment, considerable money and potential were wasted in the investment firm's endeavor to make money. Not only did most of the small businesses they invested in fail, but so did the investment firm. Apparently, their one-out-of-thirty goal did not work.

When capital and control are infused into a business for "lift-off," a fundamental mistake is made by changing leadership. What trust and structure does exist in the organization at so crucial a time is taken away, and this results in helplessness and anger in the ranks. Unless dealt with openly, deliberately and inclusively, this is a recipe for disaster. But even if leadership change takes place cautiously, the environment will change; and this is an unknown by those most affected. It is to be expected that whenever power is transferred from one person to another, so a philosophy towards relationships and power will change as well.

BECOMING A SUCCESSFUL ENTREPRENEUR TAKES HARD WORK

All entrepreneurial efforts, as long as they are legal, moral, ethical and principled, have the potential to do "good" beyond just achieving goals. Since most people who try to walk this path fail, it may be of value to isolate the laser-like characteristics of the true entrepreneur who does succeed. Also, will education and the efforts given to raising a budding entrepreneur's awareness levels make a difference? Perhaps, in the process, it is better to weed out those who are unable to make the full commitment before dedicating time, resources, and physical and emotional costs to being entrepreneurial.

It may be a stretch, but making a commitment to do physical exercise, for example, makes for an interesting comparison. People join health clubs all the time, but how many hire a professional trainer, learn proper exercise techniques, and alter their eating habits, diets and lifestyle? And how many then continue with the program for a lifetime, or much less, or even for the membership period they signed on for? The majority who appear to commit soon quit. Making promises to one's self to commit to exercise and then stay with it is a waste of words and empty of substance for a considerable number of people. Simply saying I want to be an entrepreneur is much the same, and the people are probably similar.ow wis

One hopeful entrepreneur gets up at 8 in the morning, has a cup of coffee, reads the paper, organizes the day, plans what to do and whom to call and may even have decided that certain actions are too aggressive or presumptuous. Another is up four times during the night to write down what will not leave their head. This person rises at 4:00 in the morning ready to do what needs to be done. For this entrepreneur there are only the challenges to make something happen and to move forward as soon as yesterday.

Do true entrepreneurs actually operate in this dynamic manner? Without question, true entrepreneurs do exactly this because the vision becomes so pervasive that any and all possible pitfalls that may be waiting along their path simply do not exist for them. Only the vision, the dream dictates their actions. If being present and in the moment is a big part of living and good psychological health, true entrepreneurs are perfect examples. When events blow up in their face, they have to deal with the event, now and creatively. They do not speculate on "what ifs" and doubts that brake forward movement. "Get it on!" and "Do it now!" are their mantras.

In comparison, pseudo-entrepreneurs do not go blindly forward at the rising of the sun. Most of these entrepreneurs attempt to piece the puzzle together before time and effort are seriously expended. Real barriers and those not yet seen become hills and mountains, both real and imaginary, to climb over or go around. And, what is the effect of naysayers who are sure to add fuel to doubts and resistance that the budding entrepreneurs already feel?

There are a great variety of entrepreneurs. Some dream dreams but never get out of the gate or bed. Others do get up and out, but stumble and fail because of being slow to learn and/or give in to frustrations and despair. Others burst out with great speed and energy only to give in to fatigue in a short distance. They are fast, for the short term, but soon run out of gas. Also, there are people who, like true entrepreneurs, are determined to do what they must to achieve their dream. But in this case, it is becoming a professional that drives them; and they, too, similar to true entrepreneurs, pay a huge price in commitment to their goal. Their vision is to become a doctor, lawyer, engineer or any of many professions that require discipline, formal education, considerable cost, time and effort; and they, too, are true entrepreneurs. How different are dedicated students/professionals from social entrepreneurs and business entrepreneurs if they are true to their vision and goal? Not much.

ENTREPRENEURS NEED MENTORS

Mentors need to be considered necessary for true entrepreneurs whether they are working towards the business they dream of or becoming a professional. An experienced mentor with essential stories and ability to teach from what they have gone through personally is best. Mentors are sought by student entrepreneurs in order to maximize their self understanding as well as to provide effective relationship tools. It is through relationships where trust and accountability are established that entrepreneurs become exponentially more able.

When I operated in an entrepreneurial mode and at the same time tried to lead our camp organization, my wife would continuously admonish me for being too much in the future. That is, I was not tending to what was at hand and being present as she believed necessary. What I was doing is giving considerable energy to what was to be my next step rather than dealing with what I had on my plate. Another way of saying the same thing: I would identify the issues; and once action was initiated or set in place, I would leave it to others to take care of the details. As new issues kept erupting from the ones already dealt with, new and challenging tasks would take me there—and the unknown "there" was most attractive. A knowledgeable mentor would have had a strong influence on my behavior, especially if I had been wise enough to seek mentors instead of letting experience and hard knocks be my teacher. As fortune would have it mentors did pop into my life and their influence and impact on the paths I followed made my work and, ultimately, this book possible.

POWER IN THE HANDS OF TRUE ENTREPRENEURS

This chapter is about true entrepreneurs as differentiated from those who simply claim the title. My concern in this chapter is not the common entrepreneurs who do what they do in order to make a living or to create work when work is not easily obtainable. These people make up the majority of what are called entrepreneurs, and I applaud what effort they do give to taking control of their lives. Common entrepreneurs are found throughout the world. They are not unique to any country, culture, age or time. Although some cultures nurture an entrepreneurial spirit, there are cultures that do their best to stifle and restrict anything that smacks of being different or challenging to the status quo. Our concern here is to awaken and nurture a true entrepreneurial spirit because the benefits, when realized, may be considerable to all.

A hidden but exciting potential are the entrepreneurs who lie buried within the organization for which they work. There are budding entrepreneurs everywhere, but many will not place themselves in jeopardy by speaking out. By choosing to be anonymous they play the role of compliant employee and yet possess an immense potential to contribute to their organization. These individuals need to be discovered and nurtured to be their creative best, to innovate, to problem-solve, to break out of the box in which they have been confined or confine themselves. If discovered and nurtured, that is, given the opportunity and resources the true entrepreneur within takes over; and they and the organization reap the rewards.

When potential entrepreneurs hide or our hidden as "worker bees" in firms, believing or fearing that they do not have the capabilities to make it on their own, they may be fulfilling a self induced belief or one imposed on them. Regardless, what they do possess are ideas and visions about making things around them easier, better, more efficient, productive and even innovative. As employees, they have much to offer their employer but are rarely appropriately nurtured or even discovered so that they can make potentially valuable contributions to the firm.

However, when reluctant entrepreneurs are discovered and nurtured the possibility exists that they just might bring unique value to the firm. Quality leaders know and seek this from those they lead. An enlightened leader will make full use of this very human possibility. It is also likely that the uncovering of one creative person will lead to others being found. The "good" of an open and nurturing leader has a way of spreading throughout an organization. Evolving from monologue to dialogue and its vital importance to relationship is made starkly apparent throughout the book.

ENTREPRENEURS HAVE EXISTED FROM THE BEGINNING OF HISTORY

Throughout humankind's history there have been individuals who challenged the envelope they lived in. They may have lived in a cave but decided that living outside and closer to water was better. It may have not been safer, but this did not stop them. They took great risks but survived, and others followed the original risk-taker. Fortunately for humanity's growth, a few people will always push the envelope. Simply stated, the true entrepreneurs among us dare to think and act in innovative ways that often break into completely new territory. They are special people who will challenge cultural conventions. Such people bring change when successful; and often, even when they fail to achieve their goal they leave a path so others can follow in their footsteps. True entrepreneurs are the path makers and creators among us.

Most of us know the frightening challenge it is to dare to think and act differently when we live and work in environments that suppress individuality and creativity. This problem has always existed. But some humans, despite restrictions, go fearlessly into the unknown and fight against what keeps them from being. Too many in positions of power attempt to shape those they lead and to corral the free thinkers. Conflict happens, and this is particularly true as babies attempt to explore and know the world around them. But it is also true of political, business and social organizations that too often suppress the entrepreneurial spirit of the people who serve them. Acting in an entrepreneurial manner may push against walls and expectations of those in power; it is often dangerous for those individuals who choose to do things in ways that challenge existing rules and borders.

Sometimes a story turns out to be a spectacular example of how important entrepreneurs, in one form or another, are to others and their organization. It is totally unlike the paragraph above that refers to environments in general. I worked for a considerable time with an unusual owner/leader, a very willing and bright student who shared the following story with me. Experiences like this ought not to be an exception, but the rule.

He had just earned his Ph.D. when he was offered a job with a Silicon Valley firm. It wasn't long before he was given projects to work on that others had worked on, but had failed. This particular problem called for a certain but expensive and precise tool he believed essential to the possible solution to the project he was assigned. Being relatively new with the firm he was reluctant to ask for this new technology though he believed without the instrument he was unable to go beyond where he was. One day, after taking a few deep breaths he approached his immediate boss and explained what he was trying to do and that he needed a particular, but expensive tool. The boss did not hesitate a moment but told him to order the instrument. Although the cost of this instrument exceeded the young man's yearly salary, his boss, a co-owner of the business, emphasized his full support of his employee. "Don't worry about me or others giving you approval to do what you need to do. You decide what you need, when you need it, and get it."

The purchase price proved to be totally insignificant compared to what resulted. The young engineer had invented something a much larger publicly traded company wanted so badly that it purchased his firm for a huge price. The firm he worked for gave him a large bonus for his work, but also invited him to join a new company they were building as a partner. In a few years his new firm was purchased by another public company, and he and his wife became instant millionaires.

What needs to be pointed out is that although he was the inventor and triggered what followed, without the attitude and instant support of his leader none of this would have or could have taken place. If entrepreneurs and innovators do not make themselves known and speak candidly, which requires safe-enough environments, their potential will never see the light of day without someone to lift and support them. So much is lost when people are treated as powerless objects as compared to being treated with respect, as equals and thereby empowered to maximize their being.

GROWING FROM ENTREPRENEURS TO LEADERS

Let's assume that a successful series of moves, hard work and some plain old good luck leads to achieving a business goal. Does this mean that the vision is complete and that everyone lives happily thereafter? This rarely happens because everything takes longer than expected, and problems will arise from unlikely and unanticipated places. Until an idea that is brought to life begins to generate its own capital/resources, more of everything is almost always needed. More capitol may be required, but by seeking outside capital, true entrepreneurs often experience unforeseen consequences that enter into their plans and actions. What may occur is a conflict having to do with power and control between the entrepreneurs who create and the people behind the money. It is, after all, my own story.

When outside money is involved, protecting and insuring all involved may result in serious problems in the relationship between the entrepreneurs and the providers. In this case, the investors may want their own person in a position of overseeing and leading the operation. By embedding outsiders into the entrepreneurs' organizations, particularly if the positions of power and authority conflict with the entrepreneurs, dysfunction is more than likely. To attempt to take control over entrepreneurs' creations while they still hold the position of authority is to miss the essence of who they are as a person. It does not work.

This is why dialogue, and ultimately Genuine Dialogue, between entrepreneurs and those they work with and those who have the resources are so essential. It is also why an outside mediator/mentor may save the day. The problems I discovered and worked to facilitate as a consultant were that all parties had their own views and expectations of the organization and the part they played in it. To make everyone's expectations known and to come to an understanding and agreement on the power structure, the funding and continuing support, as well as the direction the entity needed to take was fundamental if probable barriers were to be identified before hand and possibly resolved. Too frequently, the barriers between entrepreneurs and investors are known but hidden. Is there a better way than placing every possible issue on the table for basic *face-to-face communication* and actually listening and understanding each other? Is agreement likely to take place before a problem actually becomes full blown or after? We all ought to know the answer to that.

I may have been a true entrepreneur during certain periods of my life. My behavior certainly gives me cause to believe so. I know that I used whatever resources I could harness to arrive at our ends. Like true entrepreneurs, who do not see or expect any tigers or lions waiting in the bushes to pounce on them, I was unaware and did not fear the jungle that I strode through because I wore blinders. I focused only on the end goal. Once the goal was realized other needs came into play. This is the story I relate in chapter six where we build and operate a large youth facility, but the property values increases considerably and the investors want to sell the property for a quick profit. The investors and I did not become an Inner Circle nor do I remember ever having experienced anything approaching Genuine Dialogue between us. I think it was at this time that I came to understand what is meant by: "Business is business."

Personal experiences such as the story that unfolded in Las Vegas underscore that there are important differences between the common entrepreneur and the true entrepreneur. Both need plenty of resources in order to bring their dream/goal to reality whether from their own pockets or that of others. They must tap every lead and person they know often before reaching their goal; and too often without knowing what will be needed once their goal is reached.

Common entrepreneurs will do what others may ask or demand of them including giving up their power to influence and control decision-making. True entrepreneurs are incapable of being bought. Ceding control to someone else for any price does not exist in their makeup. Both true entrepreneurs and common entrepreneurs may sell what they have created; but true entrepreneurs are incapable of selling themselves whereas common entrepreneurs do so easily. This is an important distinction between them.

Common entrepreneurs will employ almost any means to acquire financing, but true entrepreneurs, as defined above, have unyielding attributes. A true entrepreneur will not place themselves in a beholden and subordinate position to one who does not have their vision. For this visionary it is much too difficult for them to witness changes being made to their philosophy and reality and not have the power to intercede and make it their own.

MORE STORIES AND LESSONS LEARNED

As touched upon in Chapter 1 on Power, my wife and I created and operated a children's program in a resort-casino for a major corporation in Las Vegas, Nevada from the late sixties to the early seventies. It was from inception planned to be the finest examples of a children's program to be found anywhere in the world at that time and place. The cost to build, staff, train and operate the program was never an issue. With the full support and blessings of corporate officials and the powerfully placed and supportive chief operating officer of the resort, we did not fail to deliver as promised.

Within a few years the resort's success led to its being sold to a major hotel corporation. Interestingly, one of the sales points was assurance that our children's program and its creators/operators would be included in the package. In fact, it did not take long before the head of marketing and sales, and second in command, of the purchasing corporation approached us with intentions to recreate the youth program in every one of their family resort hotels located throughout the world.

With this goal in mind we were asked to travel to the Hawaiian Islands in order to check out the resorts located on different islands. We were given complete freedom to research all aspects of each location including availability of staff. We not only identified excellent resorts the corporation operated, but improved on the pilot program in Las Vegas by turning each youth program on the islands into a cultural experience for its visitors to be. We envisioned and described a time machine that took each visiting child into as authentic a Hawaiian/Cultural experience as possible. We sought to nurture and revive the Hawaiian culture and at the same time create an educational as well as a recreational experience for our visitors.

Before we could present our vision, the Vice President of the Corporation who fully supported the development of the program had a massive heart attack. He passed away and so, with him, as we soon discovered, did our vision for the Hawaiian resorts. This was the one person in the corporation who had the power and the desire to making it all a reality. The person that was placed in his position had no time to read or hear of our plans for the corporation. It was all put to rest without an airing. How important is leadership? The cultural vision and concept did not die, but was to be revived a year later through another corporation in Fiji.

The person that became the new operating head of the hotel-casino in Las Vegas also was the one who canceled the idea of youth programs in other resorts, He also made it plain to me that he knew all there was to know about children, and, indeed, took control over the youth program and any thoughts of future expansion. He wanted us, the creators and operators of the original program to become his employees and that he would make all decisions henceforth having to do with our program. He made it quite plain that control over us and the operations of the program was his intent. Needless to say, the lines were immediately drawn between us, and as I was to learn very concretely, where power is, that's who wins the battle.

We were offered many reasons to remain with the corporation, but the ones not offered by this leader was control our own philosophy, the program and hiring and training staff. Entrepreneurs will sell what they create, and if the price is right, even themselves. True entrepreneurs, on the other hand, do not sell themselves, and it's not a matter of price. What he proposed was immediately unacceptable to us, so we quit our relationship with the resort. The alternative was to have sold our years of experience and philosophy for some silver. Impossible!

Change leadership and you alter the environment. Is this a universal law? When leadership is changed so will relationships, top down as must the whole inner organization change. The change may bring new life and growth, or, in time, the program becomes something less than what is was, struggles along or dies. In the resort's case, soon after the program's creators left the program it began a steady decline in quality and impact even though the new leaders of the program were former and excellent staff members. Business, the bottom line, power coming from others not part of the working philosophy pulled the strings. I learned that it mattered a great deal from where the power and control comes from. Change a true leader to another or turn the original into a figure head and you change the environment. No question!

What to do in situations where there is a change in who leads and where control comes from? I suggest that when one organization takes over another it is best to allow leadership and philosophy to remain exactly as it is found. Transition time is necessary; in particular when the program purchased is "good enough" to warrant the purchase. Allowing power and leadership to remain as is when taken over for a period of time is the wisest course of action. By giving the entrepreneur/leader the freedom to be what they are and do is an empowering and so sensible a way of transitioning, but transitioning over a period of sufficient time that events are allowed to dictate when to make any changes.

Another entrepreneurial story: Prior to my wife and me setting out on a quest to discover, own and build our own children's summer camp somewhere in the mountains north and close to Los Angeles we willingly gave up the successful summer camp we had created and operated on leased land for thirteen years in Malibu Canyon, Los Angeles. It was nearing the end of the fifties and although leaving so excellent a site and successful operation was a huge gamble we feared that as long as we remained on the leased location our future was dependent on the good will of the people from whom we leased. Although wonderful people, they were unwilling to give us any long-term assurances that we could continue our operation for as long as we desired. Also, the value of the site made it completely impossible for us to consider making an offer to purchase the land.

We knew how to operate a camp with children ages three to teens but hardly anything about how the world of business and finance functions. We obviously did well in planning, employing, training and operating a children's camp environment. On the other hand, when it came to the business world outside of camp we were ill-prepared to take on what we most likely would have to face if we left the security of what we had and knew. It is one thing to lease a facility. It belongs to someone else and our responsibility was to use it and leave it intact and clean for the next day's use. Owning, building, maintaining one's own land and facility is a completely different world. We decided to seek the advice of the financial, legal, and other business people of experience with whom we had trusting relationships.

We asked our advisers the hard questions having to do with going it on our own. We not only wanted their approval but, hopefully, some financial help in making our dream a reality. It was clear that "playing it conservative and to doing nothing to rock a good boat" was the advice we got. It was unanimous that we stay where we were—on leased land. And as it turned out, no financial support could be expected if we went off on our own. We were fully, to put it mildly, on our own. Did that stop us? Not for a split second.

Spoken like a true entrepreneur! Yet I know that at that time I had no idea what "entrepreneur" meant. I did not see myself as anything more than an educator and an aspiring child psychologist attempting to create a philosophy and methodology having to do with a child's growth and development. But after all these years and much reflection on the life I have led I feel I may have earned my membership in this relatively small group I have labeled "true entrepreneurs."

SHIFTING GEARS FROM ENTREPRENEURSHIP TO LEADERSHIP

Successful entrepreneurs reach their goals through their own focused use of power and by using the enlisted power of others. They lead themselves and helpers during the creation and building phase of the business but require substantially different tools and philosophy when things go operational. At that point, true entrepreneurs are forced to become leaders of others instead of entrepreneurs solely driven by ideas and goals. It is here at that interpersonal and communication issues come to the forefront. My own experiences speak loudly that effective entrepreneurs do not make particularly good leaders. This is so because the demands placed on the shoulders of an entrepreneur are vastly different from the demands placed on the shoulders of a leader. Entrepreneurs are visionaries, problem creators and solvers. Relationships with others have to do with overcoming barriers and they are, essentially, unilateral in their decision making.

Leaders are significantly different. They are communicators and require excellent relationships with their significant others. They also seek to arrive at consensus with their key people, and the better, wiser leaders' desire attitudes and behavior that is akin to ownership from those they work closest with. This does not happen quickly and their approach to issues is through dialogue, mutuality and cooperation as compared to monologue and an attitude of "this way or the highway." The entrepreneur is all about the goal and the leader is about relationship and communication. What the successful entrepreneur and successful leader have in common is that they are both excellent students. Differences are significant. The entrepreneur is the point of a spear, the cutting edge of a blade; a leader is a teacher of attitude, behavior and empowers others to lead, not through words alone, but also as a role model. The leader is part of the body of the spear, not its point.

Tools and Being

History overwhelmingly supports that learning to use tools is relatively easy and why people choose this path over personal growth. This is true despite the oft repeated words that "experiences are our best and most valuable opportunities to learn and grow from" and, as leaders, to influence others to grow. Too many people repeat significant errors and omissions because they do not reflect back and extract lessons from their past experiences. Those that do grow from each experience and are the wise amongst us. It is why I emphasize the importance of entrepreneurs and leaders being lifetime students and, primarily, but not exclusively, students of events and people that happen in their lives. Also, if they are students of their own life, they are likely students in general and seek mentors in order to facilitate learning and growth. (The importance of mentors to entrepreneurs, leaders and people in general is carried throughout the book.)

Can Successful Entrepreneurship Be Taught?

Again the question: Can becoming a true entrepreneur be taught? It is difficult but doable when the right teachers with considerable entrepreneurial experience and the committed students come together. For the teachers, this means life experiences, a deep love and knowledge of the subject and possessing the art of teaching, and a full awareness of their power and influence on students. But without the committed student, the teacher, with all of their experience and wisdom, cannot and will not make someone be what they have no intention of becoming.

If a person simply wants to learn tools and techniques for the purpose of becoming an entrepreneur or a leader—and my experience is clear about this—they can; but this will not change who they are. What these people do is to purchase another look, another appearance; but do not change, do not grow, and deceives no one. This is acting, the reading off a script and always return to who they really are and do not remain the character they play for long. The more important point is that no one is fooled by a person's use of tools and appearance.

GENUINE DIALOGUE IS A VITAL DYNAMIC FOR ENTREPRENEURSHIP AND LEADERSHIP

Genuine Dialogue is given its own chapter (Chapter 6), and its importance to significant relationships is impossible to overstate. It is the moment or moments of total openness with people essential to realizing an entrepreneur's vision, and even more important for a leader to operate an organization. Genuine Dialogue is clarity and purity between people important to each other and when it does occur, time, as a condition of relationship, disappears. All are present and it is only the "now" that holds each participant. This brings mutual respect to people, hierarchy is non-existent and all are one and equal while in this space. Dialogue replaces monologue and participants are heard, understood, confirmed and candidly responded to. Problem solving and creativity are never given so fruitful an opportunity. Potential is not hidden, but comes out as a contribution to the common good as well as one's own growth.

What allows this to happen is the reality of trust and safety and not simply being assured of safety by words alone. When this occurs individuals experience the leader as vulnerable and open for others to know their true thoughts and feelings. Only the weak and cowardly falsify being vulnerable which, in any case, is not the "vulnerable" I refer to, and is seen for its deceit. For the healthy individuals, being vulnerable is their truth and no strings or conditions are attached, they are the courageous ones.

The Few, the Unique, the True Entrepreneurs

In the ideal personal and work relationships, those involved with each other have an equal opportunity to be all that they can be, and hierarchy/power is temporarily non-existent. In the world as it is generally lived, this is fantasy. Equality and the freedom to be all that one needs and is able to be are rarely given to anyone, but must be fought for. To give in to what has been and is, or to powerful people and events, is the common way of too many, but not all. A few people found everywhere are unwilling to give in to those in power according to expectations and convention. These few do not accept established and traditional ways of being and behavior. This is the true entrepreneurial way and attitude and they will do what they choose to do; power and pressures may fall on them, but only "like rain upon a closed window pane." So, whether these unique individuals fail in their dreams and efforts, and most do, they still fuel possibilities for others.

Those who would insist on having more control over their lives and who do not comply for whatever reason are less influenced by the world outside of them than from the world that exists within them. For true entrepreneurs, compliance has little meaning. Their calling is to be what they choose to be and this may include doing better at what is being done or create something completely new and different. True entrepreneurs follow a different drummer and the beat begins early in their life. But so does it for all humans and yet most give up the external fight.

Many parents see a baby's need to be a unique self as a challenge to their authority and power. We know of the so-called terrible two's as a fight for independence between those in power, the parents, and the child's drive to be what they want and need to be. This takes place regardless of the fact that the child could not possibly survive without the care of their parents. Compliance is the common choice the great majority of children are forced to make because of their inability to care for themselves, and learning to become compliant becomes a lifetime issue. This fire to be oneself initially burns extremely hot in all reasonably healthy humans. Too soon, however, the fire becomes a small pilot light for most—but never to true entrepreneurs. They choose their path and walk or charge ahead self-assuredly, recognizing that they often walk alone regardless of the unknown and dangerous twists and turns that lay before them. But, does anyone really make it solely on their own?

ENTREPRENEURS AND THE INNER CIRCLE

Building a quality Inner Circle may well be the most important step any entrepreneur *must* take. I emphasize the word "must" because, first and foremost, we do not exist without an Inner Circle, or what brings us into this world? It takes two to tango in a relationship and perhaps a maximum of eight to operate a giant corporation. The point is not the size, but whether an Inner Circle just happens, which it does, or that it is given serious thought and a selection process that brings together people of substance, inner courage to be themselves and knowledge that is all about contribution. This is important enough that the Inner Circle is given a full airing in chapter five.

But for now, I will consider the entrepreneur and the value and importance of an Inner Circle to them. As stated, the Inner circle is a natural process. No one stands alone or exists in a vacuum and hence the Inner Circle begins to take form as life itself begins to form. But, our concern is not the Inner Circle via biology or through comfort and being with and depending on family or friends. The effective Inner Circle I refer to is hand-picked by the wise entrepreneur because of each person's knowledge and proven success in their respective fields. Differences are what make the best and most productive of Inner Circle's. It may not be obvious, but much is owed to a few within this circle of differences who contribute to an entrepreneur realizing their goal. Also, Inner Circles change as the entrepreneur grows in experience and wisdom. The need for expertise is what brings on the necessity for change in participants.

Assuming the true entrepreneurs reflect, then extract and grow from their experiences they come to recognize and appreciate differences. Agreement based on compliance is not what they want or seek. Still, prior to this epiphany most entrepreneurs surround themselves with family, friends and people with much in common. I know this was exactly what I did with my numerous Inner Circles. All were wonderful, loving and hard working people, but we were all too similar when what I needed was true expertise and people who saw the world from their own perspective and strong enough of character to be able to express themselves. This is particularly important: It does little good to bring different talent and experience together if the one that holds power insists on and gets only "what they want."

I learned much too late the importance of the differences between people and how those differences add depth and knowledge to one's own life. The mistakes I made as an entrepreneur affected many dedicated people, but I was totally ignorant of my errors and omissions relative to my understanding of what an effective Inner Circle is made up of. It took my becoming mentor to other professionals for me to realize the importance of this.

Given the choice an Inner Circles needs to be made up of people who have established themselves as quality in their respective fields of endeavor. And because true entrepreneurs and quality leaders are strong personalities to overcome individuals in their Inner circle must either be willing to risk disagreement and possible conflict through dialogue or their value is wasted. This is a challenge for each member of the Circle including the entrepreneur and the leader. In order to attain Genuine Dialogue between them all any insecurity or fears, personal or otherwise, must be eliminated. Without a mentor/facilitator, this may be impossible to achieve.

It is when an Inner Circle is able to have a level, mutual and cooperative playing field the Circle begins to move from the hierarchy of power, protection and competition to the healthiest of relationships. It begins to happen when the entrepreneur or leader shares their power. In fact, it is then, only then that each member becomes an entrepreneur or leader while together behind closed doors.

Growth, as compared to aging, requires intensive and meaningful life experiences that are drawn from as one draws water from a well. Microsoft's Bill Gates, Apple's Steve Jobs, and other enormously successful entrepreneurs achieved spectacularly because of near total immersion in what they did. Imagine the countless hours they gave to the "games" they played and working on some of the most advanced machines of their day and times. Not to be missed, they were sponges to the teachers, events, and opportunities they were given and met along the way. Were they present and fully into what they were doing? Did they learn? Get better at using the tools at their disposal? Were they passionate to learn more, as well as push and innovate the technology they were privileged to have available to them? And, finally, did they—do they—define what a true entrepreneur is? What else, if not this? By the way, none of the above has to do with the quality of their leadership because, as stated throughout the chapter, being a leader is a totally different animal than being an entrepreneur.

ARE ENTREPRENEURS MADE OR BORN?

Clearly, I believe true entrepreneurs are made, but not completely made without the added benefit of certain inherited characteristics. This is the profound and complex area of "nature versus nurture" that has been argued for many years. After thirty years of work with children and then thirty years more with adults in their roles as entrepreneurs, professionals and leaders, I stand on the side of *nurture*. Those with whom I worked came from every possible background, with formal education or the lack thereof; and without exception it was life's experiences that influenced them most relative to what they had become. Nature had a hand in the making, but its contribution was secondary to relationships and experience.

I know with certainty what an intensive, personal relationship means to a child and even to adults; and this holds true whether outcomes are for good or evil. In fact, and as we shall read in this and other chapters, change can and does take place in adults whose characteristics have supposedly been fixed for life. But it is vitally important to acknowledge that change takes place only if and when people are committed to their own growth through being open and unafraid of learning how significant others see and know them. For this to take place a facilitator/mentor may be essential.

As an example of the above, many people believe they are entrepreneurs; but their behavior points to not being entrepreneurial. Rather, they seek degrees of independence in how they live and what they do. They want to put food on the table and to take care of their basic needs but not to build an enterprise that brings with it the responsibility of employees and the many related issues. It takes being in a relationship and the passage of time to understand anyone's intentions, expectations and to what degree they are what they believe they are.

The actions people take, not the words they speak, are the best indicators as to whether they are what they claim to be. Entrepreneurs need to work hard to enlist as many players to their game plan as required. And if wise, they build a professional Inner Circle that gives voice to investors, legal, financial, marketing, sales, and whatever other resources that can be thought of and brought on board. Nothing that can be anticipated is left out of the mix, or to chance.

Based on the many professionals and business entrepreneurs I have known, many speak of having been woefully unprepared for the problems and demands of the entrepreneurship stages they went through prior to achieving the goal. They underestimated the time, energy and resources needed to realize their goal. In addition, they were ill prepared often with no strategy or business plan to follow. What they had is a vision, a goal to be attained through hard work, commitment and focus. Where was there help to prepare them for the operational and relationship side of their entrepreneurial efforts?

Entrepreneurs and leaders must open themselves up to personal growth and the absolute importance of relationships with significant others. For too many, events and experiences do not bring growth and no growth insures that the person commits similar errors and omissions time and again. It appears to be a condition of humankind that growth and the becoming conscious and aware, is not easy to achieve. This is due to the fact that few people volitionally seek being naked and vulnerable to anyone. It is difficult, often painful to learn about one's self from those most significant to them, but is there a better way? It is why I suggest finding the proper person to mentor and facilitate the process, or how does an Inner Circle—regardless of how thoughtfully put together—and Genuine Dialogue becomes an experience of the group?

Clearly, the wisest course of action for entrepreneurs to take when the first impulse to be on their own and independent is to seek out any and all resources available to them including the local college, the community and proven entrepreneurs. Those that aspire to this need to be independent and be the student *seeking* the teacher who understands the problems and necessities relative to being and creating something new or different. Waiting for the phone to ring or the letter/e-mail to come to them suggests some personal issues that need to be dealt with first.

Since other people are essential to any entrepreneur and the journey they take, the need to learn about the importance of communication between them is impossible to overstate. Relationships, the Inner Circle and attaining high level of cooperation and mutuality with significant others is not an accident, but needs constant attention and care. And, indicated throughout the chapter, is the seeking of quality mentors to speed the journey as well as to avoid common traps. Also, the need and ability to communicate face-to-face regardless of the technology that exist today is probably a greater necessity today than at any other time.

Finally, given success in the entrepreneurial stages and reaching "the" goal, it becomes imperative to change from that of an entrepreneur to that of a leader. This is not just a matter of changing hats, but of a true transformation from that of a "hard driving" independent individual to a teacher, student and role model needing others to join in the operations of an organization. An entrepreneur, in order to become a successful leader, must literally remake themselves, their inner sense of being and most importantly their relationship with significant others. Without this change/growth the entrepreneur is likely to harm and misuse important relationships. Clearly, entrepreneurs are driven to "get it on" whereas leaders need to enlist others to take ownership; two very different approaches to people and tasks. The reality is that most entrepreneurs remain what they were prior to achieving their goal. They are frozen in their determination to have control of their own lives and in the process the lives of others. Seeking a mentor to assist in their own journey of growth is a giant step forward, and never an easy step to take. This is so because real change does not come from pressures outside of us as much as from deep within us.

The former entrepreneurs' new role as leader of an organization has little to do with power and control and the previous role they have played. They must now confront not a creation problem—but an operational one. It takes one mind-set and immense determination to bring a vision to life and a completely different mind-set to operate what is created. The demands made on entrepreneurs to create something from nothing, as compared to leading an operation, demand very different kinds of attributes and, actually, are two totally different people with different philosophies.

Being a leader is as great a challenge as that of being an entrepreneur. Most true entrepreneurs as discussed in this chapter are classic "lone wolfs;" self-centered, self-driven, powered from within and with few, if any, thoughts about sharing of power. Whereas, our quality leaders as discussed throughout this book are selfless, teacher/students, and role models to those they lead. Their power is shared with those in their Inner Circle.

This transformative/growth process is both rare and courageous for true entrepreneurs to risk. They have been a lone-wolf on the hunt and now must transform themselves into being a role model, teacher and student. As stated above, where once they were the point of the spear, they are now part of the body. Is it expecting too much from successful entrepreneurs that they be both successful entrepreneurs and then become successful leaders, the former in order to create reality out of a vision and the latter to operate and facilitate people's growth?

In summary, the ideal education of a budding entrepreneur needs to be a mix of the real and the academic, with emphasis on the real. In every case, the true entrepreneur, whether young or old, does not hesitate to "go for it" regardless of what the many books and professors teach. For those few, the vision is all that counts. The top of the hill is "around the next bend or two," but who knows? There is no turning back.

A true entrepreneur is never finished, never satisfied with "good enough." That is, one challenge leads to another. They have about three quarters of their body, mind, and spirit in the future; and the balance has got to be in the present. "Yesterdays" are just that invaluable bag of experiences from which the good ones draw lessons from.

Again, every organization needs true entrepreneurs that ignite the quest for the next dream, opportunity and innovation. But as employees of a business or corporate setting, potential entrepreneurs need the freedom and resources to make things happen. This does not mean without restraints, but restraints that are reason-based as compared to emotional, cultural and "don't rock the boat" tradition. Without freedom to risk and resources made available to them, reluctant entrepreneurs will remain nothing but possibilities to the organizations in which they work. The story of the young Ph.D., whose invention makes the firm he works for millions upon millions and makes him a millionaire, is the exception. This is too rare an occurrence and the reason is the lack of quality leadership. The young inventor was able to achieve for the whole because of his immediate leader.

Why should society nurture the entrepreneurial spirit? It is where innovation, creativity, and the general pushing of the envelope come from. As societies age they tend to build around themselves tradition and a reaction against what is the driving force behind a true entrepreneur. This is the passion to be one's self, to do what has not been done before and to test established limits. Through their efforts and even stubbornness they bring newness, invention, create jobs, art, music, better health care and much social good. Not only are entrepreneurs essential to organizations, but to societies everywhere and, also, to the small and only world that we all live on.

CHAPTER 3

LEADERS

Influence unknown
Nurtures or destroys others
Yet so essential.

The invasion of the island of Okinawa in World War II by the U.S. Army, Navy, and Marines was one of the greatest and most devastating battles of the Pacific. There were huge numbers of casualties on both sides, with considerably greater losses suffered by the Japanese. Although the war was over, limited military actions still continued on Okinawa for some time involving a limited number of Japanese soldiers hiding in caves.

I was an 18-year-old serving in the U.S. Army on Okinawa in 1945, soon after the battle of the Pacific and the peace agreements were signed. On this particular day, our squad was on a mission to find Japanese soldiers still hiding out in caves located throughout the southern part of the island. These few soldiers refused to accept that Japan had lost the war and that the fighting was over. Also, they had been led to believe that they would be tortured if they gave themselves up, which may be why they continued to fight their war.

The caves they hid in were elaborately constructed and fortified, with railroad tracks built from one opening to another so that they could move large mortars and weapons to different firing positions. Japan had prepared Okinawa for war over a period of many years and built strong defenses in anticipation of possible war with the U.S.

Our squad had a Japanese prisoner of war (POW) who was sent into cave openings seeking possible hold-outs. If the prisoner found any Japanese soldier hiding in the cave he conveyed the message that the war was over and that they would be treated well if they came out of the cave without weapons. If no one came out of the cave, we would dynamite its entrance so that it could not be used again.

In this incident, etched well in this young soldier's mind, the POW brought three men out of the cave, and immediately the sergeant in charge of our squad yelled out, "Ogulnick, take the prisoners to the compound!"

The squad had driven into the hills beyond a town called Naha in a ¾-ton stake-bed truck, and the sergeant was ordering me to drive the truck back to the compound with the prisoners loaded in the back. This had to be one of the most exciting moments in my life because I was being "ordered" to drive a truck! Until then, I had never driven anything but longed to have the opportunity.

Being from Chicago and growing up during the depression my mode of transportation was walking, running, roller-skating as a kid, and riding streetcars. I never even owned a bike until I was 35 (and this was a gift from my wife). Also, during my teen years none of my friends owned or drove a car. The thought that I ought to tell the sergeant that "I don't know how to drive" never entered my mind. My desire to drive that truck completely overruled any reasonable behavior on my part.

When I got into the cab, I quickly and wisely read the driving instructions on the instrument panel, turned on the ignition, and grabbed the wheel. Finding a gear to drive in was the most difficult challenge for me. When I hit the gas, the four people in the back, an armed soldier and the three prisoners, fell to the floor and held on for dear life. This was going to be a drive to remember for each of us; it definitely was for me. But somehow we got down the hill without hitting anything or anybody and made it to the compound. An experience I will, obviously, never forget.

A few weeks later I was given orders to build and organize an outdoor warehouse to store the piles of various items left lying around almost everywhere. The items were then to be organized and if in good or salvageable shape were to be shipped back to the U.S., and everything else was disposed of in one way or another. I was told to use prisoners of war to help build and organize an outdoor storage yard, so I went to the compound to pick a few workers I thought looked able enough to help me do the work that needed to be done.

Sitting together against a fence were the same three POWs who had been part of my first driving experience. They recognized me as soon as I walked up to them, and we all smiled at each other over the "shared" experience we recently went through together. This, added to their surrender and obvious fear of the unknown, must have contributed to what was to become a very special relationship between the four of us. I have to believe that when they surrendered they were not sure of surviving the moment they walked out of the cave, and add to this the truck ride? Yet what began as a potentially horrific experience for each of us turned out to be one of the most powerful and enlightening experiences of my life. The lessons I learned from my relationship with the three prisoners of war remain part of what I am to this day.

I know that my initial way of leading was not a thoughtful process, but it was more intuitive and based on the good people who led me early on in my childhood and teen years. But, I clearly remember my early trust in the three Japanese prisoners to do what needed to be done. I was responsible to them, and they reciprocated by taking immediate responsibility for getting things going and in order. Keep in mind that the only way we initially communicated to each other was through our hands and facial expressions. They did not speak or understand English, and I was the same when it came to Japanese.

Kato, the youngest of the POWs, was about fourteen years older than me. He was small in stature but strong and seemed happy and willing to take on any task. In "real life" Kato was an actor. Ohara was sixteen years older than me, tall, strong, athletic, an absolute rock of dependability. Before becoming a soldier, Ohara was a streetcar conductor in Tokyo. Yamamoto was the eldest, and the most respected and honored by his fellow prisoners. He worked for a bank in Hiroshima before becoming a soldier and had become fully informed of the dropping of the atomic bomb on his city of birth, home and family. He never talked to me about this devastating event in his life, and I never imposed on him to do so. Before I left Okinawa, I did my best to help him remain there. He had no desire to return to Hiroshima upon repatriation. Although they each contributed to my becoming a better person and leader, it was Yamamoto who became my true mentor.

As we all hope to discover, none of us are islands unto ourselves. Instead, we are aided or abetted by players both known and unknown to us. It all happens as we move through life, and its various good and bad experiences grow us into what we are and will become. Too many people learn little from life which is, as they experience it, repetitive. The wiser ones know and understand that experiences and people make them who they are and who they are to become. Life's experiences, our family, the people we meet, failure and success are our best and most meaningful teachers; and most of life's happenings are left mostly to circumstances beyond our control. The only thing we control is what we take from each experience.

It seems to me there is a requirement that we be eager, even passionate students of all that we experience. If not, we simply age and eventually die without necessarily growing during the process of living. But by looking at people and experience from the vantage point of a student, we learn from what we see and then are able to move forward, to change, to contribute, to be accountable, to lead and, yes, to follow. How else ought life to be lived? It sounds so simple, and yet is so obviously difficult to do.

Back to the story: I called the three POWs by their first names, but they insisted on calling me "Mister Sy." I insisted right back that "Sy" is good enough, but they smiled and went on treating me as special. They wanted it to be "Mister," and I let it be. Right from our first working day together I tried to learn some of their language, and so we set aside time each day for English and Japanese language lessons. They would give me some essential and basic words to speak, and I would give them the same right back in English. It was not long before we were actually making ourselves understood, and we laughed a lot doing it. I smile even now as I get this story on paper.

Yamamoto became my primary mentor in many ways. He taught me lessons through his behavior, his trust, responsibility, integrity, dependability, honesty and mostly *honor*. There was no formal agreement that he would teach and that I would be his student. It was simply who he was and what he did. It was Yamamoto being Yamamoto. There was no act, no pretense and no hidden agenda that I ever saw or felt. It was obvious in his relationships with the others as well as his supportive, perceptive relationship with me. He was respected and honored by the other prisoners and was their chosen leader; and he, in turn, always showed respect for them. However, I would frequently take note that although sensitive to others' needs, he was firm in dealing with individuals and the group when necessary. I remember that he never hesitated in reacting to events and people in appropriate ways, and that meant leading or following as events dictated.

This is a story of honor, responsibility and, appropriately, high-quality leadership. I'd like to write that the story took place through intention and the conscious desire to grow myself into a better person. In fact, like so many of my stories they are accidents, happenings; but I have been wise enough to draw important lessons from them, the people and experiences. Whether my witnessing or being fully involved, superb leadership as demonstrated by a few others has happened in my youth and throughout my life and I have benefitted.

What good are our personal stories if we do not seek the possible lessons they carry within them? Not only to be looked at retrospectively, but extracted, remembered and used. Once again, I was, innocently, a student enough to find and use what I learned. It had to be those lessons that contributed, considerably, to what I was to become as an entrepreneur and later as a leader and teacher.

It took years and many experiences with people for me to realize that events and people were steps on a ladder I climbed to become what I became. One powerful example is of the three remarkable Japanese prisoners of war who were supposed to be my sworn enemies and yet contributed immensely to my understanding of people and what was to be my role as a leader.

This particular day one of POW workers, we now had twelve, was missing from role call. My first thought was, "I have a serious problem, and I'm in trouble!" and my immediate reaction was to take off after him. The last thing I wanted was to have some GI harmed by one of those crazies who believed the war was not over.

Before I had a chance to chase after the missing POW, Yamamoto stepped in front of me and said in a very firm voice, "No! Mr. Sy, I will go find him and bring him back!" and he immediately took off into the hills after the runaway. He did not ask for my permission; he just acted before I could stop him. "Now I have two prisoners gone!" I thought, and my immediate reaction was to go after Yamamoto, too—and then I realized that it was Yamamoto's safety I was concerned about more than his absence. After all, I knew that he was not running away but only protecting me by taking this action, and more as I was to learn later. He did not want me out in those hills alone. What Yamamoto, Ohara, Kato and I shared was trust and respect. Both are necessary when people live and work together. When it does take place, it makes for the strongest of ties between people.

Ohara and Kato literally held on to me and tried to reassure me that Yamamoto would be back with the escapee. My concern for Yamamoto as well as every possible disciplinary action against me grew in my fertile imagination. Two hours later, Yamamoto returned, half-dragging the escapee behind him. He then ordered all the workers to line up at attention and placed me front and center. e tehnIt soon became apparent that I was to witness a cultural event of considerable importance to the Japanese. This would be one of the most important pages I was filing away in the recesses of my mind that would much later influence my being a better leader of others.

Yamamoto proceeded to dress down the man as I had never seen or heard before. I made out little of what he was saying but strongly felt the emotional and powerful words he spoke. At the end of his harangue, he slapped the POW across the face—both ways with an open hand—and it was all over. We all, including the POW who ran away, went back to work. Nothing more was said or done. What was impressed upon me was the firmness of Yamamoto, the "letting go" of the incident once it was dealt with and most importantly, *honor!*

In time it became clear to me that U.S. Army personnel who wanted or needed to use any equipment stored within the open warehouse yard had to go through Yamamoto, Ohara or Kato first and get my written or verbal approval from "Mr. Sy." This arrangement created the appearance that nothing functioned without my leadership. The POWs were playing a deliberate game that I knew was taking place, understood and supported because they, the POWs, wanted it that way. Through their actions, essentially, we together created an efficient warehouse and support operations from scratch. Thanks primarily to the three of them, the yard was highly organized and tightly controlled. I was the boss, their ostensible, leader; but they ran the show, and made sure that I drew the applause. Did I learn something about how to work with people? You bet! And they were my mentors.

I never saw or thought of myself as a leader to anyone. What I did recognize was that I had a streak of independence that ran deep inside me. Although I was a willing participant in almost everything my group of friends did, I, early on, recognized that I was not a joiner who needed others to find identity. That is, I never thought in terms of my identity having something to do with group membership. It was a big challenge just trying to be my own person and to discover who I was. Being a member of a gang did not detract from that quest.

Before I departed Okinawa for home I did what I could for Yamamoto, Ohara and Kato. I know what they meant to me then and even more so as my life unfolded. I could not have known at that time the important contribution their ethics, integrity and principles (honor) would play as I grew into my years as an entrepreneur, then a leader and as a consultant. It was much later that I came to realize that what I experienced with the Japanese POWs was mutuality, a well-functioning Inner Circle and Genuine Dialogue. All through this expereience none of us became comfortable and at ease with each other's language and culture; but here's the point: we respected, heard, understood, confirmed and were candid with each other.

My time on Okinawa was a brief period of about one year; but because of three Japanese prisoners of war, it was life-changing for me. One of the many lessons I learned is that it's not the length of time we spend with an experience but the *intensity* of our involvement, and our conscious willingness to *learn* from the experience. Even writing this some sixty-plus years later, my connection remains clear, strong and emotionally grateful to my three co-workers and friends.

RELATIONSHIPS BETWEEN LEADERS AND FOLLOWERS ARE VITAL

This chapter is about what it means to be a leader, whether our relationship with the leader is accidentally, as in the boss we work for, by choice or the parents who give us life. We also examine the heavy responsibilities that fall on the shoulders of all leaders and the relationships between leaders and those they lead. It is important to keep in mind that no human is devoid of some contribution to any relationship he or she is in. Each part of the stew influences in its own small way the whole of the meal.

We know our immediate leaders because they have direct influence on us. They are not mysterious to us; we hear their voices and know how they communicate with us. We feel their presence and witness their behavior. We may not know their intentions, but we do know their actions. They are our parents, teachers and immediate bosses at work and in direct positions of authority over us. Many of the relationships with leaders are hierarchical, and the leaders believe this arrangement works for them. Wiser and more effective leaders have learned through experience that leadership and power needs to be shared and that there are times when leadership is completely unnecessary. In either case, it is the leader who creates and maintains a way of leading with followers whether unconscious or deliberate.

On the one hand, we may choose a friend as our leader because he or she is kind, nurturing, supportive, or strong and dominant; and we want that person to lead us. On the other hand, we may have no desire for others to lead us and seek only a mutually beneficial and dynamic relationship. But even here, no relationship is without leadership at some point and due to some event, and ideally still remains fluid and dynamic.

WE KNOW OUR LEADERS BETTER THAN THEY KNOW US

Depending on how close we are to our leaders at work, at home or a student at school, it is expected that those who lead us also know us to some degree. However, those closest to a leader come to know their leader better and usually at a deeper level. Why do I write "those closest to the leader know the leader better than the leader knows their people?" It's a matter of perspective and numbers. The leader is one person experiencing one or more people from a position of multiple responsibilities while those dependent on a specific leader view their leader as one person. Also, leaders are most likely to be "center stage" with their words and behavior constantly influencing the environment and those within the environment.

Beginning with our parents we can expect to have many leaders in our lives, but the leaders we need to be most concerned with are the possessors of a power, invisible or otherwise, that influences our behavior. That is, there is no other person above them to whom they are required to answer. In the parlance of the street they are the "boss of the bosses." They are at the top of the hierarchy; and instead of being held responsible to a board of people, they are free to make whatever decisions they choose to make. They are also where the "buck" can go no further. They hold the power, and all leaders and followers below them know this.

I write that these individuals have "true power" and that they be understood as not having to seek help, guidance or approval from anyone. And if they do, it is not a question of being told to do so by others, but of personal choice seeking advice from others. Obviously, I do not refer to a CEO who must answer to a board or one holding a political office. Even the President of The United States is accountable to the people and can be voted out of office. This is not true of an entrepreneur, the owner of a business who is definitely the leader, and also our parents when we are babies and young children.

I also believe that our most ambitious and goal-directed entrepreneurs have this power, know it, want it and will not give it up. So, whether entrepreneur or leader, getting to the true power person is absolutely essential for the purpose of making this particular philosophy of leadership work. It does not and cannot work bottom up. In fact, it will do little or no good for leaders who are subordinate to another above them to exercise and may actually be dangerous for them. This book is for those that hold power and those, as students, who desire to be powerful over others. It will show that power, when used properly, builds and grows individuals, relationships and organizations or, when used improperly, will destroy individuals, relationships and organizations, including the one in power.

This chapter, then, is about leaders who hold true power and not about any leaders beholden to another for their job. Considerable experience with leaders of relatively small organizations brought this to my attention. What I slowly became aware of is that if change and growth are desired for an organization or personal relationship, it is the true leaders who *must* be committed to their own growth, first and foremost. This commitment cannot be made on the behalf of others the leader wants to grow or change, but is made for one's self and through this personal transformation to influence and possibly grow others.

Without a person's willingness and courage to open themselves up to the perceptions of others who know them best, I believe significant change is too difficult for people to achieve. Even with professional help it is almost impossible to bring transformative growth to an individual. To be vulnerable to those who are most aware and affected by their leader's behavior is a delicate operation, and there is no defense to protect from the likely pain and trauma that ensues. Yet I have discovered no better and more effective way than this process to bring about real growth. It is why I insist that if change to an organization is to actually take place, it begins at the top through dialogue and not somewhere in the middle or bottom and forced or manipulated.

Knowing people whether as leaders or anyone we live and work with takes time. How important are we to them and how important are they to us? We are "inner people" to ourselves and "outer people" to the world. We start out as one congruent baby having needs which are clearly expressed and surprisingly understood by the mother. There is no duality or conflict between what new babies need and convey to their caregivers. Duality starts to arise when the babies begin to be conditioned by the caregivers. It is at this time that a babies' needs are met by what the caregivers expect and want the babies to be. The result, and it happens to all, is that as we grow we learn what we need to do and how to protect ourselves. One example is to not readily expose what we feel and think to those who hold any power over us. Eventually, what most people have taking place in their significant relationships are the "games" we each play to best protect ourselves. Authenticity begins its journey of withdrawal at an early age.

Generally, people do a fair job of masking their feelings and thoughts. But leaders, because they are so "front and center" with those close to them, are seen and known beyond how they might believe they come across to others. In this case, assuming leaders have the courage to be vulnerable, they learn about themselves from those who know them best. What leader would not benefit from having his or her followers be volitionally candid with them? This demands Genuine Dialogue, which, as we shall learn, is achievable but not without the safest possible environment assured. At the beginning this may require a guide/mentor to lead them through a likely mine field of ancient stuff.

Excellent examples of this are the members of the leader's Inner Circle. They are familiar enough with their leader to give ample feedback to facilitate the leader's growth process. In return, and as growth is demonstrated by the leader, the environment begins to change; and the increasing feelings of safety and security eases for members of the Inner Circle to risk their own being vulnerable. In time, what was an "out-of-touch leader" becomes a more trusted leader. They are the same leaders found everywhere and under every possible circumstance but volitionally have allowed themselves to be touched emotionally and mentally by those important to them. The impact of on a leader from those close and important to them is what begins to change them and in the process the environment.

The quality and humanness that is deeply covered over and probably unconscious to leaders for years find daylight to the benefit of themselves and those with whom they live and work. This transformation would have been impossible without the genuine dialogue with others who are close to them. Quality leaders are now able to use their position, resources, authority and power to facilitate the growth of their followers. When this takes place the seeds of trust and safety are planted and in the process people will tend to risk becoming more vulnerable. What was, at the beginning, a leader's desire to grow becomes a nurturing environment for others to grow.

Even more dramatic for the more courageous leaders is their acceptance of being role models, teachers and students to their significant others. Visions, goals, strategies and problem-solving belong to each member of the Inner Circle as equals. The leaders do not carry the visionary burden alone, and ownership attitudes and behavior are common to all within their healthy Inner Circle. When mutuality is firmly established between leaders and key people, leadership roles are shared. In this case, many hearts and minds feel and assume attitudes akin to ownership and people's behavior is as one and yet more themselves.

GOOD LEADERSHIP HAS THE BRILLIANCE
AND FLAWS OF A UNIQUE DIAMOND

Leadership needs to be studied as one looks through a microscope at a unique diamond, seeking both its brilliance and its flaws. I intend to do this in the following pages and the chapter on Leadership Attributes that follows. Hopefully, the stories I share about the good and bad leaders I have worked with will contribute to other leaders' opening themselves to those closest to them. I will make the case that leadership is learned through the actual doing and being, and that people and events play a very dominant and dramatic part in why people are what they are and that when growth takes place in a leader this growth is likely to spread to others. Experience, no epiphany here, is what gives us our best opportunity to learn, to grow, and to be and become.

Books and classroom instruction on leadership are helpful in giving us information about every possible kind of leader; but regardless of the fun and challenge of reliving history in the classroom, the only effective way to learn to be a leader is by being a leader. This means experiencing failure as well as success. Both failure and success teach important lessons *and* need to be studied if one is open to becoming a better leader. However, willingness to learn from experience and significant events is exceedingly rare, which is why there are so few quality leaders. Most people go from experience to experience assuming little change, learning too little or nothing at all and remain what they were.

Most of us make up and believe our excuses for not learning from experiences. Or, experiences happen but we are not present; and if not present, where are we? What have we learned? Often an experience is like being caught in a brief rainstorm: we get wet but soon dry off, and everything is again as it was. Did we see the rainbow or smell the sweetness of washed air? When we are part of an event there are things to learn and possible opportunities that envelope us as do raindrops. But we do not look back into the event that we were part of. Where is the student within us? Being in the moment and present to it is not the time we learn. This takes place after the fact; the experience happens and we then extract from it what we find, but we must look back.

Learning and becoming is all about experiences and what we derive from them. What was the event? Who and what roles do people play in this event? What opportunities or learning made itself known because of the event? By asking questions and listening to the answers or no answers, learning takes place. And then there are opportunities to learn by simply observing an experience from the outside looking in. This type of learning is not the same or intensity of being part of the experience and why being present in the moment is so important to each of us, and the present becomes a gift.

Note, the "present" becomes a "gift," not *is* a gift. It demands that we be students to our experiences. We look back to know what took place and whether there are or are not lessons to own and use. The problem for too many leaders (our concern here) is that they are not the students they may think they are. They do not learn from experience, do not ask the right questions, miss out on the answers and repeat the same errors and omissions. Only exceptionally rare leaders look to each and every experience for important growth lessons. Why so few leaders (or people in general) take advantage of their experiences and grab hold of possible lessons in order to make things better for themselves and others is a profound question that only each person can answer.

To be sure, quality leaders take full advantage of experiences. They are students who seek to know about themselves, the people they work with, their business, and the community and world at large. A student is a student, is a student and is a student of all things that may or may not give answers to his or her infinite questioning. Whether this is the result of good parenting, accidental nurturing life experiences, or teachers and leaders who are role models "extraordinaire" to them, they are students. It is a choice made volitionally and cannot be forced by others.

What needs to be understood is that most leaders are and become what necessity throws at them and respond rarely to a conscious and therefore deliberate desire and effort to be the best possible leader they can be. Most leaders do not do what they do from a deep awareness or the sincere desire to grow as a person. They react, react and react again; and growth is a non-issue. Most problems begin with leaders, to be sure, because they are a problem to their significant others and which means they are in one way or another the problem to the answer.

The *good leaders' behavior*, in contrast, is what makes them good leaders. Being makes it so, and it is their behavior. Intention, by itself, is never enough. As a result of the actions they create an environment that is acknowledged by those they lead and is returned in kind. This does not come as a surprise to the leader nor is it based on expectation but deliberate open communication in the form of dialogue as against monologue. The better leaders understand they are role models, teachers and students to others and there is no or little accidental behavior. They are not only conscious of their multiple roles and responsibilities with, and for, others; but they intentionally create an environment in which individuals and relationship are able to grow and to be one with them.

This is the quality and wise leadership that is attainable by most leaders if they, as students, demonstrate the courage to let their guard down. This is not likely to happen as long as leaders are unable to be vulnerable with their key people. Being this with a mentor or counselor may help them understand more of what makes them tick, but it is hardly the same as being vulnerable with one's own people.

Where there is assured, good leadership there is no manipulation, hidden agenda, duality or conflict between people. There are problems and issues to deal with, and these are logs placed on a fire, but under control. This organization and the relationships within are what an outsider experiences. In this scenario all relationships are significant, and people are not related to as "objects" or as if they were invisible. Never to be forgotten is that what makes this possible is the quality of the leaders' behavior.

QUALITY LEADERS RELY ON GENUINE DIALOGUE AND THE INNER CIRCLE

The selection process to membership in an Inner Circle is deliberate and thoughtful. Enlightened leaders knowingly seek the talented who are, also, students, teachers and leaders either established or in-the-making. None may be fully developed in any specific area, but their potential leaps out at the enlightened leaders. It is relatively easy to see the student, teacher and leader behind a face and is as simple as watching their behavior. If the selection process is proven wrong, and it happens, the enlightened leaders do not attempt to manipulate growth. What happens is that quality leaders increase intensity and demands on the relationship to the point that the member either chooses to "grow or go." Enabling is not a characteristic of quality leaders. (This subject is more fully covered in Chapter 5," The Inner Circle.")

When I was an entrepreneur and then became a leader of others I did not remember ever having to consider the quality of my leadership style or how others perceived me. I did not think to ask and none, that I remember, volunteered their view of me as their boss. I did what I was called upon to do, and those I considered my Inner Circle did what they were supposed to do. Events and people dictated our behavior and not issues of power.

I do not remember being aware of the influence those who were my key people had on my own leadership style. On the other hand, I've never forgotten certain people who must have had influence on me. How important were my parents in terms of the love and warmth my mother gave so easily and the determination and fight to feed his family my father showed? And, how does the honor code of the POW's on Okinawa influence me? We are all a mix of our own uniqueness and desire to be, and the influence of others whether positive or negative.

It took the writing of this book about a philosophy of power and leadership to bring this about. Now I seriously looked at the meaning and impact people and many wonderful and painful experiences have had on my life. In this sense they are all vitally important to me as the people who have played a part in the book's creation and my life. I also know that if we are within the range of being influenced we are going to influence in return. Significant relationships are always a two-way street. Leaders are responsible for the environment they create and control, but those who are controlled are also contributors each in their own way.

One example: it took many years for me to understand that my Japanese "band of brothers" were for each of us a well-functioning and efficient Inner Circle. They taught me Japanese phrases and words, and I taught them English in the same manner. There was respect and trust between us; and even though language remained a constant challenge, it was, strangely, never a barrier. We actually listened to each other, confirmed what each was saying and doing, and supported each other. I have no doubt that we came to experience Genuine Dialogue between us. Ownership and accountability were as mutual and authentic as I later came to understand and attempted to teach to those with whom I worked.

I acknowledge that my way of leading or non-leading played a key part in initiating the environment that took place between us. I also know that it was not intentional and with awareness of what being a quality leader means. It was simply me being what I was at that time and accepting where I was. I also recognize that events brought into my life many other remarkable people, and what I am must be a result of this. The beauty of experiences and different people are the lessons and seasoning that each event and person brings to the soup pot we each are.

A QUALITY LEADER IS WHAT WE LEARN TO BE

Becoming a good leader is learnable and teachable, but it absolutely requires two fundamental ingredients. First, leaders must be a student unafraid to learn how others, who know them best, experience them. This requires that the leaders/students be vulnerable to those closest to them and, further, that the leaders share their thoughts and feelings with these key people. It also means that the leaders must hear, understand and confirm what others are saying. It does not mean *agreement*. It is a sensitive and difficult process getting people to walk in the shoes of the other person without also losing their own perspective.

Being vulnerable to significant others is dangerous waters to be in unless courage exists to learn about one's self from those closest to us. Most leaders protect and insulate themselves and, in fact, avoid placing themselves in this position. Too often, it is an invitation to abuse from those that have histories of being themselves abused by those who have held (or hold) power over them. To overcome this possibility I suggest that the leaders seek a mentor to guide all involved in this process of opening up. But, and not to be forgotten, it is the leader who is the primary student to the mentor. It is what must be established between the mentor and the leader and then to their key people. Being vulnerable without also having guidance that facilitates and controls what is to come is too often an invitation to more troubled people to try to take advantage of the leader and turn what is planned as dialogue into a cathartic rant. The problem that is first to be understood and resolved is that leaders teach through their words and behavior, including "Do as I say, not as I do"; and every action is a lesson to those key to them. With proper guidance from a mentor and a leader's full participation, their growth and, in time, the growth of others becomes a realistic probability.

For leaders, the process of selecting a mentor to help them grow says a great deal about any leader. This is because the mentor selected must also have quality, hands-on leadership experience and a mentor who is neither pawn nor manipulator. For the mentor, the more years of actual experience as a leader and understanding what it takes to teach are invaluable assets. Finally, the mentor needs to confirm before any attempt at teaching takes place that the leader is a student willing, able, and committed to personal growth.

This is a very different process from teaching leadership tools, that is, for all intent and purpose, appearance. I refer to tools on how to listen, proper verbal and non-verbal responses where people are led to believe they have been heard and understood, even how eyes connect to eyes and tone of voice. These and more are tools a leader can learn. None of the skills mentioned and many more have to do with inner growth, which is and requires a totally different approach. The one is an exterior make-over and the other is an inner transformation. Unlike Jekyll and Hyde, there is no going back and forth.

Of immense importance is that most leaders either disregard or do not know that they are also teachers to those they lead. How do leaders also take on the role of teacher when they are so burdened by their leadership role that demands so much of their time? Even leaders who are aware of their responsibility to teach all too often miss "teachable moments." Quality teachers, in comparison, do not miss teachable moments because teaching is their focus and reason for being involved. This is true of a teacher, but it is also true of leaders. Whenever the moment presents a significant opportunity to teach and the issue is important, leaders cannot afford to not teach. When are significant others more vulnerable?=

The beauty of the teachable moment is that in the heat of action people are usually present and open. An example of this is the story of the father driving into camp in his pristine, brand-new white Cadillac. Upon parking he was enveloped by a cloud of forest dirt and a large German Shepherd that challenged him. I heard Heidi's bark, came to the parked car with motor running and door closed, and welcomed the parent. He was upset with the road, the dog, his rental car covered by leaves and dust, and probably was tired from his flight and drive to camp.

The first thing that came out of his mouth was, "Where is my daughter?"

I said, "She's in the girls' washroom with her group and counselor. Come on, I'll take you there." Beyond his curt demand and my response not a word to me about how she was doing or if she was happy. He simply and directly wanted me to take him to his child.

When we entered the washroom he saw her with her head in a toilet bowl, scrubbing away. "What!" he literally screamed "is my daughter doing cleaning toilets?"

I told him that every group did their share of keeping camp spotless, including cleaning the washrooms, working in the kitchen and having to clean their cabins first thing after breakfast.

"I did not send my child to camp to work, but to play and learn!" he responded sharply. "I'm taking her home."

When the girl heard her father's voice she turned from the toilet and, without running to greet him, said, "This is my group's week to keep the washroom clean. It's our responsibility, and I am not leaving camp!"

His look was incredulous. At home she had her own bedroom and bath that a maid kept clean. She did not contribute to anything at home apart from having to do her homework .She had the material things any child could hope for and was well on the road to helplessness without others to care for her. At camp she was asked to be accountable, responsible and a contributor as well as experiencing how to take care of herself. Yet, this was a small part of what camp was to each camper. Its primary purpose was to offer relationships through small group living and a cornucopia of recreation and education experiences to each camper.

The father wanted to take his daughter home at that moment, and she was as adamant in her refusal to go home. I asked him to stay the day and see what took place before he took so arbitrary a position. He looked at me, thought for a moment and agreed to stay through lunch. The next time I saw him was after lunch, so I asked if he still wanted to take his daughter home.

His response: "I'd be a fool to take her away from her friends and what she insists she loves. She has learned so much and feels so good about herself. Is it possible for me to stay a few days with you?" He did stay with us and literally found a fountain of youth for himself enjoying activities with his daughter, her group and camp at large.

When he drove off in his very dusty car he was, as is said, "a happy camper." Were the few days he spent with us a collection of teachable moments? Actually, it was a teachable few days. I believe it was the environment that did the teaching, but the father had to have opened his mind to the events taking place. To his credit he was present and open. Did the results of this brief experience change him and his relationship with his daughter? I know so.

When problems and issues are hot and unless an emergency has to be handled immediately, to miss a teachable moment is to lose what may be a golden opportunity for growth. This is why I, as mentor, will interrupt what is taking place in favor of capitalizing on a teachable moment—even to the point of frustrating the speaker or doer. Teachable moments are quick openings for a left hook, but need to be taken advantage of or close off just as quickly.

Good leaders easily differentiate among those in a group who willingly participate and those who play pawns and passively comply. In such a case, it can be immensely important for a leader as teacher to pierce the moment by seeking any opinions from the passive pawns. The efforts towards inclusion may not succeed in changing anything, but to not have tried surely loses the opportunity presented by any teachable moment. Sometimes the smallest things temporarily open a passive person to ask a question or offer an opinion. When and if such an opportunity takes place a quality leader will jump at this, seeing it as a possible building block. Listening, understanding and confirming, it is the leader who acknowledges the speaker and in doing so, might, in incremental ways, contribute to a passive person's sense of safety. It's worth the time and effort.

Leaders Need to Identify, Nurture and Grow Other Leaders

As important as it is for a leader to be a teacher, it is equally important for the leader to identify, nurture and grow other leaders. All leaders need to be able to replace themselves or to have others as substitute leaders, such as when business owners sell their business but are interested in having its good leaders stay on. In any case, good leaders are surrounded by talent and people who demonstrate leadership qualities. Inadequate leaders are more likely to be surrounded by people ill prepared to become good leaders and are given little chance to learn what a good leader needs to be. For good or bad, it is the leaders who are responsible for what is taught to those important to them.

For a leader to not consider beyond their issues, or nose, is sure to be problematic. No one person is best suited for all things and events. Others are bound to be more capable to lead in certain situations but need to be nurtured and supported to do so. Good leaders know this and create the environment where leadership is transferred from one to another based on ability and knowledge. Also, events happen and need to be dealt with immediately. Do people wait for the leader, or do they lead? Are they supported to do so? The wisdom of good leadership is shown by preparing for this eventuality and by the quality of the people who do meet and exceed their responsibilities. History shows that this is too rarely the case.

Leaders who are unaware that they teach those closest to them through their behavior are fools who do damage to others and themselves. These leaders are out of touch with their power and lack the wisdom to understand their influence as a teacher. They are also blind to the reality that they create or contribute significantly to problems they then erroneously blame on others.

When leaders insist on being permanently in charge, always in control, I also find that the leaders' Inner Circle members accept this as a fait accompli, and the more independent individuals depart what is too stifling an environment. As a result of this, when I observe that leaders lack quality people in their IC, this is not meant as an attack on members of their IC. It is rather the leaders who create the environment and gather in those people who, in the leaders' mind, behave as the leaders want them to, which for the most part, they do.

Leaders who are unaware of their power and how they use it do not understand mutuality, cooperation, and the art and necessity of dialogue. Monologue and top-down communication is their way. Because of being the leaders, the choice is theirs to make; and they get what they want. Examples abound: If leaders deny themselves the benefits of teaching as events dictate or being students as perceived by their key people, how do they get accurate and timely feedback from others?

In a rigid, hierarchical environment, everyone loses. The many opportunities to grow oneself and others into being and becoming better leaders and participants are squandered. And such leaders complain that they have no one but themselves to count on.

Given years of crucial experience as followers, entrepreneurs, leaders, teachers and students, it seems impossible for a person to not have developed a philosophy of living. Most humans who survive birth and live a reasonably full life have many untold experiences. The question is do they make use of their experiences in as fruitful a manner as possible. A wise person does, and this is what separates quality leaders from most other leaders. They are students, who become more themselves with every experience and yet continue seeking to learn more. They are never finished as students always seeking mentors. In the ideal world, quality leaders/teachers and students seek and find each other because they have a need for each other. Relationships of mutual benefit are circular and result from leaders who teach, are a student and connect to other student determined to be the best leader, teacher and person they can be. It is mutuality at its best.

Ideal relationships are not "one-way streets" but work to mutual benefit in both directions. Again, leaders who are teachers are also students to their students who are also to be leaders. It is this authentic two-way relationship that brings a freshness and difference into the workplace and Inner Circle. An excellent example is with today's technologies that young people own and know as almost an additional appendage. Being invited to bring technology into the workplace gives many students the power to lead and influence. The organization or relationship grows from wisdom gained from the past and the innovation of the present and future.

Modern technology is changing the world, not only through the immense data instantly available but in ways simple and complex relative to human relationships. Technology may overwhelm older generations but not those of this generation. Communication between generations has rarely been easy and in fact is sure to be difficult and challenging. What I suggest is that the older, more experienced generations needs to accept the young as their teachers relative to technology and even empower them to lead by allowing specific and related events to dictate. This is what being inclusive means: not as a matter of age, but experience and knowledge that fits the given event.

Its consequences are greater understanding of each other against the historic separation of generations from each other. It is not a question of giving one thing up for another, but of acknowledging that inclusion means being open to the old as well as the new. In this case, the vital old-fashioned face-to-face dialogue way of communicating becomes more important than ever.

When tradition and expectations are set aside we enter into unexplored territory. Humans have been doing this pushing and exploring the unknown since the beginning of walking this Earth. Today, it is not territories we explore but the minutia of what makes our different environments tick. Now, and for the foreseeable future, technology has become our unexplored world; and apparently we have just scratched the surface and it is the young who own this new world of technology. Including them in is wisdom at work.

In the wise organization (meaning wise leadership), the young become leaders and mentors of what they know. But what has been hard-earned by quality leaders, that is, the ways of quality leadership, dialogue and cooperative relationships is knowledge that takes years to accumulate. This, too, must be taught to the young, who as leaders of what they know must in addition be made aware of the vital importance of interpersonal relationships and dialogue. So who amongst us is not required to be both student of the new world and of the best of what has been hard-earned about human interaction and communication? Are we able to count the ways people and their organizations benefit by being open and welcoming of both the new and the old and from sources that know and can teach?

The State of the Authentic is Knowable

Quality leaders seek and want what is real, and deal openly and honestly with others. These special leaders are pragmatic and seek what works for them and their people. They are not perfectionists but seek a utilitarian's approach. In this sense, the best leaders are neither genius nor hero but focused hard workers and nurturers of others. They are, also, superb teachers and facilitators surrounded by people who are eager students and likely want to eventually become leaders. In this ideal setting they benefit as individuals and contribute to expanding the common good. To nurture each individual to be and do their best and to have each contribute to the betterment of the group and organization is about as good as it can get.

Another important aspect of the relationship between excellent leaders and their key people: Wise leaders have an open-door policy making easy access a two-way street between them and their key people. Although leaders and students need each other, the better leaders want their people to push the envelope, to be assertive without also being aggressive, self-centered and insensitive to others. And, ideally, it is better that students walk through the door to be with the leaders than that the leaders seek them out. No assumptions or wishful thinking made by the leader; the student's openness and courage makes the point.

The motivation to be a leader may begin deep within the student, but having good role models helps significantly. Clearly, having the few memorable leaders as examples to draw from contributed to my leadership behavior and style. It is when I began to be the mentor to leaders and their key people confronting communication and interpersonal issues that I came to more fully understand how important the leader is to whom they lead. I have often considered the influence and direction changes I have gone through because of the actions of others on my behalf. Immense courage, honor, candor, humor, intensity, vulnerability, compassion, empathy, love and more that I owe to others. I owe so much to so many.

Relationships that have lasting impact become so through time, effort and many teachable moments. Trust and respect generally evolve slowly since most relationships require time and experience. Relative to this, quality leaders do not waste much time with relationships that "feel" wrong, and are either quickly corrected or discarded. This intuitive sense differentiates quality leaders from those who will continue to give time and energy to those whose agenda is about self. It also is indicative that the leader is either looking for quality and courage or to use people and actually seek the compliant.

Why are Good Leaders and Real Students Rare?

Quality leaders, teachers and students are rare not because of birth and natural selection but rather due to experiences they have and their inquisitiveness into the experiences. My experience is clear and confident that it is the power of leaders and environments they give birth to that influences behavior and attitudes of others. The human potential is hardly scratched and remains closeted in too many. It may be accidental or intentional, but if the right relationship is established between those who do hold the power to create nurturing environments what has been only potential will want and needs to see the light of day.

What quality leaders or teachers bring to most relationships are their histories and hard-earned knowledge and awareness of what this means to them and what it may mean to others. Ideally, students bring passion to learn, to question, to grow; and they each bring their own stories to share. Still, many may bring nothing more than fear of being exposed for flaws real and imagined and why their potential is more resistant to coming out. Here is where the safe and secure leaders/teachers and the environment they create play so important a role. When perceived as "safe enough," the student in each of us is awakened to possibilities. If the leaders/ teachers offer their hand, the other may reach out for it to grasp—and if not now, soon. This is no game of words or sleight of hand, but of what exists and the perception of the one who awakens or remains closed.

Personal experiences are what we learn from, and they hold our own stories we most need to study and extract lessons from. It is why I write that reading the stories of others, hearsay or being a passive uninvolved witness (as in so many classroom situations) does not make us more than what we are. Only life, our being a participant and searching for lessons out of our own experiences, provides us the best chance to grow and to actually change. It is in personal, face-to-face encounters where we earn our physical and emotional cuts and bruises. It is where we discover our true selves.

This is true of humankind: We are, essentially, what we have extracted from our personal life experiences. The less we extract, the less we have to show and be. The more we take from our own experiences, the more we are and become. Our behavior is a result of experiences. If, at the earliest, our parents and the environment that enveloped us give love, nurturing and are supportive of our need "to be," the odds are that we love, are open, cooperative and nurture others. Make our upbringing dark and restrictive, and what are we likely to be to others?

If there is a good that comes out of a negative upbringing, it has to be that what we are is primarily learned behavior and attitude, and these are not inherited characteristics. They are learned, and if they are learned they can be unlearned and be replaced by a more nurturing relationship ameliorating the damage of the past. It is why I stress the importance of being able to tell one's own stories. If an environment is perceived as "safe enough" in which to tell one's own stories, this is the beginning of possible growth. Now what is needed is the conscious, receptive and accepting space between any leader and storyteller with the result that there is a likelihood of greater respect and change. The key is the "safe enough" environment in order for people to allow themselves the courage and freedom to express their deepest thoughts and feelings through the personal story they share.

The Value of Leadership Shifting from One to Another

The more the leaders empower others to lead, the more likely it becomes that key people are exposed for their potential to lead. Empowering in this case means that the leaders trust that others within their Inner Circle have more experience and are more capable than the leaders to deal with a particular issue. Leading then depends on the event and the freedom and willingness of the "best and most able" person to take charge, to take ownership of the problem.

This is a common problem I found when beginning my work with an organization. Leaders may have wanted others to take charge but were blind to their inhibiting behavior that kept the more capable from taking charge. Leaders easily speak to the issue of wanting their people to step up to the plate but do not, initially, see themselves as the possible barrier to this taking place. Facilitating others to be the leader in specific situations, to own the power temporarily, is an exciting picture; but to get there depends so heavily on the leader's willingness to seriously give this power to another. To allow others to be in control, to take a full leadership role and for the true leader to become part of the team is no small challenge.

A considerable part of beginning work with leaders and during a workshop is to have the leaders, volitionally, place their power on the table as a resource to be taken and used by anyone in the room who feels capable of leading in a particular situation. In other words, when events dictate that leadership is in the hands of the person most likely to handle the issue best, it is this person who assumes control and not the leaders, who now facilitate the temporary leader by becoming a follower.

The story that comes to mind is about the dentist who called me and said, "I do not want to be the leader of my office any longer. I just want to concentrate on my being the best dentist I can be." He asked me to help free him from having to play the "heavy" with his staff. As it turned out, he was an excellent leader and a superb communicator but simply and forthrightly did not want the role of leader. What he clearly expressed was his desire to be a dentist and not the leader and manager of a business office. His picture of his office was that the people on his staff each became their own leader and did the best possible job they could without him, or anyone else, directing and "interfering" with them. More importantly was his commitment to this taking place. I remember him as being fearless and a remarkably receptive student when it came time for him to face his use of power as perceived by his staff.

Regardless of what he wanted and said communication in the office was, as expected, top-down. It was nothing like what he expressed to me as a desire for the distribution of power to each person on his team. His employees viewed him with respect, regard and probably some degree of adoration. His caring for them was exceptional, and not one was capable of sharing any of the problems or issues he or she may have had with his leadership style, which happened to be "parent to child." His employees each played their traditional role as dutiful employee, subordinate and child to the parent.

Bringing the staff to a level of understanding, acceptance and ownership of their respective jobs could not be forced by words alone. They each had to perceive the leader as one of the team simply doing his job. By placing the leader in as high and exalted position as they did, the thought of being equal and sharing power in any form seemed impossible. The individuals needed to have rock-solid evidence that his desire to do dentistry and not manage was, indeed, real. It took much dialogue between them all before acceptance began to take root and they all could talk about owning their respective jobs. The real "pulling of teeth" (no pun intended) came when we began to get to their feelings towards him and their relationships in the office. This is when the "rubber hit the road," and they began to accept that he sincerely did not want and need to lead. It was difficult because his personality was so outgoing and dominating. Loving and charismatic is what he was to everyone; but as I came to understand, this was not an act but the person he actually was.

What happened had to be witnessed to be believed. He was very aware of himself and his power to influence but used these attributes more as a gift and resource to others. He did not alter in any way his being a loving, nurturing, perceptive individual. What did change was his role as the dentist who did his work at the office not as its leader but as a significant participant. The staff, individually, began to take full control of their own responsibilities. None evidenced that they needed any leader directing their behavior. They each became their own leader. None of this was possible without the dentist's willingness to let go and to personally give effort and time to his and the others' growth, and which he did full out. What a remarkable role model.

Perfection Is Not Ours to Be

We humans are so obviously incomplete in our evolution that when I use the label "enlightened leader" I do not intend this to mean that such a completely enlightened person or leader actually exists. What I mean is that a particular person demonstrates superb and enlightened leadership behavior some of the time—but not all of the time. When I am in the company of quality leaders it is a pleasure to witness their considerable ability to be with and care for the growth of the people for whom they are responsible. I am also aware of their incompleteness and sense their passion to know more about themselves and others. It is as if they are aware of being unaware. This is made evident when they are not present, or locked into a position, miss teachable moments and are themselves not students. Even the best of leaders are human, and to be human is to err.

History tells us loud and clear that humankind is imperfect, and too few leaders met the challenges of their time. We know of the few remarkable leaders who during their reign achieved much, but even they lived with errors and omissions they either created or could not escape. The classic example is what usually happened after an enlightened leader's departure. Instead of preparing others to lead years prior to their departure from the world of leadership and power they leave behind ill-prepared people or none to replace them. History and my own experiences and mistakes, and working with many other leaders, demonstrate that this omission continues. To grow any person, to grow a leader, demands concrete experiences and learning from those experiences and why the existent leader needs to also be a teacher. It is why I believe it essential for quality leaders to surround themselves with people of merit, students who are also capable of leading as events dictate. I have learned that only those who are willing students dare to seek out the quality leader/teacher.

Who and What Behavior Make the Better Leaders?

Our best leaders do what they do with and for people intentionally; they are aware of what they do. This behavior is not accidental. The deliberate, conscious acts to be there for their people, to nurture their growth, to teach, to follow, to acknowledge and be the role model, and to continue to be a student to their students is rare and essential. As I so often stress, our best lessons are learned not as an uninvolved witness but as a participant in the action taking place. Experience is the vital component of learning, and getting into the thick of what *is* taking place is best of all.

In comparison, the leaders who are at best inadequate most likely think of themselves as effective and even excellent leaders, and do not seek their own growth but that of others. They have the position of power and authority in a hierarchy; they sit at its peak as owner/operator of a business, as parents or teachers. The majority come to their positions of leadership blind to the power they have to do either harm or good to their followers. What they too often see are pawns waiting for instructions to act but hardly to think. To be sure, there are inadequate leaders who may be conscious of their power and, intentionally, use it for personal gain. That is, they derive pleasure from wielding their power in order to enhance their own existence regardless of the damage this may do to others. This indifference to what they suffer others to bear becomes their eventual undoing rather than the consequences they expect. What one sows, one reaps.

Interpersonal Communication Is Itself Too Often a Morass

The problems of interpersonal communication, and most problems begin with communication, are their effect on our relationships with each other. Also, there is no easy way to correct communication when it is top-down or when power is an issue in the relationship. Since our concern here is leadership and power, this is where I believe the problems between people need to be confronted and corrected. The Inner Circle is an excellent place and relationship to scrutinize. If communication within an Inner Circle is fixed (not shared), one should visualize a pyramid with a fixed leader sitting on its peak while a sickness created by the leader is spread top-down throughout the whole body of an organism, whether two or thousands. It is of the leaders' own making, and yet they are the least likely to look at themselves as "the problem to the answer." Leaders influence their key people, who in turn influence their key people, who in turn influence their key people. And so it continues throughout an organization or a relationship between only two. (Chapters 5 and 6 deal directly with the issues of communication, the Inner Circle and reaching Genuine Dialogue.)

As indicated above and throughout the book, true leaders control the power and use it as either a destructive or a building tool. Leaders who do not see themselves as the creators of the environment they participate in and therefore as the most responsible one for what they have wrought fault others for their problems. This makes matters worse because by doing so, leaders justify their way of using power by making their shell harder to break through. Regardless of reasons and results, inadequate leaders are differentiated from quality leaders by the attitudes and behavior of those they lead. The differences are evident in so many ways at work through the success of problem-solving, creativity, productivity and the sense of ownership people demonstrate. One organization explodes in positives and growth and the other struggles to maintain and may not succeed at all. The former is led by excellent leaders, the latter by leaders out of touch and unconscious of their heavy-handed and controlling leadership style.

Titles do not a leader make although many claim the title of leader. Quality of relationships and performance sets one apart from the other. Inadequate leaders have communication issues that unless dealt with get worse. How can it be otherwise given that communication between people in a fixed hierarchy is not level? In comparison, a quality leader diminishes the separation between themselves and their key people. They accept and nurture that events, not people, dictate who is to be the leader. It is all about communication with others and the making of talk as level, mutual and authentic as possible and that leadership is only necessary when an event dictates so and not the leader.

LEADERSHIP AND CONSEQUENCES

Some people seek and willingly participate in an environment that is dysfunctional. They have a need for power and control, and satisfy this need by associating with inadequate leaders. Leaders who accept power-hungry people believe they are empowering themselves and not the competitors. Yet they are complicit in a game that is a competitive and even a survival-of-the-fittest environment. It becomes more about position and control than how well the organization does. Those not in the power game accept this state of affairs and its consequences as a matter of survival, particularly when they believe they have no choice and must conform in order to pay the bills and put food on the table. In dysfunctional and competitive environments people hide, choose sides and protect their backside. Any expectation of mutuality and cooperation does not exist here, distrust does. Eventually, conflict among players for power and dysfunction, as with any illness, sucks the energy of the organization and places its existence in jeopardy.

Communication between people is the problem to the answer if based on competition and power. It is not about solutions, innovation, creativity and inclusiveness. It is trouble with a big T when communication between members of the leader's Inner Circle has to do with protection of each member's position and the feathering of his or her own nest. Not only is communication warped, but each member's own Inner Circle becomes a bastion against the good of the whole. How does any organization or relationship function when its key people are each vying for power and control? And in how many different ways do they, then, influence the whole organization?

All Inner Circle members, whether aware or blind to dysfunctional communication that begins with their leaders, carry the message and germs of dysfunction to their own groups. Yet the leaders, who are the creator and initiator of the problems of communication, and accept no responsibility for the important role they play in this. It follows that problems and issues that need to be dealt with are often buried, avoided or altered to fit mood and temperament. Inadequate leadership is the first cause of dysfunction, and a cycle of despair and failure is its ultimate end.

At the positive end of the leadership spectrum, where communication is open and even attains a level of people being vulnerable with each other, growth is inevitable. With growth come creativity, spontaneity, dialogue, cooperation, mutuality and the quickest and the best responses to problems. Here power is shared, and people are empowered to exercise their own power—to contribute, to problem-solve and to grow. The resources and nurturing that quality leaders bring to their Inner Circle facilitate each becoming a better leader in their own Inner Circles, and therefore the whole of the organization benefits in positive and profound ways.

The environment, when positive and nurturing, is a creation of quality leadership working well with key people who themselves are leaders to others. I stress that it all begins with the leader; but without the Inner Circle members carrying the philosophy and methodology to their own Inner Circles, all of this would be for naught. The aura and influence of inclusion, respect and the invitation to open dialogue moves out to every corner of the organization. Communication is not the problem here. And more importantly, problems are seen as opportunities for innovation and growth.

There is also the case of leadership that does everything possible to remain invisible through assigning the public role of leader to another, and dysfunction is its result. Communication takes place between the hidden leader and the public leader, but not with the public leader's Inner Circle. What message do Inner Circle members carry from this relationship? A brief story illuminates this point.

I was invited to do a workshop with a CEO and his key executives having to do with improving dialogue between them and the more effective sharing of responsibilities. Sitting off to the side in a darkened alcove was the person who called upon me to help alleviate the problem he believed to be simply one of communication. The man sitting in the alcove had no intention of participating, but he wanted to observe everything that was to take place.

When I begin a workshop in a small-group setting, I know, or believe I know, where the real power is. That is, who is really in charge: in whose hands is the power to hire, fire and make final decisions? Leading up to the workshop I thought I made it clear that this power person (true leader) must participate. I was told that this person was the CEO and that the CEO would participate in the workshop. In a private talk with the CEO before the workshop began, this appeared to be confirmed. He assured me that he was given the power by his board to lead the firm—and, of course, those at the table were his personally selected Inner Circle.

It took about thirty minutes for me to realize that the CEO was not the actual leader. This was made clear through his words and behavior, and by the other executives sitting around the table. He and they constantly shifted their eyes to the person sitting in the darkened alcove as if seeking approval of what they were saying to me and each other. How could the CEO be the leader if, as it became apparent to me, the hidden observer was being acknowledged as the real power?

I called a break and cornered the secret observer. "The CEO is not really in power," I said. "It's obvious that none of the executives in the room believe that the CEO is anything but a puppet speaking for you. With you being in the room but not at the table with all the other executives, little of value will come from this workshop. Why don't you join us at the table? It will open up the dialogue you seek, which is why you hired me to conduct this workshop; and it will help the organization."

"That's why I brought you in," he said. "I need you to help the CEO do a better job of running the firm so I can go on with other business interests."

In response I said, "Unless you give him full power and authority to run this organization, he won't and can't do so. His supposed Inner Circle knows that he is your 'mouthpiece' and flounder with him awaiting your instructions. Either you assume outright leadership of the organization or find someone you fully trust and give them the full power and authority to run it."

Trying to convince this leader, or any leader, that he or she is the creator of an organization's environment and therefore inextricably influences interpersonal issues is no small challenge. This is particularly true if the leader wants freedom to do other things while still holding on to the reins of power of another entity. In this case, it became clear that the true leader was both professional and entrepreneurial, and was seeking the best for both his worlds. He could not be tied down to one or the other. He was fully dedicated to his chosen profession as well as the best possible operation of his other entities: an impossible task if power and leadership are not properly and fully given to another.

Ultimately, the real leader admitted to and accepted that he needed to give up control. He corrected his errors and omissions, and the organization moved ahead with stronger leadership and an Inner Circle that he did not micro-manage. This story is another example demonstrating that entrepreneurial behavior is not the same or even similar to that of a leader. Be one or the other. Do not attempt to wear both hats at the same time, or both suffer.

The story above is another example of the difficulties present when dynamic entrepreneurs or leaders expect the people they depend on to handle important tasks. Most leaders do not see themselves as a barrier or problem in their significant relationships. What they do see and believe is that the people they count on and need are the problem; and the leaders therefore seek outside help, only not for themselves but for their key people. The more common ways leaders deal with problems and their key people is to exercise more power over them through intimidation and fear, demotion or dismissal. In other words, leaders "kill the messenger." Another, and more modern way, is to bring in outside consultants to do the "dirty work." But since the employees are not the problem, this approach is failure-bound.

Consulting organizations that specialize in rooting out and helping troubled executives and management deal with personnel problems may discover that the leaders are the "problem to the answer." But, as with the people they are employed to help, they too will be reluctant to inform the leaders that they are the problem. It is most difficult to "bite the hand that feeds you."

That reminds me of a workshop I did in New York City years ago. During a break a psychologist came to me and stated that, "If you confront a client with 'you are the power and primary cause of the problems in your family,' you'd likely have no clients." Obviously, my comments having to do with identifying who holds the power in the family and that he or she is the source of the problem is, potentially, too hot an issue. This is particularly true if that person is unwilling to acknowledge and accept this.

It took years of work with organizations before I realized the importance of the leader relative to the state of their relationships, whether personal or at work. It was then that I came to understand the futility of working with subordinates as "the problem to the answer." Thus, the efforts, time and expense devoted to attempting to develop more productive and contented subordinates results in, at best, a more sophisticated façade. Nothing will have changed beyond nuances if leadership does not change their own beliefs and behaviors towards those they lead.

By not dealing with, or avoiding, those who are at the root of the problems, the "professional healers" do no more than treat the symptoms. Does this solve the problem of power and how it is used or masks the problem and makes it worse? The answer is, as this chapter stresses, if leaders are the source and primary cause of the problems with those they lead, the leaders are the people who need to be helped. If this help to grow as a person is not requested and sought by the leaders, they can be taught every possible leadership tool and nothing will have changed.

In a general sense, most leaders are aware of the communication and personal problems that exist between those they lead and themselves. They feel the tension and possibly even the games being played and yet to consider themselves as a major contributor to the relationship between them and others is rare. As I have stressed, leaders are prone to faulting others and not themselves. What makes matters worse is that communication between people who live and work together is not simply necessary, it is essential to a relationship's very existence.

Whether deliberate or accidental, communication that excludes mutuality has to end up causing greater communication difficulties. The leaders' influence, and how and what they communicate, spreads as well as changes as it moves down through any hierarchy. It is similar to the game "telephone," where people whisper a brief story to the person next to them, and each person repeats the story to the person next to them. When the game is over, the story told by the person at the end of the line is likely to be a totally different story from the original story told. At what point, and person, does the original story get almost completely altered? It does not require many people to sufficiently alter a story so that it is hardly recognizable from its original telling. This is an innocent and fun game at a party; but at the workplace or in relationships if safety, trust and respect do not exist, the consequences are considerably worse and certainly with no laughter either.

The Subgroup

When an Inner Circle's communication is dysfunctional, which takes place when the leader is unable to make timely decisions and is perceived as weak or too strong and controlling, a subgroup is likely to form. The subgroup's creation is not about building a better and more successful organization. The subgroup's agenda is to serious undercut and damage the well-being of an organization because the motives of the members are self-centered and self-serving. The subgroup leader and the subgroup suck positive energy from the organization in order to satisfy the subgroup's own needs and goals.

Subgroup leaders will build their own, exclusive, Inner Circle while also working deliberately and consciously to gain the true leaders' trust and respect. They usually hold important positions in the organization and are good at what they do, that is, they play to the needs of the leaders. A primary example of this is that the inadequate leader usually sees the subgroup leader as one of their key allies and supporters. Why not? This environment actually fuels the power and influence of the subgroup leader. However, what the subgroup leader seeks is not ownership or the responsibilities that come with leadership but the strings to control the supposed power of ownership.

Reluctance to Grow Personally is Ubiquitous

Whenever leaders are unwilling or resistant to accepting their considerable complicity in the creating of an environment, how can the environment change without a leader's departure or admission of the need to personally grow? What exists between leaders and those they lead is difficult, if not impossible, to alter without the leader's permission and full participation in the process.

Our leaders, including parents, teachers and bosses of every kind not only build the environments we live and work in, whether aware of doing that or not, control what they build. How does the baby or child go against their parent? How do students go up against their teacher? How does an employee go up against the boss? Some try, but lose. And those holding the power win battles—but all suffer the cost of the war.

This brings to mind another page in the story in Chapter 1 having to do with my experiences while at the Las Vegas resort-hotel.

Although employed as a consultant to do a specific job, I was asked to participate in all executive meetings during the period of construction and operations that lasted close to four years. The president/leader wanted me to be at every meeting for reasons to be discovered at a later time. Beyond knowledge in my specific field, I believed I had nothing to contribute or to gain from the executive meetings. I was so wrong!

When it came to leadership lessons and the uses and abuses of power, the meetings proved to be immensely important to my understanding of leadership. As it turned out, being witness to the machinations of the leader who oversaw the construction and operations until the casino-resort's eventual sale to the public corporation proved to be an invaluable series of lessons on leadership, power and consequences. Taking full advantage of the experiences I had there, I learned a great deal about leadership and use of power that was far beyond anything I had previously experienced. These are the life experiences that not only teach, if we would wise enough to ponder, but cut deep enough so that the lessons become indelible. What I witnessed, then, clearly influenced my own leadership style. The experiences also enriched my ability to inform and teach other leaders the necessity for their own transformation as people and as leaders.

Some meetings were held at 2:00 A.M., and everyone had to be fully dressed with jacket and tie. Being present and ready regardless of the hour was critical if an executive wanted to keep his or her job. You may ask, and I did, "Why 2:00 in the morning?" On the one hand it could be argued that we were all so busy during the day doing our respective jobs that we had to meet at such an ungodly hour. On the other hand, it was an effective way for the leader to demonstrate his power. I did not question his motives, but I always believed that the timing of these meetings was more about power and control than any other reason.

At one never-to-be-forgotten meeting, the leader made a few opening comments about a very expensive marketing program and asked for feedback from each of the executives at the table. Each person had something to say, and most comments seemed to clarify issues and agree with what the leader had suggested in his comments. When it came to the marketing director, however, he stated unequivocally, "I disagree with the program. I think it will fail. It won't do the job. It is a huge sum of money I believe is being poorly spent." The leader waited for more comments from the marketing director, who neither said anything more nor offered any alternative approach.

Silence in the room was deafening for a period of two to three minutes when the leader literally jumped out of his chair and began, verbally, to tear the marketing director apart. It was the most violent use of the English language I had ever witnessed. The words, mixed with anger and disrespect, came quickly, cut to the bone and had everyone squirming in their seats. I was blown away by the destructive nature of the barrage the leader leveled directly at this talented and experienced person. On my drive home after the meeting, I went over the dramatic events very carefully to try to understand what and why it all took place. This disturbing confrontation baffled me as to why it was so verbally violent.

This same leader and I met most Saturday mornings in my office, initially, to discuss my program and related issues. He was a great listener and a candid responder to issues and questions I needed answered. In fact, I would have to say that our relationship became about as open and direct as I could hope for. Today, I know that he and I experienced Genuine Dialogue. Fear, status and authority never entered the room. Between us, particularly in private, we were always in a mutual relationship. Before too long our relationship turned, for him, into a close approximation of "his" therapy session.

We spoke of everything from his work issues to his family issues. Even without my probing nothing seemed out of bounds for him to share. In time, this would include the occasions and happenings that I personally experienced in the executive meetings that left me confused. As I remember, he did not "justify" his words and behavior; and he easily answered all questions I asked him. His response was always clear and seemed reasonable to me.

Keep in mind that from the beginning of our relationship I was aware that his power was beyond any I had ever experienced before. Initially, it must have kept me from being more candid with him about some issues but never about what were my responsibilities. As time and our dialogue progressed, his power disappeared during our conversations. We were more like two friends talking and sharing our day's experiences. Nevertheless, I never lost the sense that I wanted to understand him as a leader. He had unique attributes I needed to know more about.

It may have been unconscious, but relative to power and leadership I became his student as opposed to being a buddy, judge or jury. In retrospect, since we were so different I know I also became his teacher. The issue of relationship and what takes place in that "between" space always mystifies and compels me to try to understand how it works. In my office our relationship became mutual and dynamic, and we were equals. In his office, I always felt he was the president and I a hired consultant.

Much later on when I began to teach about the Inner Circle and its unique dynamics, I tried to make it clear that what an Inner circle is and experiences behind closed doors does not remain the same as when the door is open and others are involved. The reason is that tradition and expectations are very hard to overcome. What takes place in privacy between people is not always what takes place in public or other venues. Only lessons and possible results are carried outside.

Back to one of our Saturday morning sessions: I candidly asked the leader about the 2:00 A.M. meeting where he verbally attacked the marketing director. He answered me without hesitation, "We had to make a decision that morning about a considerable outlay of money in preparation of our opening party. When I asked for each executive's thoughts on the subject, I was looking for creative suggestions including problems anyone anticipated in the program, why and suggested solutions. In fact, I welcome disagreement but want a better or another idea attached to any criticism."

He shared a critical lesson with me: when seeking the opinions of others he welcomed disagreement and criticisms—but with the caveat that attached to any disagreement is an idea to make things better. I mentioned to him that I never heard him say this to me or anyone else. He argued back that "any executives worth their salt should know this." I said nothing more but thought immediately of the marketing director and his destruction. What would have been the marketing director's response had he understood how the leader expected disagreement to be handled? *Expectations* between people, without being brought out in the open and clarified, are "land mines" of trouble. If and when they explode, all within range are harmed. That was the case here.

This is not an uncommon problem. Leaders do not, generally, discuss their expectations and invite discussion with subordinates as to how interpersonal communications need to work when they are together. More importantly, most leaders simply fail to set the example for how discussion takes place in actual practice. I never heard anything about what I call the rules of engagement, but I learned much later on that this is rare in any case. Did I knowingly do this when I played the role of leader? I have an uncomfortable feeling that at the beginning of my leadership roles I may have taken establishing rules of communication for granted. But I learned that this is essential between people who live and work together if communication is to be effective and inclusive.

Another short story, somewhat, connected to the above: At the resort I had a secretary who was, initially, as fragile as anyone I have ever worked with. Every time I approached her with issues (properly typed letters, appropriate notification of appointments, etc.), she broke down and cried. If I entered the workplace without acknowledging her, she broke down and cried. She was sure that I had ignored her because she had done something wrong and was going to be dismissed.

One day I called her into my office and told her that I wasn't any different from her. I was a person doing my job, and she was a person doing her job. I told her that I did respect and care for her, and that if I forgot to say "good morning" it was that my mind was somewhere else. My body was there for her to see, but I didn't see anything but the issue in my head. I added that I simply wanted us to be there for each other and the work we had to do—and it was okay to treat me as any other person.

I repeated this as often as possible until it was obvious that she "got it." One Saturday, maybe a month or two after our discussion about her fears and feelings, I was with the president of the resort having one of our "sessions" when, unannounced, she came into the office and asked if the two of us could possibly quiet down because our voices were interfering with some activity talking place in a room near us. We immediately did so. Later I thanked her for her service to us and her concern for the needs of others. We both came to understand each other and, not so incidentally, she grew as a person and as a secretary. I smile now even thinking of her many years later.

Early in my leadership education I may have assumed that through my behavior others would know and understand me. This is leadership acting on assumption. It is a constant responsibility of leaders to make clear what they want and need from their significant relationships and in what form communication between us works best. Also, leaders need to verbalize their intentions and expectations because taking things for granted leads to trouble begging to happen. In my many years as a leader and then as a mentor to other leaders, any expectations I or they had were identified as quickly as possible, clarified and openly dealt with. What is left unsaid so often speaks too loudly.

Leaders who expect their followers to be open, candid and better all-around participants need first to be open, candid and equally receptive to their employees. People trust their own perceptions and either become more open and authentic or closed and protective. Trust does neither take place as a result of a leader's words and promises nor through threats or manipulation. If trust is to be established, it depends solely on people's perceptions of each other.

Quality leaders are aware and intentional in what they do; and the bad apple sees this and drops from the tree. Talent and potential flourish in an environment that invites and resources honest participation and encourages open dialogue, the taking of responsible leader-like actions and definitely facilitates personal growth. Leadership whose philosophy is about power, self-aggrandizement and exclusivity inhibits talent and potential from others coming out into the light of day. People have considerably more potential that is hidden than what they allow to come out, and this is due to their perception of the "welcoming committee."

Back, once more, to the casino-hotel in Las Vegas: The original president and leader of the Las Vegas complex led each phase from construction to successful operation to its eventual purchase by a public corporation. Clearly, he knew what needed to be done and employed the right people to make it happen. From the beginning he was given a "free hand" and unlimited resources to take the project from design to a fully functioning operation; and he, deservedly, earned great recognition for his accomplishments. He successfully brought a vision to reality, including bringing on board the best available talent to manage the operation from gaming tables, restaurants, rooms and convention sales to the finest entertainment available at that time. Finally, he had the foresight and courage to experiment with a first-of-its-kind family program designed for children pre-school through teens for guests of the hotel.

It was during our Saturday morning sessions that I came to know and understand this powerful leader. It was then that I became more than his employee (as a consultant, builder and operator of the children's project); we became equals. Away from my environment, elsewhere and with others, the operational hierarchy reformed and controlled our relationship; and we both played our parts. It was an important lesson to realize that his relationship to key management was, for the most part, a fixed hierarchical structure. In public he presented a picture of power, fully in charge and permanently fixed in place. The question I often asked but found no answer: Did his hierarchical relationship change behind closed doors as it did with me on Saturdays?

We learned much about each other only when he set his power aside. As equals we talked to each other person-to-person. It was a very different feeling and environment when compared to our being with others and his taking on the role of authority and me as the subordinate. But I knew he listened to and understood me even when I was in my subordinate role, and he demonstrated considerable trust in what I had to say. During the construction and the following operational stages I believed him to be a brilliant leader. At this time in my life he was my role model of what a leader needs to be and do in order to get the job done and at its highest possible level of quality. But what did I know at the time? Not much but the education and recreation of children and the training of staff.

I pose the following questions retrospectively. Was he as wise and good a leader as I believed him to be? What have I learned since that might have made him a better leader? For example, did he receive from his Inner Circle members all of the best of what each brought to the table? I also know that he needed to communicate his expectations and have more open dialogue with his Inner Circle. Had I understood then what I discovered many years later, I believe that he would have heard and understood my words and warnings about his errors and omissions having to do with his expectations and communications style with his key people. Perhaps, more importantly, he needed to understand that his words and behavior in front of his Inner Circle either "lit their fire" or kept them mostly operating at a moderate and self- protective burn. To this day I believe he, they and the overall operation would have gone to still another dimension of quality if enough safety and security existed between them. It was obvious to me, even then, how much others held back their opinions and feelings on almost every subject they had to deal with at those meetings. It was all the opposite of the experience we both had in our Saturday morning sessions. How safe he and I felt with each other when in my environment as compared to being in his environment. As leaders, we all have much to learn.

Quality Human Relationships Require Tending

Given quality leadership, what happens when relatively enlightened leaders depart the scene? Thoughtful, good leadership, as I define leaders, prepare for this eventuality. They have trained others, certainly at least one, to replace them because without this preparation, and which may take years, a vacuum is created when that leader leaves the organization. Unless others have been well prepared for this, there is a strong likelihood that competition and breakdowns in unity will take place and chaos may follow. We go from periods of light and growth to despair too quickly. History is replete with these examples.

Wise leaders who build a healthy Inner Circle do not necessarily select a specific leader to replace them. This is possible when an Inner Circle functions at so high a level that leadership changes as it needs to change, depending on events and the personal experience one has in order to take charge of a given event. An inclusive and pragmatic leadership philosophy nurtures the growth of leadership beyond the leader and is available to all within the Inner Circle. And not to be forgotten: a leader is necessary only if the event calls for leadership and, if not, each person is his or her own leader.

The problem as I frame it is that an organization or relationship is less its body or limbs but is what comes from its head. This is where the true power is to be found. Quality leadership confirms this through a quality Inner Circle, the level of dialogue and that each member is empowered to lead, to take ownership of a problem. Does a committee do the job as well or with the same efficiency? This comes directly from my own history of leadership. I always had effective Inner Circles, but they were much too narrow in their world experiences. Did this place me too frequently in having to be the leader?

What I did not do is seek out and enlist entrepreneurial types. I did not isolate and educate one single person to be what I was, and that is entrepreneurial. I selected those I believed to have excellent leadership qualities. This insight to identify the one person who would and could take over my role as an entrepreneur came much later, actually not before I became a mentor to other leaders.

We know that the true entrepreneur gets it on. We also know that quality leaders surround themselves with quality people in order to operate and grow an organization. In line with this I discovered that a troubled relationship or organizational problems have at their core troubled leadership with results spread throughout the body. All are symptoms of bad leadership. It takes being an unattached but perceptive witness to an Inner Circle's interactions to realize the truth of this.

The message received is that it is extremely difficult and complex to fix relationship and dialogic issues unless the leaders accept being the key problem to the answer. It is the leaders who must be open to their power to influence and therefore to seek personal growth. They cannot demand this of others but only for themselves. And yet, it may be too difficult if not impossible for any person to volitionally come to this by and through one's own efforts and why the need for a mentor.

Leadership is ubiquitous and exists in every possible human relationship, whether involving two or thousands, and is part of our existence from conception to death. Parents are immediate and important leaders to their newborn child. Yet through the vagaries of life, parents become as children losing their power and role to their children. Where are leaders not found and not necessary?

Whether as parents, teachers or as leaders in organizations that humans build, we lead ourselves, lead others or are led. The ideal is that leadership is self-achieved, dynamic and shifts to those most able to lead. Parents initially hold and use their power, but over time the parental powers wane even to the point that those they held power over now hold power over them. In the proper and healthy Inner Circle, every aspect of leadership is found and used. Events dictate this.

In any case, humans are biologically in hierarchical relationships and usually to a leader whom they rarely choose. For the most part, life and the luck of the draw do the choosing for us. If our leaders, beginning with our parents, happen to be aware and conscious of their role and responsibility towards us, there is a strong likelihood that we will be nurtured to be what we are meant to be. In other words, love and nurturing will be given us with few expectations, and we learn from our earliest relationships that the world is good, safe and secure. Generally, this translates to being more independent, to leading one's self and respecting others to lead themselves. Does this nurturing environment help make us better leaders? I strongly believe so; but again, this is a matter of learning not of blood.

For many, probably for too many, all that happens is that they are fed but not nurtured to be themselves; instead, and worse, they become what others choose for them to be. And if born female in certain cultures, they may not live to see many days. For those who do survive childhood, expectations, whether from the parents or the culture are too restrictive, and rare are those who break through their past conditioning. Those who do, do so with the help of others. People really do need people.

Expectations influence a relationship; they are too often silent and almost impossible to confront. Left unsaid, expectations are powerful vibes extending out from those in power to those dependent on that power. And when expectations are spoken without any room for understanding and dialogue, expectations are exponentially more powerful and breed discontent. A classic example is the parents who expect their child to become a doctor. They pay the cost of the best education and surround the child with an environment meant to facilitate everything going in the direction the parents have arranged. But the child grows to love music and the guitar, and dreams of being a musician. Are the parents talking to their child? Do they recognize the child's love for music and the creative arts, or are the parents dreaming their dream and the child his or her own dream? Does the child, now a person, live the life chosen by others or the one chosen by him or her? Have parents and child/person ever come close to genuine dialogue with each other? How is this extremely important problem between them to be resolved? Being a leader either by choice or accident can never be taken for granted. The influence on others a leader is responsible for may often be invisible, but has the potential power of a "knife through one's heart."

A REVIEW

It is worth reviewing the multiple roles a leader has as stated in this and other chapters: leaders are teachers, role models and students to their students and followers. This is what leaders are whether they accept this or not because in the eyes of those they lead this is what and who they are. To be unaware of this responsibility misses what all leaders bring to significant relationships and why the potential of people being led too often remains just potential. Whoever said or wrote being a leader is fun and easy? I believe it to be the "father or mother" of all responsibilities. How does anyone refute this?

Having leaders in our lives at the beginning has to be a biological necessity in order for humanity to survive. How do we exist without relationship to others in every stage in our journey? As we age and move from the world of our family and its influence, we continue to be influenced, and influence in turn. Apart from parents, family and friends, we meet teachers, classmates and numerous authority figures. There is leadership somewhere in every one of our relationships whether it comes from us or others. All play a part in who and what we are, and are to become. In turn, we use our learned behavior and attitudes towards power and leadership in all of our relationships. No one is simply at the effect without also becoming an effect.

Finally, the most important lessons we humans learn do not take place in a classroom or the reading of a book, but between us in our relationships. It is in this space that we experience each other and where the greatest impact and influence take place. Yet, most of us are blind to the power of position to influence our relationships whether as a leader or as a follower. At one time or another most humans are bound to be one, the other, and probably both.

What can we learn about ourselves through relationships? A great deal! But, if this is to happen, it is essential that Genuine Dialogue occurs in our important relationships. It is difficult to make happen but so is climbing most mountains and they are climbed every day by thousands. Most important and probably the biggest and most difficult metaphorical mountain to climb is the one I label Genuine

Dialogue. It cannot happen unless people, in significant relationship, want this for themselves and the other.

One person must lead the way, and this one has to be the true power person. The true power person does not demand that another be genuine, and only through their own courage and vulnerability do they demonstrate this to others. Then, and only then, are people willing to risk openness, honesty and being vulnerable themselves. The leader is the key to trust, respect, Genuine Dialogue and love between people who live and work closely together.

It is true that we learn how to protect ourselves from those with power over us; and in the process of building walls, we are also walling ourselves in. It is also true that nurturing and loving relationships help us to be ourselves and to tear down walls. This comes early; it may come late or not at all. This depends on those we meet in our life's journey. And since humans are not cast in concrete we are able to unlearn and learn anew. Being and remaining "the" student is essential to our final breath. It is how we learn to know when to close ourselves off and when to open ourselves up. Leaders need to take note of this since they hold the key to doors people choose to open and close. It is always a matter of perception. The wise take advantage of the "teachable moments." The unwise do not even recognize the opportunity.

The chapter that follows is about attributes that quality leaders possess to one degree or another. People are not born with the attributes I refer to, but they are learned from nurturing, understanding relationships with people who are our leaders and teachers. With good fortune, we meet people who have influence over us who continue to facilitate our growth; and we become what we desire to become. In the process we take on attributes as if they are us. In fact, attributes are not possessions but are acquired through our relationships to others.

We each have the power within us to be what we choose to be, but it helps immeasurably to be assisted along the way. Good parenting, teachers, friends and our leaders all play a big hand in our growth; but the final responsibility is ours and ours alone, and this demands an immense amount of courage "to be" and to seek out those who will help us be.

CHAPTER 4

ATTRIBUTES OF RELATIVELY ENLIGHTENED LEADERS

Most anyone can learn
Head and heart are one unit
Being is necessary.

He came across as if he believed himself to be omnipotent and omniscient. When he spoke his words came, not as a comment, but a definitive statement that required no further discussion, no exchange of opinions. We met at a dinner party of a mutual acquaintance. When the acquaintance introduced us he also briefly described the work that we both did and that "I think you two have much to talk about." We did and as we discovered it had to do with his view of power and how he applied power. Our philosophies were worlds apart.

He told me about the retreat that he and his "followers" had built in a desert environment far from any neighbors or the intrusion of strangers. The purpose of the community was to bring clients seeking psychological help in to their totally encapsulating community for resolution of their emotional issues.

Clients lived at the facility for as long as he believed necessary and his approach was to slowly and deliberately eliminate a client's defenses and to make them dependent on him as the only voice and guide. He provided his clients with the appearance of love, concern, sympathy and conveyed immense confidence that he knew what his clients had to do to correct an, apparently, grief ridden and lonely existence.

He seemed interested in knowing more about the philosophy of leadership and power we lived by in our firm, but as I discovered, not because he was open to learning about another viewpoint, but rather his desire to establish his philosophy as dominant and preferable. As it turned out our relationship continued more out of his desire to destroy our "myth of leadership and power" than his desire to consider alternatives. It was hardly a question of dialogue between us, but his justifying his approach to power. Although any sort of agreement was out of the question what intrigued me, and why our dialogue continued were his attributes that were so about control.

He was confident enough in himself that I was invited to observe the way he communicated with his followers who numbered approximately fifty. No question but that he was charismatic, intense and bright and demonstrated these attributes in every public opportunity. He definitely wanted people to view him as special. He clearly loved the role of guru, and the power and influence he knew he conveyed that others looked to from him. He expressed the fullest confidence and capability of providing love, security and wisdom to any and all that came to him. But, being human, his needs and agenda soon enough began to reveal the pretense and charade behind the aura he attempted to create.

At first it was a single client's complaints and criticisms of what they had gone through. Soon it became others and when problems began to appear in his community amongst his followers the organization quickly unraveled. It was weak foundation built solely on shallow attributes and the leader's charismatic behavior. The leader's Inner Circle was made up people whose needs were as considerable and dysfunctional as many of his clients. They were so obviously dependent on him and no one that I met appeared trained or allowed to take a leadership role. The people who were closest to him were themselves in need of the security and love. When the ground he stood on began to weaken, to be questioned, his followers began to look elsewhere for another "rock" to stand on. The life time of the therapeutic community was brief. His attributes may have shined brightly for a time, but wore through to the truth quickly.

What I witnessed as an outsider was a person who loved power and the playing of "master" teacher and the only leader of his flock. The attributes he showed his followers and clients were finely sculptured and made to fit him perfectly as long as he was on stage. Off stage, when relaxed and not doing his thing, and this with few and select people, the attributes he used with his clients and followers were quickly set aside. Interestingly, he would laugh and make light of the way his followers and clients deferred to him when he played his role as "master."

The preceding brief story has much to do with negative and destructive attributes and, in this case, deliberately worn as if clothing to cover, what turned out to be, a warped mind and abusive use of power. But exterior attributes, that is the playing of roles, are common among many leaders and are exemplified above and in the story that follows. Also, the roots of the story below are told in Chapter 1 and should be easy to recognize and connect and why continued here.

I was invited to attend a meeting held by a former camper, teenage-worker and employee who had recently become the owner and operator of a business. He wanted me to meet and observe his having a meeting with his staff, which I was pleased to do. I remembered that although he was remarkably self-sufficient and extremely confident in his ability to accomplish tasks, he was a loner who did not appear to have mutually nurturing relationships as a camper and teenager. And this was not easy to do since seven or eight campers, counselor and junior counselor lived and shared most camp experiences together. Regardless of efforts of his counselors and my own intervention to deal with his socialization within the group, he never became one of the "gang." In spite of this, he returned to camp year after year and never, as far as I knew, appeared discontent or caused problems.

Why did I expect (be careful of expectations) different behavior from him as an adult and, eventually, as a leader? He grew into adulthood what he was as a young boy and teenager—a self-sufficient loner. But, as I was soon to witness and learn about him, he knew he needed others, primarily as additional "hands" to make his dreams a reality. And he, too, as with the opening story in this chapter, sought out needy people as needy people tend to seek out those who will care for them. If there is a form of mutuality here, it is that the former seeks extra hands as tools and the latter willing to be those "hands" as long as they are cared for and protected.

I believed or wanted to believe that I was invited to observe an interesting hour or two of excellent communication and leadership. He told me prior to the meeting that "It was the philosophy of camp I'm using in my organization." I was hopeful that it would be inclusive, nurturing, empowering and he, as leader, valued dialogue and each person as unique. Why did I believe he would behave that way despite his being a loner at camp? I hoped that his many experiences at camp did, in fact, influence him to incorporate a philosophy of cooperation and mutuality to new heights.

In a matter of minutes it became obvious that his style and philosophy of leading had nothing to do with the philosophy of camp. He was in control from the moment the meeting began. Dialogue was non-existent because his interest and focus were on his vision alone, and input from others was not invited. He was in charge and spoke in an almost "messianic" manner of what the employees must do in order to create the "better" organization and world he envisioned. There was no exchange of ideas, agreement or disagreement; and there were no questions.

In those few moments of listening to his words and watching his body language, I, not surprisingly, realized that this was still the child and teenager I knew from camp. Only at this time he was the adult in charge, bright, capable and definitely charismatic and determined to achieve. He came across as if on a white horse leading his army charging against an enemy he saw before him. He was still the loner, but now with a very strong singular vision of what he wanted. He was clearly in power, and he coveted and loved that power. Not only did he relish the role as a charismatic, hypnotic leader, he obviously enjoyed stroking the strings of the needs his staff members brought to their relationships.

I was disturbed for a number of reasons. First was his obvious need for power; second, a philosophy that had little to do with the personal growth of his staff and others; and third, his world view. In essence, he was not about contributing to what exists or making things better, but rather he was attempting to escape what IS for a vision he believed ought to be. What came out as soon as he began to speak to his staff was his self-centered belief in him alone. And, also, I realized that what he wanted from me were tools, not a philosophy of personal growth. To this extent he was and is a student, but having little to do with personal growth or the common good, but to better control others. His focus and determination to have it his way, whatever it would take to realize his vision, he was willing to pay the price, as long as he pulled the strings. And, he did.

From the beginning of our relationship, I misread him. Yes, he did excellent work with the tasks presented to him, but less for the job required and more to gain points and respect from those in power. I bought in but eventually learned another invaluable lesson having to do with why people do the things they do. Later on, many bright and high-achieving people would reach out to me for the same reason. They wanted to be more effective as leaders but not necessarily to grow themselves or anyone else. If a tool seemed good enough to increase their effective power and influence over others, they wanted that tool. In words having to do with this chapter, people will do much and pay a big price for attributes that facilitate winning, but not to go through the most difficult process of personal growth that demands being vulnerable.

The differences are glaring between leaders who seek tools in order to become more powerful and manipulative as compared to leaders who sincerely commit to their own growth and that of others in their lives. My experiences were instructive and I came to realize that I had to separate leaders who seek power tools (attributes) from the leaders who volitionally seek to grow as a person and in the process try to nurture others to grow. It was not long in duration before I became aware that many who invited me to conduct workshops having to do with office communication and relationships mostly had in mind "their people" and not themselves. With this realization I began to make sure, up front that the leaders hear and understand that I hold them responsible for a major part of their organization's interpersonal issues. To the credit of many once this was made clear most accepted the challenge to be a student and not in control. Being vulnerable sets attributes aside and role playing is replaced by the "real" person.

In the two stories above, both leaders appeared to have attributes that were dynamic and magnetic. Both were bright, charismatic, loved power and control, and were able to gather people who needed what they, apparently, offered even if deceptive. They also created environments that met the needs of those seeking a charismatic leader. They both focused on mind and emotional strings in order to induce supportive behaviors on the part of their followers. Yet they both failed to build anything lasting or substantial. Neither was capable of building an effective, well-functioning Inner Circle and nurturing Genuine Dialogue. This could never have happened due to the leaders' controlling behavior. Both leaders did not surround themselves with people of merit and the courage to easily and candidly express their opinions and knowledge. What they wanted and got were followers in need of a false sense of security and, perhaps, power through association with dominating leaders.

WHY THE "RELATIVELY" ENLIGHTENED LEADER?

The fully enlightened leader does not yet exist in real life. Humans are imperfect; leaders (historic or present) are human and therefore, regardless of what some of them might have thought or done, are imperfect. When I describe the attributes of a "relatively" enlightened leader I do not intend attributes as something inborn but rather what is learned and acquired through life experience whether accidental or deliberate. What follows are positive attributes attainable by most people if they are willing students and seek or are gifted a wide variety of experiences with people and events, and that they learn from their experiences.

A major problem for humans is that we do not see ourselves—however our behavior is witnessed by others. And, because we are not witness to our own behavior, we do not know ourselves as others close to us see and know us. The view of one's self is too subjective to be accurate. In fact, thinking we can be our own witness to what we say and do takes us out of the present and places us as an audience to ourselves as actors. Is this a form of madness? It is why I write throughout the book how important our relationships, whether personal or at work, are to each of us, that is, if we want to grow from within outward. In other words, we need those significant to us to help us know ourselves and to become more ourselves.

Also, by choosing the "Attributes of the Relatively Enlightened Leader" as the title to this chapter, I intend degrees of enlightenment not enlightenment itself. High-quality leaders I have worked with have many excellent attributes, but all (as does this mentor) have failings and weaknesses mixed with our more positive attributes. What they have in common is being students and all have a thirst for personal growth and experiences. They hear, understand and accept that they must be open to their own growth if they are to facilitate growth in those with whom they live and work.

In the coming pages is a partial list of attributes that I believe provide the essential groundwork to being and becoming quality leaders. All leaders are people and most people can learn and use any of the attributes identified unless they fear knowing themselves through the eyes of others. I have encountered a lack of courage to grow, but more common is the degrees of apprehension of what this may mean; it is, after all, an unknown.

What needs to be understood is that "expectations" of what is to come needs to be set aside because growth is unpredictable in how it is to take place, if it is to take place. Also, and more reason for eliminating expectation, is that others in their group may not choose to participate and what they will not share may be important building blocks. The process to help a leader grow had everything to do with the willingness of subordinates to share their perceptions of the leader. This requires a level of safety that people must feel is "ironclad" and this requires so much more than words and promises.

People who seek to grow and hope to grow others in the process need to be aware of the complexity of this challenge. It is why I suggest that they seek outside mentors to facilitate their search for growth. The wise learn from experience that they are unable to grow their own sense of self without help and "objectivity" and this comes best from outside their own world of influence. The odds are that this seeking for relative enlightenment is due to issues of communication, relationship and, also, that of power. Problems of communication, relationships, and power are not academic or intellectual problems. They are problems of self and others in relationships each trying to be and become. Somewhere along the journey true students give up seeking easy answers, personal protection and the protecting of others.

WHERE QUALITY ATTRIBUTES COME FROM

The lucky among us are born into environments and relationships that nurture our becoming the unique individuals we are in the first place. We meet these lucky ones in life as more enlightened people and they could be our teachers, friends and bosses. Who does not remember that special person who respects us as we are and treats us as the unique being we each are supposed to be? To be born into a family that lives and shares respect, power and leadership via love, dialogue and behavior. It is here that the individual's uniqueness is nurtured and at the same time so is membership in and responsibility to the family and community. How necessary to humankind.

The family is the initial crucible that makes us who we are but not necessarily what we are to become. Humans are not cast in concrete; we remain clay to be shaped and reshaped throughout our lifetime. Potential may initially be severely restricted simply by those who are supposed to be caregivers and nurturers because they, themselves, have not known love and nurturing. The parents may not have learned and or possess the attributes that truly nurture another. This is not a permanent state even if begun badly. As we age we have no way of knowing who we will encounter along our journey. All humans are a potential gift to another and may trigger a pilot light to at last burst forth in full flame. People who have acquired certain attributes are capable of "gifting" them to others assuming those others are open when they interact.

It is difficult to seed and grow enlightened behavior in an individual who did not have a family that provided consistent love, nurturing, respect and an environment "to be." Also, there are people throughout the world who believe that our lives are pre-cast in stone. That is, we earn a better birth and life through how we live our present life, and that the sharing of love and kindness to those we meet on our present journeys predicts our next.

I do not challenge another's beliefs, but know what I have personally experienced. People are capable of growth and do change regardless of what their childhood, youth or adult behavior is like. It takes place in relationships and openness I call "being vulnerable," It can happen in personal relationships, at work, friendships and accidental as I have personally experienced a few times.

Growth is often a matter of good fortune when a person who has power and influence over us happens to be compassionate, understanding, loving, nurturing, and is and teaches mutuality. This is a level of being that people are capable of, but how does it happen without mentors or role models showing us the way? This is intentional and desirable, but the facts for too many are that most events and people that might cause us to be open and possibly grow are accidental. And if we are not fully in the present the opportunity passes and we remain as we were. Our earliest lessons go deep and are foundational and if we allow them to rule our existence growth is not impossible, but unlikely. In any case, I know that what we have learned is not permanently fixed, can be unlearned and potential to change exists in every human and therefore every relationship. As we mature from child to adult, our opportunities to meet those who might influence our lives expand. It is important to realize that events and relationships have the potential to bring about change in humans.

An example of this: We do not select our first mentors, nature does this; and for the most part, as children and young adults we have no vote in the matter. Our needs are such at this time that our ability to make decisions on our own behalf is questionable at best. This is particularly true when in a dependent relationship with our parents. It becomes less so in our relations with our teachers and even less so as we develop friendships and our relationships at work. As we mature and move as independent individuals into the society at large, however, it is then that we do, to a considerable degree, control our own destiny.

The human "need to be" is never fully suppressed. As young adults we are more likely to rebel against those in power over us who do not see and treat us as individuals. Some seek personal choice, freedom and independence at all costs and others do not fight, but submit. These are the extremes since most do not fully battle, but do not fully concede, either. It is acted out in many ways. We may be entrepreneurs or simply try to have a voice as to who shall lead us. Some people actually recognize the importance of role models and their need to grow and deliberately seek out the more enlightened leaders. But for the multitudes it is acceptance of their lot and yet it appears that technology may be changing that attitude around the world.

Important question to consider: are we aware of differences when we interact with quality leaders as compared to inadequate leaders? Do we recognize the attributes of our leaders as favorable or dangerous to our own being? Do our leaders acknowledge us, respect us and treat us as unique individuals or as just another part of the crowd? Our questions are answered through a leader's behavior. Good leaders recognize "students" in groups they interact with and can also pick out the "bummers." Quality leaders separate the students from the indifferent ones and increase pressure on the latter to "grow or go." It's not an accident that likes are attracted to each other.

On one side of the coin, where there is good and nurturing interaction with our leaders, it is their attributes that influence our own behavior in positive ways. Their needs as well as our own are being fulfilled, and we confirm this to them through our behavior in responsible ways. The other side of the coin is also true: When attributes convey an indifference to us, what does our behavior demonstrate? Depending on our experiences with those who lead us, we tend to respond in kind. Attributes are not innocent accoutrements but influence us, as do words and actions.

GENERAL THOUGHTS ON ATTRIBUTES

As previously stated, some people are less flawed than others and bring much grace, warmth, and respect to their relationships. The attribute of mutuality appears to be as natural as breathing to some. Others, with little awareness of mutuality and other positive attributes, bring pain and abusive power to their relationships. Regardless, if positive attributes are rare or non-existent coming from a leader, people are able to adapt and to an extent protect themselves. It is when a leader is inconsistent and certain attributes appear and disappear that people live and work in apprehension and tension of what may or may not come next.

Being witness to the problems brought on by inconsistencies of leaders' behavior and quality attributes—one moment on and the next off—are "land mines" to relationships. When this occurs, it is obvious the leaders allow their emotions to rule their behavior. It seems not to matter that this issue is discussed prior to an initial workshop. At the beginning stages of work with an organization, the leaders generally have difficulty accepting that they are responsible for the poor communication and troubled relationships within the organization. As leaders, most agree that cooperative and happier employees are more productive and that most of their interpersonal issues would disappear if and when employees improve communication amongst themselves. Most leaders are convinced: "the problems in the office have to do with my employees and their personal issues with each other."

The leaders with whom I worked did not lack the attributes that make for an excellent leader but were, generally, unaware of their own attributes as witnessed by those close to them. Most, initially, believed their problems to be "the others" and not what they were responsible for creating through their behavior. What they sought from me as mentor was to solve "staff" problems, a not uncommon diagnosis made by those who lead. "It's the other guy" or "them who are the problem" and pointing their finger. This belief was commonly held by most leaders even if it was made clear during our initial conversation that they, the leaders, were responsible for the problems they blamed on others. How often do we hear only what we want to hear?

The workshop slowly strips away the façade that is often carefully crafted around an apparent enlightened leader. The obvious truth is that "good" attributes and troublesome ones exist from the beginning. By being a witness to the leader's Inner Circle most issues are made know quickly. Where are individuals empowered to lead, to express thoughts and feelings honestly and candidly, and where is listening, understanding, confirmation and candor? Where is mutuality and to what degree cooperation? Most important, where and what are the attributes the leader shows? If hierarchical in fact, and the leader probably does not see this, but expects an attitude of ownership on the part of the people involved, this is where the true journey begins.

To understand human potential is to realize that it does not manifest itself by itself, but needs someone to show the way. This means that the quality attributes of a leader are the key and road map gifted to their significant others because potential needs considerable care if it is to see the light of day. Enlightened leaders ARE considerably more than talk. They back themselves up with consistent behavior and which is imperative.

Since enlightened leaders are more aware, intentional and conscious of the "how, what and why" of their behavior and positive attributes, they quickly "tune in" on those to whom they relate. Quality relationships with most people, even as a potential, are given the space, resources and opportunities to grow. As growth happens, so does the change in relationship between an enlightened leader/teacher and the student. The fixed hierarchy between leader and follower is flattened and becomes more dynamic as power is shared. When this happens, the leader may become the follower and the student the leader, and it is events that dictate which.

Healthy relationships are a result of healthy environments and healthy environments are the Petri dish for human interaction and change. This is created by the true leader. In this type of environment choices are made individually that enrich the relationship and expose illness. No one can long remain hidden. Participants whose agenda is about gaining power, prestige, position, financial rewards and other self-centered attributes do not belong and they know it. People are forced by events and their own ideas about power and control to make decisions. To either "grow" or "go" is unavoidable due to the transparency, authenticity and consistent attributes of the leader and the environment they are responsible for creating.

RELATIVELY ENLIGHTENED LEADERS HAVE HEALTHY RELATIONSHIPS

Relatively enlightened leaders are neither foolish nor fooled in their relationships. They are the people with attributes that are obvious and consistent, and they have no desire to manipulate others and their behavior. They seek, through experiences and interpersonally, to know themselves and courageously are open to this from those with whom they live and work. They assume, with full awareness, their roles as the model they seek for others: They are also teacher, student, facilitator and contributor to each person's own choice to grow or go.

It is through quality leadership we have quality experiences and in the process have the potential to acquire, for ourselves, positive attributes which we then convey to others. The "good" in this case is likely to spread to others that we live and work with like any other contagion. This is a magnate to people who aspired to power for what it means to them on a personal level. They are students and may seek personal growth, or to fulfill a personal agenda having to do with power and seek effective tools in order to control others. True students do what they believe is best for themselves and not what will please another.

To restate a prior observation: although we find positive attributes in most people and leaders, none anywhere, and even historically, are without flaws. Humans are simply imperfect animals. Relative to this, it is the journey we are on and the evolutionary process that slowly and hopefully moves humankind in the right direction. We anticipate the future but cannot know with any assurance how, what and when it will arrive. We want our "expectations" to be fulfilled, but we also know that expectations come with no guarantees and more importantly cause troubles between us. It is much better that we deal, primarily, with what "is" and making it better. This we can do and it may influence the future. The alternative is to be stuck in the past or fantasize the future. In either scenario we lose what is our present.

Humans who do not relate to and deal with the *present* apparently choose not to grow, to change and acquire new attributes. The problems for them become similar to those of Sisyphus, a king in Greek mythology, who was punished for being deceitful and abusive of others. His punishment was to push a boulder up a hill only to have it roll back to the bottom again, and again, and again—and never to succeed. It's the story of those who confront their problems in the same old way they've used in the past, expecting different results each time. Such is the bleak outlook for those who choose not to grow or to acquire new and positive attributes.

ESSENTIAL ATTRIBUTES FOR THE ENLIGHTENED LEADER

I have identified a number of attributes that I believe should be embodied in our more enlightened leaders. The attributes that follow are important markers against which to thoughtfully measure ourselves. We all have role models, leaders, teachers and others that possess the attributes I refer to here. The goal is to incorporate in ourselves as many positive attributes as we can. It is not easy to do.

To complicate the issue of attributes even more, we are the least likely to know the self that we project to others so how are we to know what attributes others witness us wearing? We may think we come across in certain ways, but we are unable to evaluate ourselves as others do. It is our family, friends and the people at work who witness the attributes we wear and know our behavior best. Why not ask them?

Integrity

A sense of wholeness and that what you see is all you need to see. The example of integrity I will use is the story in Chapter 1 of the eight-year-old hyperactive boy who was so disruptive at home and in school that he had to be on a drug to calm him enough so he could be with other children. The condition under which we accepted the boy to join us at camp was that when and if I believed he could be off the drug, we could and would stop giving it to him.

One morning I watched him sitting quietly on a rock, patiently fishing and he barely moved for over thirty minutes. I sat at a distance so that he was unaware of my presence. Keep in mind that this child came to camp unable to concentrate and be still for any amount of time without being held hostage to a small pill that literally turned him into a passive pawn. Yet it was not many days at camp before his behavior in his group began to evidence a health and awareness of him as a very capable and positive contributor to his group and the camp at large. I informed the counselor to be particularly observant of his behavior as I weaned him off the drug.

There were no negative consequences the counselor observed. When I watched him fishing he had been off the drug for a week.

At camp, among his peers and participating in exciting, often challenging activities, he had become a fully integrated human. The environment, relationships in his group and at camp had to have made it possible for him to be whole. The question begs to be asked: Why was the drug not necessary at camp but necessary in his other worlds? Why integrity and a fully integrated human at camp, but not elsewhere in the life he led at home and school? The point here is that I believe "integrity" is a learned response and therefore an attribute that comes out of an environment that nurtures being one's self and at the same time "in relation to others." And, yes, he became a leader with his peers in his group. Clearly, at camp he became a "whole" person.

Moral

Knowing and intentionally doing what is right and desirable for self and others. Many years ago I had an employee who was a prince from a Middle Eastern country. He was enrolled as an engineering student at the local university. It was during a summer in the early 1950s when he worked as a counselor in our summer day camp with a group of seven-year-old boys. One of our programs was for teenagers who were training in certain specialties and activities or, if old enough, to one day become a counselor. All counselors could and did make use of the teenagers to help them in certain activities with their group.

It was during one of those training situations that a precocious teenage girl became involved with the counselor/prince. It was quickly rumored that he and she were seen kissing, which she was thrilled to confirm with her friends and me, apparently "taken" by his being a prince. In minutes this became the hot news in camp, and I immediately went to the counselor/prince to check out the circumstances surrounding the rumor. He did not deny that he, in fact, did kiss the teenager. But he did not see the innocent kiss as a moral issue. In his culture, he explained, it was acceptable that a young man take an interest in an attractive teen of the opposite sex. In his eyes and cultural upbringing, she was an attractive person, not a child. He added that he had forced nothing on her and thus felt that his behavior was perfectly normal. In fact, he explained that he kissed her to thank her for the good work she was doing with his group of seven-year-old boys. But he finally agreed that what he had done was not right at a camp, as he qualified it, "in your country."

Based on his and the teenager's accounts, nothing more than a kiss took place; and he voluntarily agreed to leave his position that day and apologized for any problem this event may have brought on her, me or the camp. A few days later a beautiful box of exotic fruits was delivered to me with a note, embossed with his family crest, apologizing once more for behavior that he understood as possibly causing harm to the camp. His intentions, he assured me was no advance on the teenager and no harm to our reputation.

The lesson I derived from this: what is moral and considered right in one culture may be looked upon as a serious infraction in another. It is best to know and understand the culture you find yourself in and to accept it as your own while living in it.

True moral behavior comes out of being conscious and intentional in being one's self and choosing "right" action over "wrong." As in the story of the camp counselor above knowing and being aware of the culture one is in is tremendously important. Being moral accidentally is not good enough and may actually lead to misunderstanding, expectations and confusion. True moral behavior happens out of a full awareness of what one does any time. Being moral cannot be an attribute turned on or off, but may be acquired. This point of morality is particularly important for a leader because the leaders' attributes become the standard for their followers' behavior.

If truth is in the eyes of the beholder, what is the positive influence of moral leaders on those they lead? I know it to be considerable and good. On the other hand, the costs to leaders claiming much too loudly and frequently of their moral righteousness when in fact they do not hold themselves accountable, and worse profess one thing and do another, do damage to their relationships. Moral behavior must be a conscious result of leaders' intentions and desire to say and do right actions. Consistency and dependability are key.

Wisdom

Making the best use of knowledge gained from experience and used for both self and the common good. Beginning in 1974, I was asked to assist professional offices and small firms to improve the level of dialogue between employees who worked together.

The problems I heard expressed almost always had to do with "them." Rarely did anyone of those that employed me consider, publically, that are "the problem" in their organization. It was always "they" the others are the problem. Did I consider myself a cause of the problems I had with people who worked for me? I don't think so or remember my taking responsibility for problems between people in my own organizations.

At the beginning of my work with other organizations I gave workshops essentially to deal with the problems of communication between staff. The leader/owner part was incidental. The workshops had to do with the relationships and communication between employees and not the leader as part of the problem. But success in the eyes of those with whom I worked did little to satisfy my own curiosity. What troubled me was I felt that all I was able to do was to apply band-aids and distribute aspirins to seriously dysfunctional workplace environments. The people with whom I worked may have been enjoying a cathartic experience, leaving them with the feeling that peace and harmony was achieved. But was that true? Hardly! What good that was done through our demanding workshops had too short a lifespan.

It did not matter that I believed the information and processes I shared were effective, and this was confirmed by the feedback I received from the leader. I always sought the best of what the leader hired me to do as necessary to healthy and productive communication between co-workers. The perplexing problem to me was not what we did during our time together, but why so little of what we achieved during a workshop actually continued beyond a few weeks or months at the longest.

I kept asking why change in a work setting seemed to vacillate from "all is well" to "we've got problems." I almost always approached a workshop concerned with whether or not any of what we did was doing any permanent good. I would leave a workshop feeling confident that the group as a whole and individuals were in healthier communications shape than before the workshop. But when I returned three to six months later, I would discover that much of what we achieved the last time together had to be repeated. I did not ask, "What are they doing wrong?" I would ask of myself, "What am I doing wrong?"

Elsewhere in this chapter I tell the story of the epiphany I had while flying home after a week of work. It was then I remember clearly seeing the answer.

It flashed across my mind: *Power and how used by the leader is the answer to the problem*. Within days of getting home I wrote a brief paper on this and suggested that the one in power may be the key to the resolutions of interpersonal problems within an organization. And, that if they we are going to resolve the problems that exist between people that work together the leader must become part of the process. I did not know yet the depth of control and influence a leader plays in the human relationship drama. It would take much work before I uncovered the whole truth of my epiphany.

Certain leaders I worked with were open and sponges to the whole idea of personal growth. They wanted it for themselves, and they wanted it for others. But, and here is the core of the problem: unless the leaders, the ones in true power, want this for themselves and then for others, it will not take place in their relationships. My task was clear in that I needed to become a student of power and control. I needed to read anything and everything on the subject. I needed to talk to my wife and others important to me about this whole subject. I needed to become wiser in as many ways as possible on the subjects of leadership and power.

Ideally, wisdom comes through personal experiences which happen accidentally or deliberately, both are potentially valuable. In my case I had plenty of experiences of both kinds to reflect on and most taught me things I needed to know. Those with acquired wisdom know that every experience may offer gifts but that have to be uncovered. The seeker of wisdom has to be vulnerable, that is, open to new "truths," even if painful when they replace other and previously believed "truths." The wise amongst us personally seek knowing and understanding and question endlessly in order to discover value.

The more enlightened are also thoughtful in their decision-making. They see the "big picture" when viewing any scene, any event. They understand what it means to be and live in the present and do so intentionally. They are the perennial seekers, students and accept the tough truth that they are role models and teachers to others whether they choose to be or not. They do not fall hostage to false gods and dreams but seek truth. The wise are realists who respect, understand, nurture and support the creative and questioners among them. There is little or no duality in their lives and know it is by being present that this is possible.

There are many stories of the wise we can read about, but how much better to learn if we meet them in our daily lives? How fortunate we are when the wisdom comes from our parents, teachers, bosses and friends; but this is impossible if they treat us as "things," and we respond in kind. The wise facilitate the giving of their knowledge and the sharing of their experiences. They understand the importance of giving of themselves and their hard-won wisdom but do not force themselves on anyone. Yet, the wise are accessible and all we need do is to ask, and persist if necessary, if we are to receive.

We have numerous opportunities presented to us to gain wisdom; but, surprisingly, it has been my experience that unless made easy, most people do not grab the moment and the lesson. Instead, what many people seek are cures external to themselves wishing problems away but with no change in them. They do not choose wisdom and understanding, but mere "band-aids" to their problems. They do not seek growth for themselves, although they often want to see change in others. Unfortunately, *assured* ignorance and continuing *failure* are what they get for an unwillingness to be accessible to life.

The wise leader grasps and accepts that power is meant to be shared. People important to each other need to candidly communicate up and down the organization and, most importantly, directly and mutually to each other. This is not achieved upon demand or wishing it to be so. It is not a group choice but that of the leaders who make this a reality. Wisdom is evident when the leaders understand this and sets aside their role as leader and shares this power with the Inner Circle. They allow events to dictate where and to whom power should go.

When those in power begin this journey of learning about themselves through the eyes, feelings and stories of those who know them best, they begin a journey that is unpredictable, but invaluable. When personal awareness moves from the unconscious to the conscious, in particular, as experienced by significant others, growth invites growth. With guidance and reason confronting blindness to one's power, the experience of being vulnerable in significant relationships begins to shape perceptions of those involved. At that time, and not before, what others have come to expect from their leader and defenses necessary to protect themselves begin to be altered. When it is assured that the leader moves from being power to sharing power, everything shifts and only the physical surroundings remain the same. In fact, as a leader grows more conscious and self-aware, the only rule that now works is that openness becomes fact, not fiction. Wisdom becomes contagious.

Intentional searching for wisdom relative to one's power is rare in the vast majority of leaders, even if we erroneously believe that leaders because they are leaders want to grow. What most leaders want is success, more productive relations with their people, fewer problems and recognition. They most certainly do not see themselves as "the problem to the answer." And although wisdom is a wonderful gift everyone wants to possess, the wisdom I speak of is not gained through birth, inheritance, position, appearance or even formal education. It comes through willful participation in life, suffering its consequences, and being students to each and every experience and the people we meet on our journey. If wisdom were an intellectual process we would have credentialed wise people, Ph.D.'s in the "art" of wisdom. Lectures we attend and books we read do not make us wise. Experience, and where we totally immerse ourselves and are present, does.

Wisdom surrounds us and is everywhere and anywhere even if it comes in small, seemingly insignificant packages; and so much comes from the unexpected. People with wisdom exist for all of us, but are we open to them when they enter our lives? To what degree are we receptive? To what degree do we seek the wise amongst us? Like so many things in life that are presented to us, yet we do not see, hear and establish a connection. How can we know what we miss when we are not present in the moment and to the other person? But that is another cave we will leave behind in the chapter on Genuine Dialogue.

On one side of the coin, I can go on almost endlessly about those I have been blessed to meet and know, and have accepted their gift of wisdom. The other side of the coin has to be, how many opportunities to learn from others have I missed? Too many! ow wiseHow wise to connect and not be overly cautious or pre-judge people and events that may or may appear to be of value to us. To be wise is to be present and extract from each moment and experience lessons that might possibly aid us in our journey. Most people seek to accumulate material wealth, but it is wisdom we really need to accumulate.

Courage

The moment and event dictates behavior, and nothing can impede them. Courage was demonstrated by the POW on Okinawa when he took off after the prisoner who tried to escape. And, what of the seven-year-old boy (the same one who was required to take a mood-altering drug in order to go to school) placing himself between the dog charging towards another dog at camp, or the camp director and the mob? It may be spontaneous action, or it may be thoughtful, but how often do we hear a courageous person say, "I just did what I had to do"? Clearly, events dictate the exercise of power, and by whom.

Some people have courage in "basketfuls," and yet events still control their behavior. And some, even if trained to perform courageous acts, such as rescues during an emergency, may find themselves without courage when it is most needed. As for the Japanese POW, I know that thought preceded his actions. He knew what he needed to do and where to go and did it without a moment's hesitation. He also felt that had I gone out to those caves I might have placed myself in serious danger. Note that he told others what he was going to do and prescribed the action or non-action that the others were to take. The young boy saw the dog break from his owner and charge towards the smaller dog, and simply reacted before anyone else did. And the soldier throws himself on the grenade in order to save his fellow soldiers.

Leaders who possess courage do not shy from decisions or problems that call for them to take action. They do what is necessary in the moment. More often than not, events dictate the action that must be taken, as in when fire breaks out. If the fire can be controlled, almost everyone involved joins in the efforts to put it out. But if the fire is out of control and lives are in danger, it is the saving of lives that comes first; and it is the courageous ones who do what must be done without concern for themselves. Doing what needs to be done seems easy, but during emergencies and other difficult times we see the separation of those with and those without courage.

In subtle or gross ways courage is taught, as is cowardice and these lessons are learned early in our lives. It is in our initial caregiver's behavior; and we tend to incorporate this as our own, they the teachers and we the students. That is why so many of us were placed in cages, restricted to a limited space and given select toys and stuff considered not to be dangerous, or allowed the freedom to explore and test our environment.

Since attributes are learned, and this is one of our blessings, we can choose, or life chooses for us, to unlearn and relearn behavior that is more appropriate to what we are inclined to be. As an example, courage to act under emergency conditions is taught in the military, law enforcement, firemen and first-responders in medical emergencies. Organizations create training situations that simulate powerful examples of what people may be called upon to do in various situations. The intent here is to remove as many unknowns as possible relative to one's ability to handle events that are out of the ordinary.

If leaders are students as I continuously suggest they must be, they learn through the various experiences they have and the people they meet. If wise, they knowingly create this opportunity for those they lead. By not being unhinged by events and showing courage in confronting events leaders not only learn more about themselves, but so do those close to them and in the process have a model to draw lessons from.

Regardless of the preparation and talk, courageous behavior is difficult to predict when events just happen or are out of our control. Whether made manifest or not depends on many factors. As stated, our histories play a major part, but also the degree a person is present and in the moment. Courageous behavior comes out of being in the present and not being in the past or the future. In fact, we could postulate that we are no where if not in the present.

Decisiveness

Using one's power to decide or to act on what is decided: As an attribute, leaders who equivocate are not good leaders. These are the leaders who fail the decision-making process because they either wait too long to make decisions that need to be made or (and potentially worse) are the leaders who make decisions too quickly. Without enough and accurate information gathered through relationship with others, leaders who act alone, prematurely or too quickly often compound problems. Many leaders (and people) literally press the trigger before they aim, or freeze in the middle of the process. Whether leaders are too slow, too quick, or take no action, influence on those they lead is one of frustration, confusion and a sense of helplessness. In contrast quality leaders are decisive, thoughtful, and given the time, seek the input and assistance from others.

If a decision is demanded *now!* so be it. In this case, quality leaders take action, but also aware that other problems may arise as a consequence and remain alert. Generally, good leadership works to create an environment where issues are anticipated, investigated, information shared and balanced decisions are then made. This requires open, safe and spontaneous dialogue, and proper due diligence from many voices that bring as much information to the surface as possible while even considering alternative plans of action. As in most other situations, the value of a well-functioning Inner Circle is priceless. Wise decisions are more likely to be made if they are based on sound discussions and knowledge as compared to the limited perspective of a single person or a group of people held hostage by a single person. Here is where the leadership hierarchy desperately needs to become circular (power shared at the round table) and level rather than up/down and restricted. By being mutual in one's Inner Circle quality leaders not only make better and more appropriate decisions, but so do their key people who may, then, take leadership. Decision-making is not left to the one true power person but also to those that have been empowered to do so. This is merit-and-experience based and when any Inner circle works best and most effectively.

Which brings to mind my very inadequate decision-making process during the land purchase in Northern California, I tell in Chapter 2. When I first saw the land sitting on the horse in a heavy rainstorm, what I saw was all I could have asked for and the purchase price was too good to be true. I was so taken by what I saw and the owner's offer that I literally was afraid to asked any of the many questions I should have asked. It was enough that I actually believed it was our dream come true. By not asking any of the questions that needed to be asked, I soon discovered that all was far from perfect, in fact, potentially a "no gamer." The source of the spring water was not on our land, the only road into to the property did not assure ingress and egress and electric power service was problematic. But! It was virgin forest and meadow surrounded by thousands of acres of wilderness and it was all I needed to see; all other issues did not matter. However, had I been accompanied with others whom I trusted, would someone have asked the right questions? And, would the answers have made any difference? Maybe and maybe not.

The obvious point of the story is that my decision-making lacked a thoughtful, due-diligence approach. The property was not going away, and time was not of the essence. I needed to know more about the property, the water, road and electric power. I needed to meet with my Inner Circle and present what I had discovered and then listen to their questions and recommendations. Perhaps a trip with others of my IC was warranted. A thoughtful and more perceptive approach would have uncovered the major issues that needed to be resolved before purchase. That we were eventually able to overcome each problem is not the issue here, but that my decision making was seriously flawed and could have led to problems beyond our ability to fix.

I was to learn much later on that the existence of a more varied and experienced Inner Circle would have enhanced timely and thoughtful decision-making. Just pure speculation, but was my own decisiveness unwise and what differences would it all have made had I sought the thoughts of others? Would answers to problems I was totally ignorant of have kept me from a purchase that ultimately brought such good to so many? What decisions and what actions do not have consequences?

Compassion

The desire to help others is easy; it is in the being and doing that compassion counts. Enlightened leaders are compassionate with those they lead. People are not "things" and "objects" to them. They sincerely care for those for whom they are responsible, but emotions that are part of caring do not blind the leaders' capacity to lead. It does not give the heart power over the head, feelings over reason; it is reason that remains dominant. This is difficult and complex for leaders who care.

What is the compassion of which I speak? It is not sympathy but empathy and respect that also offer moral and material support and which is confirmed through listening, understanding and doing. Compassion is demonstrated in what one does with and for others. It is not a weakness or implied agreement but may be misread as such. A truly compassionate person does not require recognition or expectations of appreciation for what they do. There are people (and leaders) who come across as compassionate, but use compassion as a manipulative tool which they then use as a way to obligate others. To act as if compassionate while actually not caring does harm to a relationship and how lasting and effective is pretense?

The story I chose to tell here has to do with the compassion demonstrated by a twelve-year-old boy. The time was early September 1956. My wife and I had taken a small group of boys and girls ages eleven and twelve on a backpack trip in the High Sierra for a week. A trail sign had been deliberately turned in the wrong direction, and without checking our compass and topographical map, we followed the altered trail sign. Our goal for this day was a lake about a six-hour hike from where we began and could easily have been reached by late afternoon. But because of the misleading sign, it turned out to be not a six-hour walk in the park but about a seventeen-mile hike over an eleven-thousand-foot mountain known as Cloud's

Rest. With a hardly discernible trail and many hours of unanticipated uphill hiking and each of the kids carrying about a 45-pound backpack, it was hardly a hike for the young or even the mature hiker.

The problem was not that we were lost (it takes much ignorance to be lost in the Sierras) but that we were running out of water. One little canteen per person is hardly enough for a unanticipated grueling hike. It soon became evident that water would be a problem for us as we discovered we were hiking a narrow granite trail taking us well above timberline with little or no water to be found. When I did realize that we were heading towards Lake Tanaya, up and over Cloud's Rest, we were well past the point of no-return. Our only option was to find water and settle in for the night, but this was not to be because there was no water to be found anywhere. Worse yet, we would be hiking in total darkness (it was a moonless night) if we were determined to reach water or the lake and a place to camp for the night.

As it got darker, we used a rope to tie everyone together with my wife at the back and the ten boys and girls strung out between us. I led the group by flashlight on the granite trail. Lots of songs and stories kept the need for water from becoming our only focus. Also, the dry foods we carried made our need for water considerably more important. Being without water and at the same time doing things that demand water is an experience people need to avoid.

Not one camper panicked or acted out that they were frightened or even concerned. But in between songs, stories and jokes there was silence as we concentrated on listening for the sound of water, or anything else for that matter. About 11:00 p.m., in pitch darkness, I stopped the group and suggested that they all camp for the rest of the night while I went on ahead to find water. Unanimously they voiced that they wanted to continue with me and that they were fine. How could anyone not love a bunch like this?

We continued for another hour or so, everyone sucking on pebbles, until one of the kids shouted out that he thought he heard music. We stopped walking and breathing to listen, and sure enough off in the distance we heard music coming from somewhere below us. Following the trail downhill, we saw firelight through the trees and heard the voices of people sitting around a campfire. Do I need to describe how good this felt to all of us? Careful not to trample anyone in front of us, we charged out of the forest onto the shores of Lake Tanaya. This is one of the more beautiful lakes in the High Sierra that one passes driving on the Tioga Road heading west from Tuolumne Meadows towards Yosemite Valley. But scenic beauty was not the issue only water and rest.

We found a place to drop our backpacks, and in minutes everyone had drunk their fill and climbed deep into their sleeping bags. Because our trail food required water we ate almost nothing during the hike and I needed to get some warm liquid down each of them. I began gathering wood to make a fire and heat up some soup. I intended to awaken each hiker and see that they took a few swallows before going back to sleep. When the soup was ready and I began to feed the first one, I became aware that one of the boys was helping me tend the fire and bringing soup to his friends. He did not have his own sleeping bag unrolled but had helped me without saying one word from the moment I started the fire. I was doing my job and he was being compassionate. Through his behavior he defined the very meaning of compassion and empathy. Incidentally, early the next morning I woke up to the kids building a raft of logs and preparing to explore the shore and lake. A magnificent High Sierra day was spent on and in the lake and the beach. A day later we hiked nineteen miles to the floor of Yosemite Valley and enjoyed a grand dinner celebration. Ah, youth!

Candor

To be what one thinks and feels without the intent to harm, but to share one's truth: Babies are candid, at least at the beginning, but for most humans candor, depending on conditioning by caregivers has to be learned all over again and why I refer to candor as an attribute. Candor is an important attribute and must be included in this list although it is discussed in Chapter 6 (Genuine Dialogue). Candor is honesty, sincerity and authenticity in the moment that when experienced is felt as a breath of fresh air. It is commonly experienced in environments where we find good leaders. When leaders are candid they invite a candid response. This is so because candor usually happens in an open and inviting environment which is the making of the leader. Candor is not meant to control and is heard and felt in this way and invites a candid response. Also, the more that candor is experienced coming from a leader the more likely it is that candor will be reciprocated by those who initially fear being candid.

As important and essential as candor is between leaders, followers, and people in significant relationships, candor remains a rarity where there is concern for the relationship. When candor does occur between people it is likely that creativity, spontaneity, sharing of power and mutuality are also taking place. Candor is one of the four cornerstones essential to Genuine Dialogue. The others are: Respect, Being Present and Confirmation (see Chapter 6).

Important to emphasize that candor does not occur between people accidentally, but thoughtfully and when trust and safety exist. People learn to what degree, if any, they can be open and direct with others close to them. Candor is being vulnerable since it is one's truth and sends a message that welcomes reciprocity. In comparison, where candor does not exist between people in supposed significant relationship, whatever keeps them together will likely fail them in trying times. When candor is lacking between people we find monologue and instead of the sense of community and the sharing of "ownership" a sterile environment.

A story of candor and unexpected reward: the co-ed summer camp we built and operated in the mountains of Northern California was without electric power for five years. At the beginning, we dug and used a deep pit covered by a canvas cover as our "food cooler." We soon replaced the "hole in the ground" with a walk-in refrigerator powered by a small gasoline generator that also enabled us to provide a limited amount of light in the evenings until about 10 p.m. At that time, I had been informed that it would cost us around $10,000 to hook up to a power line that was only one mile away but would have to be brought through a thick virgin forest. Although we believed electric power to the camp was necessary to its well-being, we also recognized that its cost was way beyond of our ability to afford at the time. Still, I persisted in the need to pursue this with the electric company even if the money or other problems stood in our way.

For five years I made numerous polite visits to the electric company's local office, wrote letters, filled out forms and had face-to-face meetings with representatives of the company. Nothing I did moved the huge electric utility company to action. It was, more than likely, my dumb and numb response to their request for money up front. Nevertheless, I pursued; and they continued to ignore me and the camp's need for power. At no time did our communication become strained or rancorous, but remained cordial and understanding.

One midwinter day I decided to take this problem to the very top of the utility company. I felt that candor, even if only on my side, was absolutely demanded of me. All that could happen was that I would experience what I had become accustomed to—and that was indifference and denial. So I took a few deep breathes and phoned the president/CEO of the electric company at the home office in San Francisco. I first spoke to a receptionist who listened to my story. She, in turn, gave me over to a person who also listened and then turned me over to the secretary of the secretary of the "boss of bosses." I told her the story, and she also listened dutifully to what I was saying; and at the end of my story and her questioning, she asked if I would mind holding for a few minutes. "No problem," I cordially responded.

One thing was clear throughout the conversations with each person, and that was my candor. There was no equivocation on my part. I wanted confirmation that each person understood the problem and my feelings about its importance to our camp. Also, and just as clearly, I sensed that nothing trivial was going to get through an established and well-organized company "filtering system." I sincerely believed that if I had any hope of success at all, the message I delivered had to be emotionally and intellectually honest. In other words, *candid!*

After an hour-plus of climbing over human barriers, I found myself speaking to the CEO of the giant power company. He listened, asked many questions, and promised he would look into the issue. In about two hours I received a call from the CEO as promised; and before the coming summer we had poles, lines and electricity into camp and, miracles of miracles, all at no cost to us. Maybe, just maybe, he figured that we had paid our dues over the previous five years of hassle. In any case, it proved to me, in very concrete terms, the value of candor.

Had I not had the courage to go directly to the top, getting electricity may not have happened for many more years. Although I acknowledge that I risked failure in my quest, my job was not at stake, I was not dealing with my own boss, and I was not in danger of losing anything I already had. As good fortune would have it, I was candid with four people; and each was open to hearing my story. They each had the power to cut me off but instead made immediate decisions to forward me to a higher authority. I believe it was the combination of the story, a children's wilderness camp, my candid presentation, and most important, receptive listeners, any of whom might have altered the outcome.

A particularly important lesson is that candor, when conditions are favorable to being candid, has intrinsic value, and incidentally, may be rewarded. However, iIf conditions are unfavorable being candid is likely to result in negative consequences. Unless safety is assured, candor as with walking on thin ice is a dangerous risk to take.

Love

Love means many things to people. I intend love as a feeling and actions towards another and is demonstrated through deep caring and nurturing so that the other is or becomes all that they are capable of being and this without expectations on the lover's part. Ideally, this attribute is found in parents relative to their child and in the process also teaches the child to love. This may also happen with the child's earliest teachers, friends, and as adults in relationships. Quality people, healthy and together in mind, soul and spirit show this attribute by the way they relate to the people significant to them. For them, others are not regarded as simply mechanical cogs or tools to use as they see fit. People are respected and nurtured as the self they are or choose to be. Everyone is important; but particularly with those close to them there is sincere fondness, cooperation, mutuality, security and therefore love. Whether with family, friends or at work, the only difference between them is intimacy and intensity. It is living in relationships guided by the belief that each person has value as the self each is.

To put it as questions relative to our issues of leadership: how can leaders not give respect to and honor those they immediately lead and depend on and in a relative sense, love? And, how do leaders expect—even demand—relationships of support and cooperation without this? If leaders have expectations of their followers, but lack love and related attributes towards them they give up any possibilities of authentic participation. They work against each other and not for each other.

If relationships are to work, degrees of love as defined above needs to exist in what goes between those in relationships. What leaders actually sow and tend to, and not any hidden intentions or expectations, will be returned to them. A relationship without love is a relationship between things, not people, and results in what? The answer, at least where power is concerned, is compliance, or worse. And when is compliance a quality relationship or results in quality outcomes? How does this compare to being there for each other, and full and mutual cooperation and participation? Love cannot be demanded or expected but is given without conditions, in particular, by the leaders to the ones who are led. Remember, the leader creates the environment where love exists or does not. Also, love is NOW. Love is not a future promise for good behavior and compliance and expectations in any of its many forms do not exist.

The following story is different and "other worldly" in many ways, and yet my wife and I experienced in real time, over a 24-hour period, what we felt was love from a complete stranger. You be the judge.

We were exploring Mexico back in the early 1970s in our wonderful Pop-Top Volkswagen we called Donka. It was late in the day when we entered the outskirts of Villahermosa in the southeast area of Veracruz looking for a place to camp for the night. On our right we noticed a fenced area that enclosed what looked at first like big basalt balls, some as large as 7 feet tall and weighing as much as 20 tons. To our amazement and pleasure, we recognized that what we were seeing were Olmec Heads from a pre-Columbian period dated at least as far back as 900 BC. Years earlier we both had taken a class at the local university in preparation for an earlier trip to Mexico to study Pre-Columbian art and history so we were somewhat prepared for what we hoped to see at some point in our exploration, but never for what followed.

We screeched to a halt to investigate, but since it was getting dark the gate was locked. While looking as best we could through the fence, a tall, heavily built man approached us from inside the fenced area and said in almost perfect English that he was waiting for us. He opened the gate, and we entered an outdoor museum that happened to be the largest collection of Olmec Heads in the world. And then, as if prearranged, he took us on a private tour of the facility with rich explanations about the carved heads, and their supposed origins and meanings. It became for us a walk among "spirits" of the past. As the curator spoke, the heads came alive and the eyes followed us. Lights and aura seemed to emanate from some of the heads. It was an experience that brought awe and a sense of being that is difficult to explain even now.

An hour or two may have passed, but time did not matter. At the conclusion of our trip into the world of the Olmeca, we invited the curator to have dinner with us; and the three of us walked to a restaurant in the village. It was early evening now, and *all* of the many people we came across on the road greeted this man with great deference as if he were a king walking among them. The waves of people actually parted for him and for us to walk through. Even when seated in an outdoor patio restaurant deeply involved in conversation about the Yucatan and Mexico, people walking by as well as the restaurant staff showed deference to this remarkably charismatic person. At the end of the meal no bill was presented, and neither he nor I was allowed to pay for our food and service.

We parted with the promise to meet the next day for breakfast and more talk. He said that he had important "things" to share with us. We camped that evening on a quiet dirt road and spent an hour or so going over the strange events we had just experienced: our (accidental?) visit to the museum, the Olmec Heads that came alive and the powerful presence of our guide. It was all beyond our familiarity level and left us perplexed. What had taken place? What would come tomorrow?

We met as promised; enjoyed breakfast together and an intriguing few hours of dialogue about history and the people of the Yucatan. We sat at an outdoor table where we witnessed his acknowledging of everyone who walked past us, and they of him. Clearly, he was respected and loved by the people of the village, and he cared for them as if they were his children. Once again I tried to pay for our meal; but again no bill was presented, just plenty of smiles, good food and service.

It was obvious that he was a man of considerable power and influence, but what we most felt was a love between him and the villagers. Perhaps he read our interest in knowing more about him, so he asked us if we wanted to visit his home. As we walked through the village to his home, the people walking towards us would again part clearly in deference to him. And no one seemed to showed concern over the two gringos, just warmth and a welcoming smile.

This unusual experience got even stranger when we reached his home. He lived on the roof of an apartment building in a small shack about ten-by-ten with a cot in a corner, a small washroom, no kitchen, and a cord line in another corner that held two shirts and a pair of pants. That was it! But if we have ever met a "rich" man, a powerful man, it was our host, who seemed so content with what he had. It was clear that he had everything he needed even if it seemed to us as nothing. And yet it was also obvious that he was a leader to the village people and that a feeling of love existed between him and them.

Before we left him to continue our exploration of the Yucatan, he asked where we were planning to go. Up to then our trip was on any road that looked inviting and usually less traveled. He pointed out a road that we could not take as "too dangerous for you"; but that in any case, "You must go to a small village near the ancient site of Palenque to meet" a certain person with his assurance that, "It would all take place once you get there." Before we drove off he gave us his picture and a hand-written poem, a tiny gift to my wife, and a few final words. Looking directly into my eyes he touched my chest with his finger and said, "You are on an important journey; and what has taken place, and is to take place, are not accidents." And looking intently at my wife told her "your task is to take care of him and keep him safe." I always thought that was my job with her?

The Poem: "*The Wandering Man*"

I have no name, I have no home, I am just like the breeze that blows from place to place. I don't know my mother, I don't know my father but I live with Nature, with the birds and animals, and the music of the Flowing streams, the sound of life which thrills me so. I cannot think but I believe I know. I worship the sun, the moon and mother earth which gives me All the happiness I need. She produces the nutrition that Men need. The air, the food and the water. I only wish that every man would feel the same as me. Then we would live in a paradise. I'm not from here nor from there. I go from place to place. I live from day to day. I don't think of tomorrow but I think of today. All I can say is "LOVE AND PEACE FOR EVERYONE."

L-ights
O-f
V-ibrations
E-levated
—Raul

After we returned home from our trip to Mexico we sent him a large box full of many things but never heard from him or that the box was received. Nevertheless, the two-day experience was profound, and amazingly continued to influence what took place and the people we met over the next ten never-to-be-forgotten days. It was and remains a spiritual and loving experience that is with us, just as strongly, forty-plus years later. The journey continues.

To this day we do not question what took place and occasionally still talk about the events that happened, beginning with meeting him at the closed museum and the people we subsequently met. We witnessed his relationship to the villagers, his lack of "things" and money. The love that existed between them all was palpable, as was his love towards us. Also, his "knowing" of the people we were to meet, and without any question on his part, that it would all take place. There is so much we do not understand.

It was an example of the magic of love that I believe, maybe idealistically, ought to exist between people. More particularly to this book, I believe it should be between those who lead and those who follow. The power to influence is considerable and reaches deeply into each of our lives. The benefits to both the recipient and the giver of love are immense. Conversely, where love does not exist what does between humans?

Knowledge through Experience as an Attribute

True knowledge is gained through experience and is where wisdom is found. Having knowledge gained through experience is how attributes may be acquired and where true wisdom comes from. Ah, if we could but grow from books, lectures, and hearsay, and learn the lessons of life that others have lived. I believe this highly unlikely because true knowing cannot be acquired second-hand. Accumulating data, the amount of which today is phenomenal, is not true knowing but simply the gathering of what may or may not be facts. Only experience leads to true knowing, and that is restricted to those who have the good fortune or misfortune of actually living through experiences and then extracting any lessons found in the experience. This may or may not result in attributes being acquired. It depends to what degree one is a student. Some people seek to learn and to grow through personal experiences, and others seem satisfied with what others tell them. Which of them has richer and more meaningful attributes?

When claiming the title of student, people may believe they are experiencing emotional and intellectual lessons from which they gain knowledge and hopefully acquire quality attributes. This may or may not be true, but reality paints a complex picture. My experience with many leaders is that they, first, seek tools from me and other consultants; that is, not inner change and growth but ways of leading more effectively with the goal of compliance as a result. In other words, they were not concerned with themselves as "the problem to the answer," but how they come across to others. This is not the deeper and healthier attributes that come from being true to one self and is paramount if a leader hopes to influence those close to them to also grow.

If we were to study leaders' resumes, we would find that most have the requisite degrees and credentials that stamp them as students. And, many seek continuing education, enroll in numerous workshops, and devote much time and energy to sharpening their skills. As with the preceding paragraph, most of what they learn and do is meant to enhance their use of tools as well as to stay abreast of the latest techniques. Few are motivated enough to nurture their own personal growth and which is difficult, if not impossible, to do through ones' own efforts.

The work I suggest as essential is not about tools but rather trust, safety and the willingness of the leader to be vulnerable. As this develops and is perceived by important others, it also generates an environment that invites others to become involved. As this takes place the level of trust, creativity, spontaneity, and sharing changes and growth is facilitated from within each to each other. This growth is not a group process, but personal to each person. Some will grow and others will decide to not risk opening up; and they will, volitionally, depart the scene. There are people so deeply damaged that in their mind they are worthless. They do not seek knowledge, but security and assurance that they remain hidden and safe from discovery of who and what they believe they are.

The following story is all about discovery and gaining knowledge about one's self. It all began on an LST (Landing Ship Tank) heading towards Okinawa after the atomic bombs had been dropped on Japan and the World War II was officially over. About midway from Hawaii to Okinawa, it became apparent that the beautiful weather we had for days was about to change. As a matter of fact, it was about to become one of the greatest typhoons on record; and it appeared that the storm was heading right at us. Changing direction of our fully loaded ship with a top speed of about ten knots was apparently meaningless given the broad coverage and speed of the storm. Everyone on board was informed that we were going to be hit dead-center by a huge Pacific storm.

I was part of a small contingent of army personnel on board responsible for the chained heavy equipment and machinery. Ordinarily, I was required to do little beyond checking the chains that secured the heavy equipment. I read a lot and contemplated the vastness of the ocean—and my insignificance. Of course I had no idea how this event would permanently impress upon me how helpless we are when events we cannot control or escape take over.

The huge typhoon was beginning to take shape across the Pacific Ocean in front of us when, as anticipated, an announcement came over the boom-box that, "All personnel are to gather in the mess hall for instructions," followed by, "The chaplain on board will be holding services for all faiths." I thought that since it was possible I might die in this storm, I wanted to participate in the event with my eyes wide open and fully experience the experience. The thought of being in an enclosed and secured room with others and being thrown about without any sense of the tumult going on outside had no appeal to me.

I found a way to the forward bulkheads and discovered that I could get outside. The hatch I opened was roped off, but I had enough space between myself and the lines to stand outside although it would be impossible to go on deck beyond perhaps one foot between the bulkhead behind me and the lines that secured it. Wearing full raingear (as if it mattered) and at the fore of the deck, I was prepared to witness what I thought would be my end.

At first the calm of the ocean was unreal; and then long, low cigar-shaped clouds began rushing towards us. The ocean began to grow in swells, not breaking waves; and soon it began to rain. The rain grew to sheets of water coming horizontally right at me. The ocean swells continued to grow. For a second or two I saw no water anywhere around me and then, just seconds later, water was everywhere, including over my uplifted head. I soon realized that the LST was bobbing up and down like a cork. Sometimes we were at the top of a mountain of water with nothing but air around us, and then we were in a huge valley with walls of water and waves obscuring everything.

I may have dozed off or was put in an altered state of mind, but I do not remember anything except being witness to the awesome power of nature. I do not remember going inside during the height of the madness and chaos of the storm. I also do not remember feeling fear, but only awe in the remarkable, natural event being played out in front of me. Eventually, perhaps twelve to fourteen hours in duration, the typhoon began to slowly diminish as it moved off to the west. The Pacific began a slow process of becoming "Pacific" again.

The worst part of the storm was over, but the damage left behind is recorded in history.

The experience remains with me as if it all occurred yesterday. But beside the pictures and sounds, what did I learn, not just remember, from the experience? I discovered that I do not fear death or the unknown and have had this feeling confirmed a few times since. I also know that I do not give in to "helplessness" but choose instead to play a hand in my own present and future. I "know" this because it has been my "real life" experience, and not a story or feeling I have dreamed. Experience is the only way to true "knowing," and it demands reflecting and extracting from our personally lived experiences.

Firmness

The simple act of doing the right thing at the most appropriate time is not so simple. The right amount of firmness at the most appropriate time is a difficult challenge for any leader. It is easy to be firm when a decision is a must and understood. An example is a fire at work or home. If at its first discovery we are able to put it out we do. If not, we alert the fire people, save lives and our own. If it is not an emergency and time is available to us why not seek more information and input from others? To not be firm enough when firmness may be called for is a common error as is being too firm too soon. I have known a few leaders who were incapable of firmness even if the issue, obvious to others, demands an action or resolution immediately. I have also known leaders who acted too impulsively with their problems and key people; these leaders would "fire before taking aim," and too often with disastrous results.

When leaders are firm and resolute, the behavior needs to be appropriate to the event. If it is not, and they have not sought input from others involved, people feel unimportant relative to what's taking place around them. This is an example of exclusive use of power as compared to others being empowered and is indicative of a strong and controlling leader. Conversely, if leaders are perceived as weak when it comes to making and enforcing decisions, this results in confused, erratic, disrespectful and indifferent behavior on the part of subordinates. When possible, the wisest course of action is dialogue and inclusion of those involved before decisions are made.

Where, when and how does wise use of firmness work? The story of firmness (and honor) in Chapter 3 that proved to be right and appropriate involved Yamamoto. He was the Japanese POW on Okinawa, and how he dealt with the escapee who he went after, found, returned and then dealt with in front of me and the other POWs. It was immediate, to the point and quickly over with. This happened without explanation or much, if any, dialogue; yet it was an action that was understood by all but me until it was resolved. I not only learned about firmness, I also learned about honor, which in certain cultures continues to be important. Yamamoto was firm in meeting his code of honor. Another lesson recorded.

Another example also found in Chapter 3 took place prior to the grand opening of a major casino resort. The operating president, who expected creative brainstorming ideas from his executives, and in particular, the marketing director, opened the meeting by expressing his thoughts on marketing a grand opening. When the marketing director criticized the president's suggestions but suggested nothing further, the president verbally destroyed the marketing director. Why? As I learned, it was not because the president objected to the marketing director's disagreement but because the marketing director did not follow up his negative comments with any positive ideas. Unlike the honor issue that took place on Okinawa and its quick resolution, this meeting proved to be a disaster for the marketing director. Both are stories of a firm leader taking immediate and firm action, but they are "worlds apart" in terms of the lessons learned and each event's lasting impact.

One more example: I worked with a professional and his office staff for many years. Considerable growth took place with him, his co-workers, and as a carry-over, his family. In fact, his professional practice came to be recognized as one of the finest in the country. He is an outstanding student, absolutely fearless about learning about himself and those with whom he lives and works. He is as principled, ethical and moral a person as I have been privileged to know. He is intelligent, strong, solidly secure and at the same time amazingly vulnerable. I have been his mentor for years, and he has been mine in return. In the process of our working together, we have become close friends.

In between our workshops and fun days of golf when I visited we would often speak to each other over the phone. Generally, our calls were more about staying in touch. But once in a while he would call to discuss a serious issue that might have to do with the office or his personal life. It was a specific issue that he needed to work through. I'd listen, ask questions and confirm my understanding of what he was sharing. I might even offer what action I would take if in a similar situation. But I never suggested or told him what to do, but only what I might do. Invariably, he would say, "I knew you were going to say that." As we got to know each other he could anticipate my responses to his issues. He always knew what he wanted and needed to do but used me as a "sounding board." Our conversation would close with the decision that he had made much before he called me. Apparently, our speaking to each other helped clarify and solidify in his mind the action he knew he had to take. The value of emptying one's mind and having a trusted listener and sounding board to bounce "stuff" off of cannot be over stated.

Did he lack the attribute of firmness? Was he unable to make the "right" decision in a timely manner? I answer that in the negative. His mind was going through many possibilities and consequences in anticipation of taking action. Unless it was a matter of life or death, all else required examination before action. To his credit, when he did take action it included what he also believed was best for others. He is a wonderful example of a quality leader, excellent teacher, solid student and superb role model.

The Attribute of Aiming before Firing: Reason Dominates Emotions

Quality leaders know where they are and have a strong vision of where they want to go and how to get there. They know what they know but never cease being a student in order to know better and more. They acknowledge their need for capable and committed participants in order to succeed and are not alone in what they do. Strategy is carefully laid out and the road map that is created is one step at a time, from the initial vision to the goal. They also include in their thought process frequent check-points along the way so that all involved remain well informed about the status of the journey. Meetings to talk over any and all contingencies are planned and ad-hoc as the need may be. To the best of their ability nothing is swept under the carpet and issues are taken care of as they arise.

This is worth another look at our casino/resort experience in Las Vegas, Nevada: In mid-1960, the operational president of Las Vegas resort hotel about to be constructed invited my wife and me to present our vision of what a youth program in a Las Vegas resort hotel needs to be. To the best of our knowledge, there were no children's programs in any hotel anywhere beyond babysitting services. After listening to what the hotel leadership had as their vision and goals in this exclusive program for hotel guests and VIP customers, we wrote a paper for their consideration titled *Instant Involvement*.

We stated that for the clientele the president wished to appeal to, activities were relatively unimportant because the economic level the children lived in undoubtedly provided every possible activity that money could buy. The children probably attend the best day-care programs, private schools and summer camps; and many may have a swimming pool, horses, tennis courts and just about everything else related to education and recreation available to them.

Because of the visitors' affluent lifestyle and probable ownership of unlimited "things" we envisioned each activity as a way to connect people to people. Yes, activities had to be appealing and fun and would, we hoped, teach in the process; but of primary importance, as we saw it, was the relationship between people that had to be the main attraction. We believed that this relationship between other children and staff was the magic that most recreation programs lacked and therefore was sorely needed. We felt that because of the relationships quickly established— and not activities alone—children and teens would want to stay involved in the program and return to whenever their parents visited Las Vegas.

This approach to a children's program was considered so unusual that differences between what we proposed and what several universities recommended brought the following response from the president of the hotel: "You're either a genius or a mad man, but I'm willing to gamble to find out." And it wasn't a small gamble considering the value to the hotel of well over 10,000 sq. ft. of interior space that could be used instead for income-generating purposes. We also had a big outdoor recreation area and a small bus for excursions. In the enclosed facility were activity rooms for different ages, soda fountain and food area, and even sleeping quarters for a limited number of children.

The program proved to be a huge success and was said to be the finest example of a children's program to be found anywhere in the world at that time. We were told by those most important to its support that the value in dollars alone to the casino resort, not including the impact at other hotels in Las Vegas, exceeded $12 million in gambling-generated revenue during its first year (that's

1970 dollars). The program was not intended as a profit center, but it did cover its cost of operations and more importantly added to the reputation and success of the whole project.

Clearly, this provides a classic example of how one person's vision is brought to reality. It may begin with talk or a dream state; but eventually, if it is to grow beyond the vision stage, leads to establishing a goal and beginning the journey. This required numerous important steps as part of our strategy. We created a road map and stepping stones toward our goal of a "Youth Hotel." This included turning a vision into a picture; presenting the concept, design and construction; employing more than fifty people; providing intense training; and eventually initiating the best possible quality program and the "instant involvement" it promised. It touched thousands of children, relieved the anxiety and guilt of parents, and became the seed for a whole new approach to family recreation.

Moderation

The attribute of temperance, balance and living "the middle way." Moderation may seem to be an odd attribute of quality leadership, and it may be rare in most leaders. However, moderation is essential when leaders are at the center of storms. This calls for delicate control that is neither too strong and emotional, nor too loose and "cool." It is the avoidance of the extreme, but it is not the avoidance of action. And moderation does not imply the avoidance of decision-making. There is a consistency in the behavior of the moderate. Such leaders perform due diligence as required; and when immediate action is necessary, they lead or follow others who are better able to do the task at hand.

Moderation is strongly allied to wisdom and to having a "sense" of the best action to take in the moment. This is amply demonstrated in the story about the POW's actions relative to honor and other stories to be found in the book. An event that may seem to be out of control and an emergency by some is approached thoughtfully and moderately by others. In other words, they do not make matters worse.

"Events dictate the exercise of power" and, ideally, our behavior. This is an epiphany I had years ago and the more I worked on this thought the more I understood that it explains what I mean by moderation. One of its meanings is that moderate leaders do not always lead, but that the event will often point to who shall lead. The talent and experience that moderate quality leaders seek and build into their Inner Circle enables them to allow others with specific experience to take the leadership reins. Moderation is not a "now and then" behavior pattern. It is a constant in the life of quality leaders.

THE LEADER + TEACHER + STUDENT + ROLE MODEL

Being which at the appropriate time calls to the quality person: Leader, Teacher, Student or Role Model? Events call out to us to be one or the other of these attributes when we are leaders. The best leaders teach from their own past experience, and the way they are and live this moment. They teach, not as in a classroom, but in as natural a manner as breathing, through words and behavior that are without duality and conflict. They do not imply or suggest: "Do as I say, not as I do," but are the living example of their words. Our best leaders grab the moment and opportunity to teach a meaningful lesson. Teachable moments are invaluable, but they can come and go in the blink of an eye. Grasping and using them when they occur is a "learned" art form, and the better leaders do this constantly.

Quality leaders are both student and teacher, one being inseparable from the other. The student in the leader becomes the teacher but always remain the students in every aspect of their lives. For these special individuals the search for knowledge and truth never ceases to exist because the more they know, the more they know they do not know. What they also seek are authentic relationships with others they respect and confirm and are respected and confirmed in return. None of this is based on *expectation* or that "I'll scratch your back if you scratch mine." Genuine Dialogue is beyond importance between them and is essential to the leader's existence as a person as well as a leader.

Finally, relative to quality leaders being Teachers + Students, they are the most powerful role models to those important to them through everything they say and do. In fact, it is impossible for any leaders to be other than a role model to those they lead. It is imperative that a leader be aware of what and who they model to those important to them. It is why integrity, honesty, accountability and so many more positive and loving attributes and characteristics of a leader are important and need to fill the environment.

If leaders are less than authentic, do differently from what they say, live duel lives, what is their impact on those they are close to and responsible for? The people who live and work with the leader know the leader best, as I have discovered, better than leaders can know themselves. This is why I emphasize throughout the book that if the leader is to ever become more aware of themselves, their power and influence, they need, almost as much as humans need air, Genuine Dialogue. Not from strangers or accidentally, but from and with those who know each other best.

This brief story exemplifies what I mean: Recently I had a conversation with a former camper, eventual employee, member of my Inner Circle, and always a dear and trusted friend. We were talking about the book and the philosophy of power and leadership. I expressed to him that I strongly believed he understood and could teach this philosophy to others. He appreciated my confidence in him but disagreed that he could teach it to the people who need it most: powerful people, established leaders. But he did qualify what I said by agreeing that he understood it well, that it was part of him and he would thoroughly apply it if he were the leader of an organization. "Why do you feel this way?" I asked. He looked at me and told me, "You are fearless in the face of powerful people" and that "intimidation is simply not part of your make-up. The teacher must be a role model to the leader and to those in the leader's Inner Circle. How could anyone teach this philosophy of leadership and power being, in any way, intimidated by their student, the leader that hires you? I would be and you are not."

"When you teach you are in charge; you take control of the environment and, slowly and appropriately, transfer this power to everyone in the room to take responsibility for their thoughts and feelings. The leader of the organization cannot take this from you, but you relinquish your power to the leader and others the more open they each become. Without your being the temporary leader, controlling the power in the room, student to what is taking place and role modeling the proper use of power, how else would it happen? Leader + Teacher + Student + Role Model: knowing when to be which is not always apparent, but you intuitively go there. This is what I have experienced with you."

In closing this chapter: I have mentioned but a few attributes. There are many that I might have described, but choose to let them be. The point is that attributes are learned and are not unique to any one person. Also, that positive attributes that migrate to one's gut, heart and head contribute to the growth of one's self. Once owned by the leader attributes finds ways that contribute to the growth of others. Conversely, negative, abusive, insensitive attributes whether deliberate or blind do harm to relationships including to the one in power. There are no winners when power is badly used.

CHAPTER 5

THE INNER CIRCLE (IC)

One with each other
Yet unique as one self is
Better together.

I think fondly of the time I worked with a particularly bright, kind and sensitive owner and leader of a manufacturing firm. When I began the task of mentoring him and his key employees relative to communication, it was easy to see that they sincerely cared for each other. Also, it was good to observe that his Inner Circle was made up of people who were experienced in the specific work each was doing. But their main problem was that as the leader he had trapped himself into being perceived as their parent and father figure to his Inner Circle members. He was a "caregiver extra-ordinaire," and his IC treated him as their beloved captain of the ship. More unconsciously than not, he controlled the way they related to him and how each responded to problems of the firm. They appeared so careful and sensitive to his feelings that challenging what he said or opined was like pulling teeth. Thus, little real dialogue took place, and innovative problem-solving recommendations and "the taking of ownership of problems" by members of the Inner Circle happened too infrequently. At the same time I felt confident that he was committed to his own and the growth of his Inner Circle members and that Genuine Dialogue between them was attainable.

We met, initially, at three-month intervals until his Inner Circle began to (individually) accept the leader's openness to their observations and recommendations. It was essential that they each experienced him as one of them as well as their leader that had empowered each to lead as events dictated. Mutuality was our goal.

The transition from his being fixed at the top of the hierarchy to becoming one with his Inner Circle was what he sincerely wanted. But his history and years as an officer in the US Navy played against his desire to be one with his key people. He would take command of a situation easily and allowing one of his IC to step into a leadership role was a major challenge for him. As it began to happen he showed wisdom and grace in the ways he supported and nurtured their growth.

His commitment overcame his past conditioning and he began to open up, to listen to them, perhaps as he had never listened before. As this was experienced by them they each began to talk openly about problems that needed to be resolved if the company were to grow. Leadership qualities popped out from one to the other. It was not long before they looked at and spoke to each other as owners of the organization. Person-to-person dialogue began to occur between them in what, for all intent and purpose, became a conversation among equals. A true sense of "ownership" replaced the traditional hierarchy I found when we first began. None of the Inner Circle had experienced this level of being themselves without fearing that they had overstepped a boundary. Instead of "walking on eggs" during any gathering of the Inner Circle, the workshops became an experience of mutuality, people working together, and, most importantly, having common and agreed-on goals.

The changes that took place in the company were remarkable. In fact, as the business grew so did the desire on the part of the leader to grow to a larger facility. At the same time, the leader was a member of a local business group who would often invite speakers from nearby universities to lecture and lead discussions on business tactics, increasing the bottom line, cutting cost, and personnel issues.

They were a conservative and traditional group of business leaders and generally sought out speakers that dealt essentially with broad financial matters.

As luck would have it the speaker at a luncheon was from a major business school. He spoke directly to what my client was beginning to look for and that is to grow his company to be a major player in his industry. After the meeting the professor and my client spoke privately about his vision and goals for the firm and my client agreed to contract with the professor and his group of consultants in order to go to the next level my client now believed was reachable.

The business owner thanked me for the work that we had done together and the growth that had taken place, "Your job is finished and you have helped us get to where we are, now we intend to grow much bigger and need business help." He had decided that what he now needed was the expertise of financial consultants from one of the great Southern California universities. I understood his need for financial guidance, but did not anticipate the actions the academics would take.

It was not long after the team of consultants arrived that they brought a major change to the Inner Circle. The members I had worked with—the very ones responsible for the growth of the company—were pushed out and replaced by "numbers" people. The new people were unfamiliar with the actual business but, supposedly, knowledgeable in the science of expanding a business. Long story short, within a two year period the whole business plan and the business itself failed, and all the growth and good that was achieved failed.

This is a classic example of the value of the "right" kind of members in an Inner Circle and the importance of open dialogue between people involved. They must have knowledge about what the organization does and the culture in which it all happens. This means considerable hands on experience in what each is required to do. And they must be able and ready to take a leadership role in order to implement needed changes and are resourced to do so. This was all undone by the replacement of experienced Inner Circle members who were responsible for the growth of the company by academics who understood a spread sheet, but not the culture.

Theory is fine and even necessary, but it needs to be carefully tested prior to the heat of battle because once the battle is being waged theory goes out the window. What we did together was not a test or experiment of a theory. It was pure "down and dirty" leveling talk to each other about the work at hand, and, in time, about the future. The people involved knew the game they were in. They were educated in it, earned scar tissue in it and understood, as fully as possible, its culture. The productive Inner Circle team that the owner/leader built was eliminated because they did not have the academic credentials: they only had Ph.D.'s in experience.

The owner's training, heroic war experience as a Naval Officer, and big heart showed him to be a student and superb role model. He had been a wonderful leader during this time of our working together and he had a remarkably effective Inner Circle. But he also valued status and wanted this for his company, which impelled him to believe he needed business professionals to take his firm to the next level although he already had a proven Inner Circle made up of the right people to make this happen. In fact, what he should and could have done is to bring into his Inner Circle financial expertise. If that is what he believed he needed he simply could have added one or two people with strong financial experience to his battle hardened Inner circle. The culture he lived in influenced him differently, and the story ended badly. It cost him and the others who were similarly committed to growth what they had built together.

What is an Inner Circle? Visualize the Inner Circle as the crucial point on which relationships and organizations, like an inverted pyramid, sits. This pivotal point is the power person and the Inner Circle people on whom the leader depends. It supports and nurtures a relationship as well as an organization to grow and prosper or through dysfunction to atrophy. The Inner Circle is the brain and heart of all human organizations whether two or many. Inner Circles are comprised of those who hold the most power and influence—leaders and those (usually) few people leaders trust to do their bidding. Ideally, good leadership translates in to a functional Inner Circle where Genuine Dialogue is likely between them, even if accidentally experienced.

History and personal experience has shown that most ICs (Inner Circles) fail, and because they fail so is the organization they represent going to fail. Yet ICs, functional or not, are a phenomenon necessary to the creation of, and the survival of an organization. As the old saying goes, "can't live with them, and can't live without them." And often, even if badly led and dysfunctional, organizations still manage to get by (*malfunction* might be the better word) regardless of the malignancy existent in the IC. Because of this state we find on-going turmoil and a severely limited lifespan.

Regardless of how an IC functions the IC is a biological necessity to the creation and existence of humans and their organizations. An IC is given life because people do not exist in a vacuum. We are each dependent on others. It is this dependency that brings with it degrees of power and domination of one over the other and which is either dynamic and changing or fixed. If dynamic there is no fixed hierarchy formed or necessary and power shifts to one or the other depending on abilities and events. But most IC's in history and today are deliberately formed, have a fixed leader and dysfunction is not accidental but built in by the leader of an IC. We will find out why most are dysfunctional and what action needs to be taken in order to maximize the value of ICs.

Another point that needs to be emphasized is that in a relationship of two each will likely be in or lead in other ICs. In organizations of many people whether political, economic, religious or social there is a 'head" or leading IC and each of its members again have their own IC as does each of their members with family and friends. Clearly, ICs exist everywhere and anywhere we have people living with people. And power is, therefore, as ubiquitous as is the Inner Circle and neither is a problem unless used for negative purpose.

Although I state throughout the book that leaders are the key to the primary issues that influence whether a relationship or organization grows or withers, all IC members are co-contributors. Every IC member is obviously responsible for their behavior and as carriers and interpreters of what takes place within the workings of the core IC to every corner of where they live and work.

What is rarely understood and appreciated is that the individuals included in the leaders' IC simply by association have considerable power in the eyes of those outside the circle. Also, they are each indispensible to the leader relative to operations and, at a minimum, to do the job they are there to do. Regardless of whether a leader is an entrepreneur struggling towards a vision or the leader of an ongoing organization the more able and free each IC member is, the more individuals and the organization benefits.

What the leader is uniquely responsible for is *who* their IC members are and the quality and values they each bring to the table. A leader selects members for many reasons, and they are dealt with in the following pages. But the point needs to be emphasized that ICs are a creation of leaders and are chosen due to the leader's own needs, intentions, and expectations. The more aware the leader is of themselves, the more vulnerable and aware of their short-comings, the more likely it is that the leader selects talent and experience different from the leader.

In the opening story of this chapter the leader's IC was ideal for the industry they were in, and the better the IC communicated with each other problems were more quickly anticipated and resolved. Appropriate decisions were made and supported by each member and each took on an ownership attitude and behavior.

When the owner/leader wanted to grow in to a major player instead of adding the talent and experience he needed to his IC in order to make this happen he turned his operation over to business professionals. They, in turn, replaced his knowledge based people who built the business with people that knew nothing of the operation and its culture. What they understood was the bottom line, budgets and profit centers. When I write that leadership "is the problem to the answer," it's what I seriously mean to say. After all, who sought out and hired strangers to his industry, but academically knowledgeable in the art of business theory, and then allowed them to replace his very effective Inner Circle with their own people?

It is a major problem that most organizational ICs fail; and if so, why do they fail? They fail due to a failure in leadership. The leader selects individuals that meet the needs of the leader instead of the organization. Read the story above carefully. The owner had a vision, invested to reach the goal, built a solid strategy and employed experienced people necessary to develop, manufacture and sell the products. The leader went farther than most and employed a consultant to facilitate the communication between him and his IC. It all worked so well that he decided to take the business to three times its size. He needed a building at least three times larger than the one they were in, and, of course, with many more employees and the latest technology.

At this point he felt considerable anxiety over the huge financial commitment he would have to make. As a former battle-hardened officer of the U.S. Navy, he understood the importance of preparation before any new and unfamiliar task. It was during this planning stage that he listened to a lecturer who spoke about growth and financial risk. This person and his firm was the answer, as he saw it, to his firm's biggest financial commitment.

It was not long after that the consulting firm placed their own people into decision making positions. The original IC members who had built the business and its successful operation were suddenly ousted from the IC and became managers of their respective departments, but without the voice they previously had. They did this or they departed. The environment was so dramatically altered that nothing was left of the previous and successful model and IC team.

Everyone brings to their relationships themselves which includes histories, biases and beliefs all combined to make how we each perceive and act in our unique worlds. Differences, as desirable as they are, are also a primary cause of conflict between most people. It is a prime reason why selection to an IC is so great a challenge to the leader, and why failure is the common end to most ICs. One thing for certain is that competition and one's ego has to be excised out of the body of an IC. The leader and members of their IC must become one body, yet made up of different, talented and strong individuals that must remain so. This is no small task to achieve.

In order for an IC to function at a high level, it must work to act as one mind, synchronized and in harmony. Simultaneously, each member needs to remain unique, special, and genuine as they make their case based on what they know and feel. It is not easy to do, but it is essential if an IC is to gain the most value from each member. Regardless, all leaders are ultimately responsible for the IC they build around themselves and how its member function. They are the model and force that creates what any IC is and becomes and, hence, responsible for the degree of functionality of the IC.

Regardless of setting and context, leaders are leaders are leaders as long as they hold power over others. This is a fact even when leaders are enlightened enough to empower, support and even to follow, as required, those dependent on them. As long as a specific leader exists, their presence and philosophy is felt and influences the IC. When IC members, often more talented and capable than the leader, assume leadership over a project they are still extensions of the leader. Even if the leader becomes one of their followers, this is situational and temporary and all are aware of this.

When I reflect on the groups of people with whom I've worked over the years, whether family, children and teens, my own employees and a wide range of professional organization, I have learned to sense and quickly evaluate the health of the environment I am in. Are people nurtured to grow and supported to do the best possible job? Is communication restricted and top down with expectations that all is well and that everyone understands? Are problems being aired via face to face dialogue and does spontaneity and innovation exist? And, most important, what is the general state of relationships with each other as well as the authority figure? None of this is difficult to uncover. Conversely, it is a, feel good, experience to witness when the "ship of state" functions well, with all hands working beneficially towards common goals as well as for each member's benefit. Watch the leader in action and listen to the dialogue between them and the reasons are clear.

GENUINE DIALOGUE IS THE "GOLDEN THREAD"

Genuine Dialogue is the "golden thread" that holds the well-functioning IC together and gives it remarkable creative and problem-solving abilities and results. The potential is there if the talent is in the room, but even here the leader always remains the key if this potential is to be realized. Even with talented and strong (healthy ego strength) IC members must be empowered by the leader to be themselves and express their opinions and feelings. If the leader is not open to leveling the playing field and abuses their power those with experience may express themselves but will lose and they know it.

Being compliant to the leader does not and cannot build the healthy and successful organization and is definitely symptomatic of inadequate leadership. Whether unconscious or conscious of what they do, leaders who do not empower their people to stand their ground and say what needs to be said lose them and are losers themselves. Those that submit to this not only are denied being, but suffer negative consequences within themselves. Needless to say, all in the relationship suffers as does the organization.

I constantly hammer at the theme that leaders are the primary cause of the success or failure of the organizations they lead. Each member of the leader's IC are as fingers of the leader's hand reaching throughout the groups they lead and influence that extends throughout the whole organization. At its worst, through a dysfunctional IC is the spread of a cancer whose root cause is inept leadership.

In sharp contrast, the good leader creates a quality IC by bringing together people of known talent and different life experiences and which becomes the basis of a dynamic Inner Circle. The leader makes it as clear as possible through words and behavior that they come together each with their own strengths and knowledge and that one's opinions are going to be heard and understood. They do not avoid disagreements, arguments, and "in your face" challenges, but at all times "show respect for each other." Participation is maximized and each IC member is as fully themselves as they are able to be. Fear and insecurity does not exist. Our histories and how we have been conditioned is faced, and if negative, are slowly replaced by our natural need to be. With good leadership and the healthier environment in place ICs members become more authentic. It is through an open, inviting, vulnerable leader that knowledge and individual uniqueness is made available to the group. Not all will join into a nurturing and safe to be environment and those that do not will leave of their own volition.

ONLY THE WISE AND ETHICAL BRING TOGETHER THE BEST TALENT

In healthier Inner Circles what exists is an understanding that there are no barriers to bringing issues and problems to the table that are work-related. Problems that affect the work environment—people, employees, relationships, customers, suppliers, financials and meeting the needs of the future—are the meat and potatoes of the IC. There is also the need to give birth to goals, strategize, assign responsibilities, initiate action, distribute resources, and seek today's various talents and experience as needed.

Most leaders create problems for themselves and the organization they lead in spite of having additional hands to help them. Their problem is that they are not given the heads and hearts of IC members beyond waiting to be directed. IC members, in this case, are not given nor nurtured to express what they think and feel and certainly not to take charge. These leaders trust no one, operate as lone wolves, and therefore believe they are the only responsible person. They are the makers of interpersonal problems and refuse to accept what they have created. When things fall apart they re-create what they have had before. They continue to surround themselves with weak and dependent people and nothing significant changes.

Leaders who do recognize the importance of whom they surround themselves with know that the first challenge they face is to identify the talent and experience they need for where they are at and for the near future. In the entrepreneur's case it may be people willing to take on any challenge so flexibility and adaptability is what's needed. In other cases an entrepreneur knows that they need specific talent and proven experience for tasks well beyond their own knowledge. What matters is that the wiser and more determined entrepreneur and leader does not hesitate to seek out talented help to join with them.

A very important part of a leader's task within the IC is to select and train potential leaders to replace them. This particular issue is more thoroughly discussed in other sections of the book, but it is in the IC where the leadership filtering and selection process works best. We witness each other so fully and intensively through Genuine Dialogue that there are no important nuances that elude us. There is no hiding or games' playing in a healthy IC.

Also, ICs need to change once an entrepreneur reaches their goal. The people responsible for giving birth to an organization may not necessarily be the best for operating and growing an organization. Entrepreneurs and their initial ICs bring a vision to reality during the entrepreneurial stage, but once this is achieved different needs arise. Entrepreneurs and their unique IC must now transform themselves into leaders and managers. Transformation from being a spear point to the body of the spear is rarely easy to do, but necessary.

It is one thing to give birth to a baby, and a whole different set of conditions to care for and raise a baby. This was our experience at the beginning of our simple day-camp operation that over a period of ten years evolved into a complex operation. We began with four people and two buses. At its peak, we owned thirty-eight buses, had 100 employees, and as many as 400 children who were picked up at their homes and delivered back home at the end of the day five days a week throughout the summer, plus additional year-around programs.

To make this operation possible, I enlisted dedicated young people and did have an Inner Circle. Not only did I not understand what an IC was, looked like or how it was to act I never thought about anything like this. Regardless, I can't remember a time when I did not have others to help me in every possible way. And, yes, we had to change from an entrepreneurs' way of doing things to being leaders and managers of what we created. It did not work for everyone, but those of us who made the transition did so because of determination and a level of personal responsibility. Failure was never an option.

In our early experiences the ICs we had (by accident, not by intent) functioned well enough, but not because of experience and proven abilities. It was due to an unyielding willingness of individuals to be personally responsible and to take risk and in the process being supported, nurtured, and empowered. But, as I learned much later, none of our early ICs came anywhere near the specific knowledge level we needed. Personal experiences are necessary gifts when it comes to building and operating an organization and probably so in all relationships, but, at the time, what did I know? Growth may happen accidentally, but is never guaranteed. It is much better to be conscious and to reflect on experiences and seek to learn more about ourselves, others and ways of being more true to who we are.

A stark example of this: As our organization grew and changed we desperately needed an experienced "business head" in our IC, but I trusted none that I came across. Because of my failings we simply did without, and this omission costs us dearly in subsequent years and entrepreneurial efforts. I was never able to take any of our programs beyond our own abilities. In other words, we never built on our successes. What might have been a strong and spreading business reality never came to be. I was responsible for keeping this from happening. I was the leader and erred in creating the best possible Inner circle to help take us to those new levels.

In its initial vision and strategic phase; from the idea to reality an IC needs to be made up of individuals who thrive on challenges and unknowns and handle multi-tasking. All members accept and work on what needs to be done. Events dictate and all the planning goes out the window. Also, each member needs to know the overall picture because in the well functioning IC no one acts in a vacuum. Primarily, at this phase they are like a wolf pack with the alpha wolf (the entrepreneur) calling the shots.

In comparison, in the up-and-running organization, the IC is all about leadership, the team, and communication. Planning and strategy still occurs, but the primary concern is operations. This means that the entrepreneur/creator and the original IC must change from dealing with ideas and unknowns to something firm in one's hand and needing care if it is to survive. As with all organisms, the IC needs to change as the environment and circumstances around it change or it dies. Once a vision becomes actualized, entrepreneurial behavior becomes less essential—never non-essential—and leaders of people are required.

It is important to restate that successful entrepreneurs are not assured of being effective leaders. They may do remarkable things bringing a dream to life, but when it comes to being an effective leader their talents and interests are elsewhere. To be sure, good leaders are rarely entrepreneurial and possess attributes that are often dramatically different from those of the entrepreneur. The entrepreneur views the IC members as tools in order to get work done. Quality leaders recognize the importance of each person in their IC and supports and empowers them to each being a leader if and when events dictate. The true entrepreneur is the power source, the quality leader is the distributor of that power.

POWER AND THE IC MEMBERS

The process of empowerment, which requires sharing power and control is one of the most difficult and complex issues a leader faces in creating and working with their IC. This issue is of such importance that everything discussed in this chapter as well as the body of the book ultimately rests on the relatively enlightened leaders and the IC they create and the ways in which they relate to each other. Leaders absolutely must understand and appreciate the meaning of power and of the sharing of this power with select others.

Members of an IC who have, as their hidden agenda, a need for power are as troublesome to an organization as is a power hungry leader. Cooperation between IC members is essential, whereas competition, which is what power hungry people thrive on, may actually destroy the cooperative and positive work of a good, but relatively weak leader. With the strong quality leader and the environment they create those who seek power are easily discovered. They are stripped of their cover and their sick, self-serving agenda is exposed. In a healthy IC these individuals will likely depart the scene or have life-changing experiences and become strong and positive contributors. It is also clear that where we find a weak leader, we find a dysfunctional IC, power, competition, and strong subgroups are major issues that slowly weakens and eventually destroys an organization.

WHO'S REALLY IN CHARGE HERE?

When power is not allowed to flow to those best able to handle certain events because it is held tightly by one or an exclusive group an organization is sure to be harmed. This was made starkly evident when I worked with a particular CEO and his supposed key people, while the actual power person sat off to the side observing the workshop. The primary focus of the workshop was Genuine Dialogue. In minutes it became obvious that the secret known by all in the room but me was that the CEO had no power. The CEO was just a mouth-piece through whom the one in power spoke, and it was the true power person who sat in a darkened corner observing and listening to what he hoped would solve many of his problems. In fact, the elephant in the room, that is, the overpowering influence, even if invisible, is always known and felt by the members of an IC.

From the perspective of each IC member dealing with the problem of a figure-head non-leader, such as the case in this story, knowing where the power actually is confronts them with a difficult and potentially dangerous dilemma. If they play at the game of pretend—that authentic communication does not exist and the designated leader is not the leader at all—Genuine Dialogue is impossible to achieve. Playing to the open secret undermines the effectiveness of individual participants within the IC and the organization they are supposed to lead. Any members of the IC who dare to directly confront the truth immediately place themselves in jeopardy with the pretender as well as the true power person.

Leadership and power need to be openly and honestly shared, and is the best and most effective way a healthy IC functions. In the effective and high-functioning IC, power moves to the person who is best able to do the job and to take charge. No leader has the cumulative knowledge to take on all issues. The quality leader knows this and easily supports more specifically talented members to take control of an issue or event.

In the healthy IC, the capacity to exercise power moves to one or another due to knowledge, not to position in the hierarchy. All issues having to do with work and leadership are on the table. Whoever takes power takes it temporarily due to the specific event and their ability to do the job. The better leaders know this and consciously facilitate it taking place. Other leaders do this intuitively, but lack the awareness of the necessity to do this. Picking the right and best people to be part of one's Inner Circle is no easy task and is one of the more important responsibilities and indicators of a quality leader.

HOW ENTREPRENEURS SELECT THEIR IC PARTICIPANTS

In my own entrepreneurial efforts and as the leader of numerous organizations, I apparently did not fully appreciate and understand the importance of specific experience and people. Expertise and knowledge is required if one is to create, then to operate, and eventually to grow an organization. I must have believed, and therefore acted on the basis that the vision and direction and implementation were my responsibilities. I thought all I needed were people capable and willing to assist me in my work; and I have the uncomfortable feeling that this was true of my initial selection of key people. I picked people who were caregivers, likeable, sensitive, empathic, and physically attractive, and enthusiastic. I sought teachers and teacher-types who would also be excellent role models and socially creative. They were the best, or at the least I believed they had the potential to do the best, for what we were doing in education and recreation.

Most of the people succeeded admirably within the parameters I set and expected. They were well supported to do so. But I failed to grow any of my organizations beyond its immediate borders even when opportunities presented themselves to grow. I accept full responsible for not surrounding myself with people of various business experiences. When we had the opportunities to go national to build youth programs in most cities not only was I without any experience for the business demands I had no one on my IC who could help take us in this direction; and I did not trust "outside" expertise to guide us.

None of the people in the ICs I brought together were knowledgeable in the world of high finance and growing a business. They were quality people, but educators and recreationists focused on the benefits to a child not the dollar. But because I did not relate to people who understood and worked in the business and finance world I failed my organization. Unfortunately, this occurs when an organization grows beyond its leaders' experience. The need cries out for different and more specific talent, and yet this leader remained blind, deaf and dumb to the obvious.

When I wore the hat of an entrepreneur I believe I was successful through sheer determination, lots of bulldozing, and perhaps much luck. My ICs were essentially the same whether we were seeking to create, to operate, or to ambitiously grow. Years later, when I began to work with other organizations to help with their staff issues and to grow the leader, I obviously drew much from my own experiences as an entrepreneur and as a leader. The more I dug into the importance of the IC the more I realized the errors and omissions of my own ways. In fact, through my own ignorance or stubbornness, I did not take advantage of the huge business and financial opportunities that were ours for the taking at the time. My ICs were an extension of me when what I so desperately needed were people from different disciplines and knowledgeable of the business, legal and, financial worlds.

A perfect example of this is that most leaders need experienced mentoring to help them attain Genuine Dialogue. Accidental is not good enough. Knowledgeable guidance is called for at every step and the wiser leaders understand this and are quick to seek talent that will assist in meeting this need. I did not understand this as an entrepreneur or leader, but as a teacher years later I realized, all too clearly, why differences in knowledge and experience are so important.

WHO AND WHAT BEHAVIOR MAKE FOR A HEALTHY IC MEMBER

A healthy IC member is an individual who either has a rich and accessible background in what they bring to an IC, or at the least is a determined, focused student eager to growth. All are cooperative and flourish in a mutually beneficial environment and of particular importance do not give up their sense of self to the leader.

When an organization grows, so does its needs for specific expertise as described in my own entrepreneurial and organizational efforts. It was obvious in the story at the beginning of this chapter of the beloved leader who turned his growing and successful operation over to a financial consulting firm and lost it all. He did what I could not do and we both lost. What we both could have and should have done is to find experienced financial talent and include them in our *existing IC*. He did this, but made the grave mistake of giving his power of leadership to an outsider and they, of course, created their own IC with disastrous results. In my case, I empowered and supported young and inexperienced, but positive people. The talent I brought together was too similar and I did not bring the business "heads" on board and suffered the consequences of my ignorance.

In the story of the silent power person in the darkened corner overlooking his "mouthpiece" CEO: He attempted to create a puppet leader controlled by him from any distance. What he failed to do is to find someone to lead the organization that he could fully empower to be the true leader. Then he needed to remain a mentor (only) to this person relative to his philosophy and its implementation.

We change the texture and people in our ICs because not all people grow relative to changing needs. It is usual that an IC member of an entrepreneurial effort finds ways of doing what needs to be done due to the fact that entrepreneurial efforts have much to do with blazing a path. Operating an existing organization is a totally different world and demands more than a strong and determined individual. Leaders and their key people must become teachers and students of others and know that they are role models to those they lead. There is no guarantee that this will happen to people who have fought the entrepreneurial fight. It appears that dedicated students of life and its various experiences ride best on the waves of change.

In any case, as conditions change in the healthier and better-led IC (the one could not happen without the other) members grow to meet new and unexpected needs. Or, experienced/talented people are actively sought out; and old-school IC members are gently helped to grow or go. Grow or go is always a deeply private decision that each member must make, but are helped to make the proper decision. This is not meant to be unreasonable or insensitive but simply what happens when events force leadership and members of the IC to change. And as different and more specifically talented people enter the scene, the environment in which IC members function also changes. Each person contributes their own kind of spice to the environment they are in.

In its broadest sense, nothing human is fixed or frozen permanently in time so change is assured. The challenge for most people is that change comes as a problem to them. If problems are seen as opportunities this is a good thing and offers many possible rewards. On the other hand, if problems are avoided, hidden or dealt with badly, unlike miserable weather which simply goes away, things tend to get worse.

LESSONS LEARNED BY ADDRESSING COMMON PROBLEMS

We designed and operated a children's facility in a large apartment complex made up of approximately five-hundred apartments. We had contracted with a major national builder to design a children's facility and to create and operate a day care program during the week, after school program for children to their teens including counseling and tutoring services and a day camp on weekends, holidays and during summer vacation. In other words, we designed and operated a children's facility and various programs from 6 A.M. to 8 P.M. each evening. From our perspective it was created to maximize and to meet as many needs of children from as wide a range of ages as possible. The developer's purpose for constructing the facility and paying us a fee for design, implementation and operation of the program was renting and filling the apartment units as quickly as possible and selling the huge project.

The program fulfilled its promise to children and due to its growing reputation rented out the five-hundred units more quickly than anticipated. It was not long before teens and young people began to form gangs and vandalism increased in the evenings. The apartment management people's answer to this problem was to hire armed guards to walk the grounds in order to attempt to suppress and disperse the gangs and hopefully to cut the cost of the vandalism to the complex. We suggested that for considerable less cost we would place a few recreation people in the complex beginning at 8: pm to 10: pm armed with basketballs, footballs and ready and able to set up tournaments, competition between gangs and just join with the teenagers using fun and games as their vehicle.

It worked so well that it saved the complex thousands of dollars each month. The complex was sold soon after. Why not? All units were rented, families were on a waiting list to rent, the preschool and other programs had a wonderful reputation, and crime in the complex had virtually disappeared. The new owners did not want to pay the cost of our program and services, and decided to turn the facility into offices and an adult gathering and game rooms. On the other hand, the original developer's wanted us to replicate this program for their apartment complexes throughout the US. I and my IC did not have the knowledge necessary to establish a mutually beneficial business relationship with the national development and construction firm. Where a long term contract was called for that included our design, operational, marketing and training capabilities the company we dealt with wanted the same loose relationship we had developed at our first effort on their behalf. Also, the economy took a steep nose-dive during this period (early 1970s) and the development firm was forced to cut back or eliminate most of their projects around the country. For me it was another learning experience that impressed upon me my own weaknesses and what I needed to do with my IC and our company.

The importance of the IC is not incidental. The sooner any leader accepts this and understands what they, as the leader, must do to build a quality IC the more likely it is they will be better protected but also to attain goals. Too often these lessons are not learned or learned too late. The story below is indicative of how well I came to understand this—that is, after my own entrepreneurial and leadership days.

A few years ago I was recommended to someone who had just purchased a local business. He knew nothing about the business he bought, but he is wise enough to secure the help of the best available people to help him run the operation. He is a student, unafraid to admit to glaring deficiencies in his own history and seeking to fill them in, and although fearless, his real courage is demonstrated through his being vulnerable. His need, as expressed to me, "I want to communicate at the highest possible level with the people I work with."

Although our working together had to do with work relationships and communication as it existed in his firm, the more I learned about him and his background the more I realized that he was the person and talent I so lacked in my own IC many years ago. Number one, he had professional and life experiences totally different than my own, and that I needed so badly. Two, he had the courage to stand his ground in the face of a strong leader. No give on his part relative to what he did and knew. He was unafraid of his truth and confident of what action to take, most particularly as it relates to his field of expertise. He was the perfect piece of puzzle that would have helped make our firm a national player, and not once, but a number of times.

Had I known then what I now know, he, his talent, experiences and professionalism would have been as much a part of my own IC as my right arm. The person I got to know and his knowledge/experience combined to make him the person that I do not remember coming across in my past. And, yes, he is completely different than those I did surround myself with, but different in a complimentary way. And, that is the point I need to stress. Differences are a blessing in an IC when brought together for creative as well as problem solving reasons. But, when differences stand only for themselves and act accordingly they do not build, they destroy. More often than not, I tended to view financially sharp people in this way. It was my problem, not theirs.

The more we worked together the more I saw a person with an understanding of money management, legal issues, contracts, banks, and negotiation with powerful financial people. None, of which, I would deal with or had an understanding of. He understood "grease," without which no organization seeking to grow can long function. He was the expertise I envision today as essential to any and all ICs. Most important to me was that he has the knowledge and courage to fight the good fight and then to support the winner.

Not surprisingly, my IC people were similar to each other in that they were, essentially, people committed to people, and why I selected them. What I needed to mix into our environments were a few pragmatists. Idealists—and we all were—need this mix to give them balance. I believe at that time in my life most pragmatists would have failed working with me because of my own biases against the more traditional and practical. I needed to understand, sooner rather than later, that what I lacked in business acumen cost our organization and its growth dearly. As the leader then, I was blind to the whole meaning of this chapter about the IC: Difference in expertise and experience is not just a good thing, it is an absolutely essential ingredient found in a healthy, fully functioning IC. Had I met this person in the story above when I was creating, operating and trying to build our organizations, would I have listened to him and let the organization be influenced by him? I will never know because it did not happen. But, I did learn how significant an IC is to any leader and to teach the importance of the make-up and best use of the IC.

It was when I began consulting that this realization came to me. But since I knew nothing of this during my time as entrepreneur and leader of my own organizations I was able to look back at the errors, omissions and the many invaluable experiences from which I drew lessons. Not theory, but pragmatic lessons were shared on how to best grow as an individual and to offer this opportunity to the key people in our lives. My personal stories became important lessons and the living proof of the efficacy of what I taught.

Leadership and the exercise of power are all about relationships and maximizing them for mutual benefit. I know this knowledge would have been impossible to acquire without the mistakes I made, and the positives and negatives I experienced throughout my journey. One of the many important lessons was coming to understand the importance of the IC to a leader and the organization. Primary to this awareness is realization that an effective IC does not come together as a matter of accidental meetings. If possible it must be deliberate and planned. This needs to be conscious because, and as stated elsewhere, an Inner Circle is natural and comes to be out of our normal relationships with others. In other words, where humans exist together, so does the IC. And for the most part, we remain ignorant of its importance and how to use it to extract the remarkable potential from people working together for some common good.

I may have given an impression to the reader that my own ICs were inadequate or that the people were weak. On the contrary, I was the problem, not those that I included in any of my ICs. For the most part we worked harmoniously, creatively and productively with each other and achieved what needed to be done. Where we were going and how to get there was another story and I drove the vehicle. They were young, some in their teens, a few with military experience and advanced degrees; but all were enthusiastic and creative far beyond my expectations. The problem was our philosophical similarities, not our rare differences and who is responsible for making it so? As an entrepreneur and then as a leader I was the "problem to the answer" when it came to taking our organization and programs beyond our four walls.

Tasks were assigned and taken on with gusto; and whether one or none had any prior experience, something was going to take place and problems were going to be resolved. Taking a chance was a common approach and whether out of pure courage or innocence we each did what had to be done. If it cost too much, we simply found a cheaper way of doing it. In this case I know that ignorance is, at times, a state of bliss, at least as it relates to getting things done, but in the end, we also learned what to do the next time. Interestingly, we all believed there would be a "next time."

The lesson to glean from this is that what I did not know, and what my IC members did not know, should have been covered by individuals who did know. This was all a circuitous way of recognizing and then understanding that the people I brought into my own many ICs were caring, sensitive, willing to learn students, but experienced in the ways of the business world? Hardly! It is clear that those I trusted the most had high energy, enthusiasm and almost limitless courage to take on what needed to be done. If I gave them the responsibility to do something, they did; and if they failed in the process, we used it as a "learnin'" experience. Differences in people and their experiences are not only important, but essential if an organization is to go and grow into unfamiliar territory.

MAINTAINING THE HEALTHY IC

This section contains suggestions that will help an IC to function smoothly and efficiently. The basis of this is the effective leader as the corner stone and initially the most important player in an IC. Replace the quality leader with a dysfunctional leader and all that is good and looks to be permanent will begin to fail. Inadequate leadership has the power to destroy a potentially healthy IC, that is, one that has been created by a departed quality leader. This will, eventually, infect the whole of the organization as well. What to do if we are to avoid this catastrophe?

Quality Leaders Are Mandatory for the Successful IC

ICs by their very nature are fraught with every possible relationship issue. Jealousy, hidden agendas, competition for power, fear of failure, need for love and respect and the conflict of trying to be one's self in the face of pressures to be like others. These and so many other challenges combine to make the reality of a healthy IC seem too difficult to achieve. But it does come about through the efforts and commitment of a quality leader. Leaders are the triggering mechanism for health of the IC and equally so, its malfunction. It is why I strongly recommend a mentor to assist and facilitate, first the leader and then the members of the IC, to understand each person's responsibility to themselves and to each other. A leader who proves to be a good student opens up to a mentor and eventually to their IC members who, in turn, become open themselves.

Specific talent is not always available or affordable, but other options exist. Young but eager-to-learn students working towards degrees in given disciplines can bring a special force to the group, if not experience, considerable enthusiasm and the passion to learn and grow. Mentoring and training programs in one form or another (formal and informal) becomes essential, and particularly so when experience is limited. Ideally, it is worth the effort and expense to seek both experience and enthusiasm in the same person. Also, it is indispensible to determine what the missing links of experience in an organization are and then finding the right person or people to make the IC's portfolio as whole as possible.

Adding to the challenge of creating the best possible IC is that a person's experience does not insure communication skills. Bringing a person of specific talent into an existent IC, in particular, a well functioning one requires an indoctrination period and guidance having to do with the unique and open dialogic style and expectations of the group. Communicating at a high level of authenticity may have been rarely experienced by a selectee. How are they to get involved without some prior education relative to understanding the relationship of the leader to IC members and to each other? One's history and prior conditioning is always a barrier to overcome or to use to the benefit of all. This is why experience is often not enough if an IC seeks to maximize the benefits experience is supposed to bring them. Being a willing and committed student as well as a teacher are equally important attributes along with experience when seeking a new participant.

That the great majority of humans are born able to communicate is obvious, but it is also obvious that in too short a time most everyone learns the importance of "selective" communication. It takes time and patience to confront our lessons of the past, our lessons of dealing with authority figures, and rules having to do with hierarchy. It is why leaders, and how their power is used, become key to the changes that all members go through if they are to make membership in the IC meaningful and positive for themselves and others. Membership in the healthy IC, and which I teach to, means the willingness and necessity to take and use resources and to be a resource to others. It also means to be candid relative to one's knowledge, and to take leadership over a problem that falls where one's strength and experience is.

Keep in mind that perception is the force that exists in each IC member. Perceptions are unique to each individual and the reality that must be dealt with. This is accomplished through dialogue, ideally, Genuine Dialogue. One's perceptions must be made public. When it comes to communication between people in the well functional IC, any hidden disagreements, opinions and, in fact, one's thoughts and feelings that remain unspoken are unacceptable and may undermine the good work of a healthy IC. When spoken aloud in the healthy IC the words are heard and understood even if not agreed with. It is well to keep in mind that agreement may or may not result from Genuine Dialogue, but mutual support happens when decisions are eventually made.

As the leader I want to be perceived similarly by each person in the room. I have an idea about whom and what I am, and I know this is subjective reasoning on my part. But I desire that others important to me perceive me in ways similar to what I believe I am. Their limited objectivity towards me is true for them. Ideally, we are not far from each other's perceptions of me as leader and person. Ultimately, in the healthier IC, this is true of each towards each other. For the IC to work well, it must be this way.

If we are to overcome our own histories that keep us from honest and forthright dialogue how do we do this without first being assured we are in a safe environment? Safety in this scenario if only verbal does not assure safety to anyone. It is what a person feels, perceives and it cannot be manipulated. Without this sense of safety the IC remains a relatively ineffectual group of individuals that are hardly themselves, but protectors of themselves. There has to be an authority with power that takes the lead in openness, vulnerability, listening, understanding, confirming, respect for others, and candor. When the leader presents this as the person they are, not as one who promises to be, others will perceive (in time) a sense of trust. Once the leader is perceived as authentic, change will take place in one and then another and another. Genuineness either attracts or frightens people. Those who are attracted are the healthier and become this, and those who are badly damaged may fear this and depart the scene. Perception of a leader's growth and resultant behavior becomes a superb filtering process.

ICs with Small Membership Tend to Work Best

An IC works best when the membership is limited to a small number of people. In this case six to eight or half that number of people might actually be the Inner Circle to an organization of eighty thousand. This is so because dialogue, when it begins to happen, needs to be spontaneous and at the same time more confirming of each other to assure that better listening and understanding also takes place. When an IC reaches too large a number of people, finding space to interject opinions and feelings becomes limited.

Members inclined toward taking a leadership role in a large IC may become competitive with others. If their agenda is about personal power, control, influence over others, or by association remaining safe, hidden and well cared for under the umbrella of a leader (subgroup?) the larger number of participants allows greater opportunity for this to happen. It is also more likely that in ICs of many there are the few who love to hear themselves talk. This may have nothing to do with personal power issues, but a desire to be heard and recognized. In ICs limited to as few as necessary any of the above may still exist, but with quality leadership this is not likely to be an issue and is dealt with quickly.

As previously stated, most ICs are dysfunctional and personal agendas advanced by individual members of an IC have the potential to inhibit healthy functioning of the IC. This emphasizes the power of each IC member to contribute to the core group, but not to the degree they influence their own IC. If the core IC of an organization is healthy, the odds favor other ICs in the organization will function reasonably well and in harmony with the core IC. It follows that the healthier a core IC the less likely there is to be a "Balkanization" of other ICs in an organization.

Since ICs are naturally formed by humans, and perhaps other animals, it follows that there will be leaders and followers. Also, if studied closely ICs are more often than not a reflection of the IC at the top of the hierarchy. If there are multiple levels, as in large corporations, the "top" may not be the top at all, but management most directly in power. They become significant to what is their responsibility. Literally, organizations within organizations and which cannot be overstated: When communication within a core IC is, to whatever degree, problematic, too stretched out or worse, core members will likely build their own fortress and private army in order to protect themselves. It happens anywhere and everywhere. Growth is hardly the message here, but survival is.

In the story earlier in this chapter of the "observer" to a workshop silently witnessing a workshop in which I found the CEO to be powerless, the CEO was a "puppet on strings" pulled by the silent witness—and that CEO's own IC members were aware of. That is a classic example of organizational dysfunction at the top that is sure to percolate throughout the whole of an organization. Even assuming the CEO decides to risk creating their own IC and applying a philosophy of leadership more open and inclusive they are in jeopardy. As long as they are held under the thumb of the true leader the CEO and their IC function under considerable stress. They and their IC know they tread dangerous waters and which, opens up to other organizational problems. Is this any way to operate an organization?

Inadequate Leadership Leads to Other Problems

A classic and relatively common problem in a dysfunctional IC is a personal agenda by an IC member who works to take over the core IC leadership. There is always the likelihood that someone will attempt to take full advantage of leadership that is experienced as weak. Such people, trusted members of the core IC, will test to the fullest the (perceived) opportunity to act on what they often say privately about the leader. Instead of focusing on issues of the organization and contributing to problem solving and growth of the organization they concentrate their energies on elevating themselves and their own agenda. Given unique opportunities made available through weak leadership, this person will further undermine the role of the leader to the point that others look to them for leadership. The damage done can be disabling to those loyal to the leader. They may fear being in jeopardy themselves by not going along with the one who seeks power. This problem has to be carefully dealt with since the leader may not necessarily see themselves as weak or that an important person to them controls more than the job they have.

An inadequate leader cannot wish this away, but requires guidance if they are to be a competent leader, a student to their IC, teacher when teachable moments present themselves and the primary role model. This is what happens when leaders are made aware of how they are perceived by members of the IC. The question is "how to make this happen?" In order to achieve this level of authentic dialogue it is strongly recommended that a mentor/facilitator be employed to guide the leader first and their IC through a personal growth process. Being vulnerable is essential to being a better leader, but for many courage to know themselves through the eyes of others is too big a risk to take. Change, anywhere and anytime, is difficult to bring about in most situations, but changes in a leader's inner self and behavior are considerably more complex and difficult.

It is never easy to look at one self and maybe impossible to know one self in particular as others we are close to know us. More than most, leaders need to be aware of who they are and how they influence those important to them. One example is the importance of the leader to *respect* others without *first* expecting respect from them. Too many leaders believe that respect should come to them first because they hold the power. Another necessity is being *present* with others and not to "appear" present. Again, leaders usually expect that others be fully present with them and too often do not give full attention to the other. Who, but an experienced mentor, is able to bring this to a leader's attention at the most appropriate teachable moment? How else is what follows to be avoided or eliminated?

A Subgroup Is a Ubiquitous Problem

In almost every situation in which I have been a consultant, as the leader and group become more open and authentic with each other, one individual is exposed as the power behind the throne, or at least believes he or she is the power behind the throne. People like this manipulate a minority to accept and support their efforts of having power and influence. They have no intention of allowing anyone to diminish their agenda and do their best to keep a weak leader, weak, or at the least, under their influence. To this end, they see any attempt by the leader to grow, for example, employing a consultant to help change the environment, as a direct threat to them. They and their supporters do what they can to undermine any outside consultant who appears to threaten their hold on the organization. They are the "subgroup" and every subgroup has a subgroup leader.

Not too surprisingly, leaders usually believe that the subgroup leader is their best and most committed employee and member of the IC. As I discovered, those who covet power and influence do not build on false ground or fake their abilities. Subgroup leaders are very good at what they do in the organization and through their achievements build the leader's support for their machinations. In other words, the Subgroup leader creates an organization within an organization. All appears calm on the surface, but underneath much energy of the organization is consumed by the efforts of the subgroup to feed itself and the subgroup leader. Growth of the organization is dependent more on the whims of the subgroup leader than that of the true leader and IC.

As the true leader becomes more student, less in control, vulnerable, empowers others and is more a participant resistance by the subgroup leader to the workshop increases. What has been and is a power hidden within the IC is slowly but surely uncovered, As this takes place, the followers of the subgroup begin to absolve themselves of connection to the subgroup leader. How familiar a picture is this?

One of the more interesting outcomes that consistently took place once the subgroup leader is exposed and leaves the organization, either voluntarily or invited, the whole body of the organization benefits. People, including those previously part of the subgroup, step into the breach. Whatever the main area of responsibility the subgroup leader had would dramatically change. Every part improved and there were few negative consequences. I could only assume that the drain of energy the subgroup leader and their covert organization had drawn from the larger organization was now available to the organization. Apparently, the subgroup leader's leaving also erased tension and competition between people and groups. The IC became immediately healthier followed quickly by that of the organization.

Time Needs to Be Given to Personal Growth

Too often leaders and their IC are so into the work at hand that setting time aside for education and improving communication between them is given too little or no time. This is not unusual at the entrepreneurial creation stage, in which the IC is often brought together to deal with known and unknown challenges and immediate demands for action. Again, this is dependent on the behavior of the leader and time they are willing to give to other than the work at hand. In this case, what dialogue does take place between IC members is often more like an undisciplined "happening." But how long can ad-hoc happenings suffice against the need for planned dialogue on which to build strategies that constantly need to be revisited?

At some point people who live and work together need face-to-face communication. Also, speaking to others without confirmation and candid feedback assures what? With each person doing what they believe needs to be done meetings become considerably more important. If true dialogue is what happens when they meet surprise and possible chaos is unlikely to occur. Modern technology, the instant communication we have with others, may appear to have resolved these issues, but does it actually make face to face interaction unnecessary? Humans need to not only see each other, but to feel and witness the other's emotions through behavior as well as words. Time set aside for personal and relationship interface is time well spent. A good educator/mentor brings both the best of the old and the best of the new together. It is not a question of "one or the other." Both are necessary.

Beware of Projecting One's History onto the Leader

A common problem occurs when the leader is made into a subordinate's parent (authority) figure. People project their histories onto the present situation, often seeing leaders as their parents. Mudding the water of relationship between leader and subordinate is difficult to avoid when the subordinate is unable to separate past from present. Or, as in this chapter's opening story, the leader unconsciously places himself in the role of parent.

During a workshop an eager IC member could hardly wait to exclaim that he loved the way his leader worked with him and that the leader reminded him of his father. Looking directly at the leader he said, "I often think of you as my father, and I want to please you and I really try to do my best to meet your expectations." How important was it for the speaker to share this, for the leader to hear this and what of the others at the table? What events and ghosts of the past are intervening in how and why people communicate to the leader and to each other? How is Genuine Dialogue possible between any follower and the leader if feelings and history (not reason and staying in the present) rule behavior? Is their talent and experience relative to the job affected? What are the benefits to the leader, IC members, and the organization whenever emotions and the past rule over reason and the present?

Our histories with authorities of every stripe are important to uncover but must be set aside in present relationships. What was the past is not what the present is and separating the one from the other is not an easy task. In effect, a person must be willing to place their past in another folder, a book of notes or a letter to those that played the heavy hand in their past. The point, unless set aside in one form or another the past does continue to influence ones behavior in the present. How can we know this of each other without the safety to expose our past and its many attachments? The assurance of safety and becoming open to one's self and the other are essential.

MORE STORIES ABOUT ICS

Workshops are not designed as "lecture" sessions with me doing the talking. I immediately invite people to be spontaneous and to share when they choose to do so. I emphasize that what they say is as important as anything I or anyone else has to say. In particular, I want to know how they experience and feel about what I am saying. Any questions or comments relative to the subject are welcome. After all, workshops are about power, leadership and communication and having people join the conversation helps direct it where it might prove to be most beneficial. Getting people to talk is voluntary; and no attempt is made to expose, entrap, or push/pull anyone into doing and saying anything he or she is not ready to say. People need to know and feel they are protected from having to expose feelings and their own truths. Safety needs to be firmly established in each individual and I consider this one of a mentor's more important task.

In this story, the leader was open to hearing how his IC felt about him. He was eager to learn and, he hoped, become as good and enlightened a leader as possible. His problem was not resistance but an obvious exuberance in his belief that Genuine Dialogue needed to happen ASAP between him and his IC. His enthusiasm was both emotional and intellectual in that he strongly believed that he, his IC, and the organization would benefit.

One of the (not uncommon) problems he had as a leader was his emotional inconsistencies. He was intensely focused, and when things went wrong he exploded at the problem, wearing his feelings for all to see. The problem was that the leader's emotional outbursts over events spilled on each IC member and through them, their own ICs. It was bad enough that even the messengers became wary of the leader. Dialogue could be elicited but whether any of it was genuine is another question. When emotional eruptions took place even dialogue became rare leaving communication to its more traditional top-down and bottom-up formats, none of which, is desirable or productive.

Although the leader vented mostly over technical problems those within his IC tended to personalize his issues believing he was angry at them. Beyond these moments it was obvious that they each felt sincere regard and respect for him. The problem for him and the firm was that his inconsistent behavior tended to keep his IC members cautious about bringing up issues they believed would set him off. In truth, he was open, receptive and wanted to know about any and all problems that might affect them and the firm.

As mentor I constantly looked for "teachable moments." Hearing and dealing with their stories was preferable to using my stories from other situations and events. When it came from them, and was about their work and relationships, this was always a more fruitful place to go. An example is the story in this chapter about the IC member that felt towards the leader as a son feels towards a loving father.

This particular "teachable moment" needed to be approached with care and the turning it into something of value to others in the room. The speaker had to feel safe enough so that we could discuss his comments. It reminds us constantly that growth is a process and not a single event, and when the door is open to extracting the lesson, it needs to be done, but with a sensitivity towards the speaker's feelings. Once a formerly closed mind is opened, a trained observer/teacher is not likely to let it be closed without first considering what's in there. In fact, when the past enters into the present, depending on the story, growth is a potential if nurtured by exposing the relationship between then and now. How can people remain the same when what has been thought, felt, hidden, and tied up with emotion is placed on the table perhaps for the first time in years? An experienced mentor will make the best use of this moment for the person that exposes their thoughts and feelings and is what happened in the workshop.

The leader could hardly believe what he heard, especially because he was only seven years older than the other man. He wanted to be related to as an equal among equals, with hierarchy and positions set aside. He did not want a relationship with subordinates who felt unequal. The leader wanted to maximize a cooperative relationship where people did not look up to where the buck stops, but took on problems as their own. A quick and passionate student, the leader grasped the meaning behind his being viewed as a "father figure," and that as long as this feeling persisted he would not be treated as member, but with filtered words and feelings. As for the one who expressed his feelings, he was helped to understand that by elevating the leader to the position of a father figure, he placed huge dialogic and emotional barriers between him and the leader.

All of the members of the Inner Circle undoubtedly were conducting their own inner dialogue in their search as to what, if anything, was keeping them from the experience of mutuality with the leader. My task was to facilitate the inner dialogue into becoming external in a manner that would allow for an awakening to take place. To do this, I went from one to the other asking them what they thought and if they had feelings they'd share with the IC. It was a time of enough safety that individuals did become vulnerable and their inner thoughts and feelings enveloped the room. It turned out to be immensely beneficial and, not surprisingly, an impressionable event for most of them.

It was following this particular workshop that I was asked by the vice president to meet with him privately in his office. Once behind his closed door he told me: "I want and need to have Genuine Dialogue with the leader/owner, but can't do this in the IC. I need to privately share with the President personal and business issues I feel I can no longer avoid." He also stated that he believed that only through Genuine Dialogue was there a possible pathway out of his dilemma. His inner conflict was near the bursting point and was pushing him to divulge whatever it was he felt he needed to say to the leader before it took its own course of action. Being second in command, a full participant in the IC and excellent student, he believed that drawing on "candor and reason" during the experience of Genuine Dialogue was the best way to save the company from a huge loss and possibly his job and relationship with the leader.

He did not discuss what he needed to say and I did not ask, but I did volunteer to facilitate and even mediate a meeting between the two of them. I asked if he would allow me to speak to the leader about this meeting taking place with my presence and the role I would play, and he approved. However, he asked me not to set a time for us to meet because he needed more time to "sort things out."

At the first opportunity I spoke to the leader about a possible meeting between him, the vice president, and me. The leader was incredulous that his close companion and trusted operations leader could have withheld anything, personal and business, from him. They had known each other for years and were, he said "like brothers." He agreed to not force or bring the issue up and to a meeting taking place with the three of us as soon as possible. By now I had become intrigued by what the VP might be withholding from the President and his friend. I knew they met privately numerous times each day, were companions away from work and that both appeared to value Genuine Dialogue.

The meeting between the three of us never happened because the VP was unable to bring himself to openly face his boss. By the time the problem was exposed, it was too late to save their relationship; and the firm suffered considerable financial losses. Would a much earlier exchange between them have altered what the future held for them and the company? In this particular case, I have to believe it would have helped in many ways. To begin, dialogue between the two would have been superior to the general conversations they had when they lunched on an almost daily basis. And had we been able to bringing them to Genuine Dialogue nothing would have been left to discover. What remedial action that might have changed the direction things were going in would have taken place. Genuine Dialogue leaves little, if anything, in the dark.

Strength and the best of an organization are found in a healthy IC. It is where problems are made known, where problems are resolved and where leadership and power is properly shared and used. Growth happens to individuals in a healthy, functional IC, and the parts of the organization each IC member represents also benefits. It is here, in the inner sanctum of the IC, that work related dialogue is at its best and does the most common good. It is also the setting for creative and spontaneous interaction between people. What results must be exponentially better than when compared to the actions taken by any one individual making decisions alone that ultimately affect others. In fact, the big mistake the vice president made was his belief that he had to make a quick decision about the project that ended up costing him everything and the firm too much.

As stated in the chapter on the true entrepreneur, there is considerable difference between an entrepreneur's behavior and that of a leader. The VP in this story acted as if he were an entrepreneur. He may have sincerely believed that what he had done was going to be for the good of the firm. But by acting as an entrepreneur he never gave the President the opportunity for agreeing to and supporting the action, denial or more due diligence. Had he found the courage to be open, vulnerable to the leader and the IC, would that have made a difference in the direction and the decisions he made that eventually were his undoing and the harm done to the organization?

The answer has to be, yes, because the subjects we concentrate on during a workshop confront any issue that might support "secrets and lies." Since it is the leader that creates the environment and sends signals as to what they are thinking, feeling, needing and wanting from others important to them. Also, when the leader is perceived as being vulnerable this has considerable impact on those in the IC. It is inconceivable for those intimately involved in an IC to not be at the affect of the leader's behavior. As dialogue becomes vulnerable and genuine from the leader this becomes the environment that germinates growth in others and the need to be one's history are over.

As told to me and I witnessed, the leader and VP were very close. But does this mean that the two of them experienced anything approaching genuine dialogue between them? The obvious answer is NO! Actually, how many people experience open and genuine dialogue with people they live and work with? People do share their more personal thoughts and feelings, but with a very select few, and these are not necessarily those they live or work with, but those they most trust or believe are most supportive of them.

By creating an environment where trust and safety are paramount it becomes difficult for individuals to remain circumspect and silent particularly in an IC where being open is made so significant. In most relationships this is simply not true. Personal communication lacks authenticity too often where it is most needed and that is with people most important to us. It is easier for people to open up when they are in anonymous settings. An example of which is talking to a stranger that means little to them and anonymity is assured. This assurance of safety and the being open and vulnerable must be the actual environment in an IC. Where there is no possibility of anonymity what is more important?

Finally, it helps that during workshops that the mentor is not perceived as a tool of the leader, but being there for each equally. A mentor's effectiveness at the beginning of a workshop has to do with perception, and why it is essential that the leader understand and accept their student relationship to the workshop mentor. The teacher must be there for everyone and this needs to be seen and "felt" by each participant. The teacher has a fully independent position, and has and uses their power appropriately, and most importantly, to the benefit of all. A mentor cannot be a tool of the leader or perceived as such.

CREATING AND MAINTAINING A HEALTHY IC IS A LEADERSHIP CHALLENGE

Words and promises mean little or nothing to actual change in an environment. The environment is not a wish or intention, but a manifestation of whom and what a leader actually is. Change of environment cannot happen if the leader does not change (grow) and this growth is witnessed by members of their IC. Change is not about changing the colors of the walls and furniture, or even the frequent replacing of personnel. Grow the one with real power, and there will be change within the environment and, in time, the people who are most involved must also change or make the personal choice to withdraw from the relationship. This is the power of leadership.

Much too often, members of an IC are so intimidated by their leader that they do not overtly contest a challenge to their sense of integrity and worth. Instead, they acquiesce in the face of inflexible and perceived abusive power. In the workplace environment of fear, regardless of experience and talent, are destructive. Candor is impossible and, frankly, the leader calls all the shots, or as the story relates, people are prone to act on their own. Of course, the leader, ultimately, bears the prime responsibility for poor decisions and results. Also, not a few IC members put up with a dysfunctional leader because they enjoy power by association. Playing the pawn by serving in a dysfunctional IC allows them to wield power in their own IC. And so it goes throughout the organization.

What does being less than honest and candid contribute to an organization's success? Not much! To be in the IC at the pinnacle of the organization, and to not feel fully secure in one's own skin and knowledge, forces behavior that is less than authentic simply to protect one's self and position. This is a leadership issue that will only be resolved as the leader becomes more open, accessible, and genuine.

Expecting that quality leadership can come from others in an IC when the leader of the IC is too weak or too strong is similar to a house built on a weak foundation. It's only a matter of time before serious troubles comes along.

If we could be an invisible observer to the machinations taking place in a typical IC, we would likely be witness to key people (leader and members) who are dysfunctional in a variety of ways. The primary problem is that too many leaders are blind to their own culpability in what is taking place around them and with their key people. Fault-finding outside of oneself is common regardless of the quality of the IC players with whom they work. Leaders need an awakening to understand and accept their own power to control and influence others. They need to learn how to set aside their power and position, and temporarily, in IC gatherings and personal relationships, become just another participant and which for many, is not easy to do.

Clearly, the answer to healthy relationships begins with leaders. Leaders not only select followers they most depend on but create the environment in which they work together. If Genuine Dialogue is to exist in an IC, it cannot come through fear and manipulation, but only through the leaders' degree of openness and being vulnerable with those they lead. As mentioned time and again throughout this chapter and the book, wise and good leadership is not accidental behavior or born within us. It is a learned attribute that is best when conscious and deliberate and as a student continues throughout their life.

SELECTION OF IC MEMBERS IS IMPORTANT, BUT LEADERSHIP EVEN MORE SO

Finally, members of a well-functioning IC should not be selected on the basis of personality or closeness to the leader. They are selected for their qualities, knowledge, and achievements. They carry with them a history and assurance and determination that they can get the job done and accept ownership of what they take on. The same potential may actually be the case in a badly functioning environment led by inadequate leadership. IC members may be equal or better qualified than those in a healthy functioning IC but are unable to bring their gifts and talents to the table. Appearing as a challenge or threat to the leader is a battle they will lose. IC members, clearly, must comply if they wish to remain in the core IC and organization. People of quality and ability do not long accept an environment that restricts them or that they are unable to influence change. Where is there a winner?

The philosophy of the leader is distributed throughout the organization because members of the core IC are not isolated from the rest of the organization. Each IC member is a leader of others, even if given little opportunity to take leadership in the core IC. It is then that each IC member conveys the leadership they experience (or are) to their own IC. Depending on the leader's behavior within the core IC, dysfunction or health is usually carried by each IC members throughout the whole of the organization. IC's, generally, are symptomatic of how the core IC functions, with the exception that a quality IC member can make a difference in their own IC where they are the leader. How? They may be a follower in another's IC and helpless to a degree, but are a leader in their own IC and will create their own environment. But, as stated earlier: since when is creating one's own organization within an organization a sign of health?

CHAPTER 6

GENUINE DIALOGUE

We hear, understand
We feel heard and understood
Candor is our gift.

I n the late 1950s I was called upon to work with a young boy who was seeing a psychiatrist for his inability to relate to any sort of structure and authority. His behavior was self-destructive and destructive of others to the point that many of the best private resident schools had expelled him. By the time he was eleven years old, he had built an unenviable record of serious discipline problems. My instructions from the psychiatrist were to work with him on social and relationship issues for a given number of hours each week.

As it got closer to summer and I was needed full-time at our coed summer camp, I agreed that he could spend the summer at camp. Combining the camp environment, a strong and perceptive counselor, and the emphasis on the small-group relationship proved out well for him. By the time summer camp was over, a "solid-enough" relationship was established between him, my wife and me that we agreed to let him live with us for a trial period.

One important condition was that we needed to get him into the local public junior high school. My wife had taught at the school and knew the principal, counselor and many of the teachers; but the young man's history was now shadowing him wherever he went. The principal agreed to allow him in—but with the understanding that my wife would be the fully responsible person to monitor every step he took at school. She also had to be in constant touch with each teacher and the school counselor.

This required that she stop teaching for the school system in order to be on top of the boy's academics, home study and whatever else in which he might become involved. She became his super-overseer, constantly checking with his teachers, and monitoring his attendance and the schoolwork he needed to do each evening. In addition, she was his primary disciplinarian. It was not a smooth journey for any of us; but with my wife's consistent nurturing and tutoring, he continued to live with us and to grow. Had this not taken place, we all questioned the likelihood that he could have made it anywhere.

At times—and there were many extended periods—we were family in the healthiest and most positive way. At other times, as with all families but considerably more intense in our case, we would ask ourselves, "Why doesn't he pack his bags and go back to his father?" There were times when we questioned our own reason for continuing with him. And this sword cut both ways because at any time he could have called his father to pick him up and take him home, or we could have sent him back to his father. But by always talking through issues as they arose, none of us failed to meet the challenges that we were each called upon to face. This demanded a remarkable consistency of openness, flexibility and guidance from my wife, which may have wavered at times but never broke. She was so clearly the leader, I in support and the young boy-man desirous of not leaving us.

In time, and not without major emotional and academic growth issues, he entered high school, where he did well enough in his grades to try out for, and make, the cross-country track team. Of course, my wife never missed an event or opportunity to show support for his efforts. She was, unquestionably, the primary force for good in his life and was wholly responsible for the immediate and essential environment in which he could, and did, grow.

When his father wanted to give him his first car, we knew it was premature for this to happen. In fact, my wife told his father that if he gave his son a car we would cease caring for him, and he would have to return to his father. The (now) young man, obviously eager to have his own wheels, accepted our decision to not let him have his first car until some later time. In fact, he handled it remarkably well, knowing the time would come when my wife felt he could handle the responsibility of owning a car. In the meantime, he spent considerable time behind the wheel with me practicing how to drive a stick-shift. I remember this as a fun time for both of us. He was a good and patient student.

How important was his relationship to my wife? He felt, he knew, he experienced that what she did for him was special and out of serious concern and regard for him. She helped him to develop not into what she or others wanted him to be, but to be all that he had within himself to be. I supported her as additional hands and eyes because two people cannot be the leader at the same time. In this sense, I was a willing participant and witness to the whole experience between the two of them. My wife was the power source, but I was there and provided a male role-model to him. In most every issue that came up, she was clearly the leader who made our family-like relationship work.

We never lost sight that our living together in a nine-hundred-square-foot house with two dogs and a cat, two bedrooms and one washroom was being done with considerable risk to my wife and me. Early on when I first began to work with the boy for the few hours each week, the psychiatrist told me that the boy was capable of doing harm to others without any grasp of its consequences either to him or to those he might harm. We never forgot this but also judged him on his behavior, which although testing at times was as good as we could hope for.

He graduated from high school, soon after joined the U.S. Army and became a member of the Screaming Eagles, the 101st Airborne, and experienced battle, death and injury to those around him and the full horror taking place in Vietnam. Needless to say, we were much relieved when he returned home and it was not long after that he married a girl he met at our summer camp years earlier. Soon after getting married he made the decision to go to college where he earned a bachelor and master degree. He has been his own person for years and is a remarkably creative and beautiful person and a gift to those who know him. It is more than likely that none of this would have happened without others, in particular my wife, who was so totally there for him.

Postscript: Our young man believed at a much later time in his life (after Nam and earning his degrees) that my wife was actually his mother although that would have made her his mother at the age of twelve. Given where he came from, and the love and respect he experienced from my wife and being part of our family, are those thoughts that unreasonable?

Just how important was the relationship between my wife and this young boy/man? How important was the genuineness and structure that she provided and that he volitionally joined into and was enveloped by? The power of honest dialogue that was always genuine and supportive, as was the environment and the family relationship all combined to successfully grow this young man and perhaps us too, into better and healthier humans.

I have labeled the communication between them as Genuine Dialogue. I did not, at that time, understand why or when dialogue becomes Genuine, but looking back I know that it happened many times between them. Understanding, intentionally teaching and witnessing Genuine Dialogue came many years later when I was a consultant to others.

The relationship and the honesty of the dialogue between them make the strongest possible case for the power of leaders to create environments that facilitate growth to happen between people. Or, if power and control are what the relationship is about, those in power diminish and possibly destroy the people they are closest to. In our particular case, being vulnerable, flexible, caring, patient and taking one step at a time, did facilitate growth in each of us. The condition of Genuine Dialogue, even if we had no understanding of the words or process, made it all possible.

Clearly, during their relationship my wife and the young man overcame powerful emotional barriers and potential disasters, but in the process a human being was helped to rediscover himself and become a contributing member of society. The experience influenced, overwhelmingly, my own belief that the power of an environment, created deliberately by a quality leader, does provide the foundation for people who choose to grow to actually do so. It is important to emphasize "for people who choose to grow." I know this to be true because without the commitment he made, or by any student to his or her mentor, how does one teach if there is no student in body and soul? If not volitional, what can be done?

GENUINE DIALOGUE IS COMMUNICATION WITHOUT FILTERS

Genuine Dialogue is more than common face-to-face communication between two or more people because the experience is timeless. Being present, in the moment, does this; and we are unaware of time moving forward or any restrictions. It is truly a borderless experience known only after the fact, never during. I often refer to this as a "happening," not because it is impossible to be planned on but without understanding of the essential ingredients, Genuine Dialogue will only be a "happening" and, therefore, totally undependable.

When Genuine Dialogue does "happen," whether accidental or planned, the people involved are in the highest state of mutuality and cooperation with each other. (Mutuality requires respect for the other and the absence of negative feelings.) When this takes place, people are vulnerable and open to each other's words and feelings. It is dialogue without filters and restraint. It is in that moment when people are most likely to grow, to learn and to change, but they are not aware of any of this because awareness suddenly makes one an observer rather than a participant. Genuine Dialogue is an experience that may lead, and often does, to ends that have not existed before.

Following is a made-up but relatively common example of Genuine Dialogue as a "happening." Three people meet over lunch and informally begin discussing politics or religion (both subjects usually loaded and emotional). They have about forty-five minutes before having to return to work. Suddenly, the conversation becomes such that all three begin to interact in ways that make each fully present to the other. They are each in the moment and the ensuing dialogue. They have lost contact with any thoughts of the food, time or what is going on around them. They only know they are there one, hearing, understanding and confirming each other. Candor explodes between them. "So what you are saying is ——?" "Yes!" says the speaker, "that's what I mean, and what I feel, and why." "Gee," says the other. "I never thought of it in this way. I always felt that ——."

Candor takes place between them, not agreement. And this is a result of all three being vulnerable and unconsciously allowing what they are hearing to touch them at their core and not, at the same time, building a response.

Suddenly, one looks at her watch (at that moment she's not in Genuine Dialogue) and screams, "Oh, my God! We've been talking for two hours! I've got to get back to work! See you later."

They all return to work. Genuine Dialogue has passed, as have two hours; but all three know that what they experienced they want to experience again. They may have expectations, but how to get there once again? It was a "happening," not planned or understood by any of them; but they each heard opinions and felt feelings they normally would have protected themselves against. This is Genuine Dialogue as a "happening" and how most people experience it.

My work was and is to make Genuine Dialogue a planned and more easily attainable experience. I acknowledge that this is an arduous journey that demands certain conditions exist between people before we can get there. This chapter will provide the recipe for Genuine Dialogue to take place through planning. It is essential to emphasis that without solid trust and safety being firmly established between those involved, and a completely committed leader, it cannot and will not happen, but only, as with the made up preceding story, accidentally.

GENUINE DIALOGUE IS DEFINITELY SPECIAL

Adult communication with other adults, as distinct from a child's less nuanced and conditioned way of communicating is rarely genuine. As in the story of the three friends enjoying Genuine Dialogue over lunch, it most often occurs accidentally. The ideal dialogue is Genuine Dialogue that can be created deliberately when needed. As we shall learn safety and trust are absolutely essential between a leader and those few people important to them and to each other if Genuine Dialogue is to be experienced. Also, participants immersed in Genuine Dialogue will know that something very special *has* happened, but it is impossible for them to be aware of it during its occurrence. This is because being in the center of the moment does not also allow for standing outside and seeing one's self in that moment. When anyone in Genuine Dialogue moves outside the moment, the speaker has a sense or knows that the other is no longer listening. Dialogue in that instant becomes monologue.

If Genuine Dialogue is that moment of free, unfettered, creative communication between people, its value to a group and individuals is priceless. What a boon it would be to a relationship of two, families, economic, political and work groups of every variety if this could be achieved intentionally. What a wonderful gift to those who lead and those who follow. During Genuine Dialogue problems are opportunities that are easily aired, clarified and prioritized; and opinions and solutions pour forth. These are truly creative and innovative moments between people. Genuine Dialogue is attainable, but like climbing a most difficult mountain requires training and commitment, and even then is not an easy walk.

Genuine Dialogue does not seek to reach agreement for the sake of agreement, and certainly not false compliance. This is because fear and concern over agreement/disagreement disappear during Genuine Dialogue. With power in the hands of each participant, there are no issues of mutuality or equality and cooperation temporarily reigns supreme.

This is a period of safety and trust between people to the degree that the reality and feelings of hierarchy and position are non-existent. These issues are set aside and power and control in the hands of anyone does not exist during moments of Genuine Dialogue. Fixed leadership is not needed and does not contribute to what is occurring. How differentow differentH are our relationships when protecting ourselves from power compared to power being non-existent? It is our differences that are needed, that come out and is fully shared with others. We are totally ourselves and yet are fully there for the other during Genuine Dialogue. How rare it is when self and the other's needs are both being met and at the same time?

During Genuine Dialogue we express our values to each other through our individual stories, opinions, ideas and feelings. But without dialogue, and in particular Genuine Dialogue, these gifts of self are withheld when safety and trust are missing from the relationship. Safety and trust come about when a person feels assured from consistent and repeated experiences that they are not going to be harmed or put down by those significant to them. Words do not make it so, but on-going perceptions do. No other form of communication offer gifts of self to the degree that Genuine Dialogue does.

EXPERIENCING THE EXPERIENCE

Meditation is an interesting example of Genuine Dialogue actually taking place within one's self. The point of meditation is to not escape from reality, but to bring us in touch with ourselves, our thoughts, emotions, our very being and to be centered in the very "now" of this instant. When this happens we become stress-free with no future or past to burden us, only the "center of the center"; and we are one with our self. There is no duality or conflict for the moment, and our clarity is total. This happens during the moments of Genuine Dialogue when we, with others, become one. Our personal and controlling agendas are, unconsciously, set aside so that what transpires between us is pure and direct. That this is possible (intentional as compared to accidental) with our significant others must be a worthy goal for all relationships to work towards.

From the leaders' perspective, how much better does the following scenario get? The leaders are surrounded by IC members who are immediately and spontaneously open to the leaders as one of them, to each other and the issues of the organization. How often is it heard, "someone needs to take ownership of the situation," and how frequently does this actually take place? Organizations benefit when problems are picked up and dealt with by appropriate people almost as quickly as problems are born. This is another of the many gifts that Genuine Dialogue makes possible.

In most cases, organizational and people problems are usually well formed by the time they are recognized. Issues are brought late—at times too late—to the attention of the people who can and ought to take action, and this generally needs to be those leaders (members of the IC) who are closest to the problem. The common course of action is that problems are confronted late or not dealt with at all. Nothing happens unless forced and the people directly involved simply live with their problems. What does this tell us of most relationship or organization where those in power, because they do not empower others, are too often the last to know but very quick to place blame? And, of course, blame is laid on the defenseless. Saying "the buck stops here" sounds and feels good, but does it actually play out that way? Rarely! Where is the communication, cooperation and the mutual dialogue that welcomes us with assurance of safety?

When does talk become authentic and spontaneous between those in the know and those who do not know but *need to know*? Without an environment in which Genuine Dialogue can happen, "communication is assured to remain a problem (the main barrier) to the answers." Wanting, even demanding to be kept informed of problems and issues does not make for quality, honest and timely communication. People learn early on in life that simply being a messenger can and does have consequences, and proclaiming "my door is open" means nothing when the person and environment are perceived as dangerous to those who would dare to enter. Demanding that people open up and be genuine is meaningless in the face of threatening authority or even what most people experience as monologue and top-down communication.

WE ARE BORN AND IMMEDIATELY COMMUNICATE GENUINELY

Look at the easy and direct way babies communicate with their caregivers. Mothers are able to not only understand what their babies are communicating and why, but they respond directly to the baby. In other words, Genuine Dialogue is initially as natural to human survival as is the need for air, food, water and elimination. Too soon, however, something happens to this natural way to communicate as babies grow into an environment that was at the beginning nurturing and mutual but changes and becomes more controlling by these same caregivers.

It is important to note that what the mother does to her body and mind during the period of gestation and immediately after birth has great influence on the relationship between her and the baby. Drugs, alcohol, or illness (mental or otherwise) may disrupt or definitely impede what ought to have been a period of Genuine Dialogue that needs to take place between mother and baby. Similarly, as difficult as it is to create and maintain the environment in which Genuine Dialogue can take place between adults, it takes only the smallest misuses of power by a power leader to destroy a safety net (feelings) when it comes to those dependent on them.

As a baby grows so do the parents become more of what they have been prior to the baby's birth. Whatever hormonal changes take place in the parents during the birthing process and for a brief period afterward begins to weaken and then disappear. The baby, so sensitive to the environment (its parents), adapts to the changing (returning to normal) environment. Babies are so dependent that they quickly adjust to changes in the behavior of their immediate caregivers. The need to survive dictates that as the environment between mother and child changes, so does the child accommodate its self to those changes. After all, who holds the power?

This appears to place a massive share of the responsibility for a child's ways of dealing with their world on the backs of their parents or immediate caregivers, but who else is responsible? Yes, babies inherit characteristics, but these pale when compared to what they learn from the world outside. This is a good thing. What we inherit is permanently imprinted in us, and nothing but perhaps severe trauma may change anything we are born with. The things and behavior we learn through experience and from others are alterable. This is what is meant by "growth." Growth happens when a person changes from within and manifests the changes without. Yes, we age and die; and most people do nothing more for themselves. To grow and therefore change is volitional and one's own choice to make. It cannot be imposed although society and those of power try hard to do so.

That we learn, adapt and grow due to loving, nurturing relationships is our best hope that Genuine Dialogue can be resurrected from our babyhood. But it takes someone who holds power to facilitate this on their own behalf and also wants this for their significant others. This is where it must come from as we age. All humans know the feeling even if buried deep in our suppressed unconscious. Genuine Dialogue is never fully forgotten; it is stored away in the recesses of our past. It is part of our need "to be" our unique selves. This need, to our dying day, does not go away. It awaits the wise and courageous leader to awaken its voice. Why? Because relationships with other humans are necessary and no person, by themselves, becomes what they become. The paradox is that only through our efforts and that of supportive others do we become more of ourselves.

THE NECESSITY OF THE PROPER ENVIRONMENT

The environment where Genuine Dialogue is to deliberately take place is created by humans who hold power over others, but have set their power aside. Properly crafted, an environment invites and nurtures Genuine Dialogue and, therefore each person as their self. If, on the other hand, we are not nurtured to be our selves, who do those in power want us to be? Not being our own self is to give in, lose ourselves and in the process do harm to ourselves and those we live and work with. Everyone loses whenever Genuine Dialogue is impossible. The dilemma, as identified throughout the book is that we cannot be or become ourselves by our self alone. Humans are required from our very beginning to do this through, with, and because of our relationships with others.

The reality is that abuse of power or manipulation at any level designed to create the impression of caring between people is a waste of time, energy and money. The efforts given to improving "person-to-person" communication remain one of the great failures of our time as is trying to grow another. And technology, at least for now, appears to be accelerating relationship issues. The belief that modifying an individual's behavior using mind games, external pressures and gimmicks will change people is a dead end. Humans grow and change not because of pressures from outside but because of pressures from inside. What the outside does is to either facilitate our desire to grow or restrict it and the rest is our choice to make.

People must feel safe and secure before becoming vulnerable, and being vulnerable is what opening up means and what growth, if it is to happen, demands. Genuine Dialogue results from being vulnerable. Genuine Dialogue does not force anything. It is as natural as breathing; but the difference between breathing and being vulnerable, and therefore experiencing Genuine Dialogue, is that breathing is self-regulating and needs no external support. To be vulnerable is also a natural state, but it needs external nurturing, support and the feeling of safety for it to exist.

The story below is about creating the nurturing environment that invites growth and its consequences including Genuine Dialogue.

When involved with public education, I would visit elementary schools throughout the district performing a variety of tasks from counseling students to giving folk-singing concerts. I was part of a small group of special teachers bringing a wide variety of experimental teaching projects to elementary schools. At one school the principle asked if I would take over a class of sixth graders that had over the years become a "dumping ground" for difficult students. By the time they were in the sixth grade, they had been filtered out of other classes until they were bunched together and dealt with as "the delinquents." The challenge, as stated by the school principal, was to "bring order, and maybe some education, to this class before they go on to junior high school."

During my first day as the classroom teacher with the students, I had the opportunity to begin placing my stamp on the classroom environment. When the bell for morning recess rang, the students all rushed to the two doors eagerly looking forward to the freedom of the playground. They jammed up against each other as if penned cattle behind a locked gate. All faces turned towards me, and I said quietly but firmly, "Take your seats." Grumbling, thirty-six boys and girls went back to their desks. When they were all seated I told them to stand, and then sit, and then stand, and then sit. After a half-dozen of such commands I asked them, "Is this how you want to spend recess?" Without any discussion or instructions, I said "Okay, line up at the doors." They actually made room for each other, lined up and quietly walked out to the playground in twos with me following.

Although other classes had finished their recess, we continued for our own full period and probably for a few minutes beyond, after which we lined up and silently walked back to our classroom. Once in the classroom I explained that caring for and respecting each other had to be better for each of us. I used the example of our enjoying recess and said that all classroom experiences would be better and more fun for each of us if we became more aware of and respected each other. I told them that I respected each of them as individuals with certain rights and freedoms, and that I hoped to *earn* their respect. I also said that it was my responsibility to earn their respect, and that I did not expect them to respect me simply because I bore the title "teacher." The immediate challenge was to make this true for them.

The environment became a nurturing one. It was safe, secure and fun for each student to the extent that many complained that "weekends get in the way of our being together." They became eager students, creative and helped each other. We became an enclave and an enigma to others and the school. Every instant that I could demonstrate by my behavior that I was there for each of them was a lesson that they also had to be there for each other. Behind closed doors we became a family and community more ourselves for sure but also more "there" for each other. They each became more responsible and accountable, and each felt like an important contributor to the whole.

The school principal was enough in awe of the changes in each student's behavior that she suggested I keep whatever we were doing under the radar screen. Other teachers were murmuring over the mysteries taking place in "Mr. O's" classroom.

I would tell the students that what we did in class belonged only in our classroom, that our group was special, and that they were each special to me and to each other. What they did feel was respect, security, acceptance and mutuality towards each other. I was there for them, and they were there for self and each other. Activities and projects took place in small groups so that they came to depend on each other, and learning from and helping each other became our modus operandi. Behind our closed doors they could and did call me by my first name, but never did this take place outside the classroom. What takes place behind closed doors is an important lesson in relationships. I somehow knew that what we did needed to be kept special and not bragged about around school. The students themselves learned to want it this way. They felt good about themselves, not in a competitive way with others but in their own capabilities to do well and care for themselves and each other when necessary.

Did we experience Genuine Dialogue? I think we did, many times. Was our environment safe, inviting, nurturing, supportive, creative and resourcing to each student in the class? Did they have room to fail and to try again and again with help at their side? You bet! As the leader/teacher I set the parameters of the classroom environment, but as it evolved each of the students contributed to its greater meaning and influence. The classroom became "ours," not "mine."

It took writing this book for me to realize with certainty that Genuine Dialogue did happen to us behind our closed classroom doors (as it did between the three POWs and me on Okinawa) and as it did in our small family. I realized how vulnerable we each must have become and that our dialogue with each other had a spontaneity and freedom that nurtured each of us. I also know that I was not aware of any unique process taking place between any of us. I only know that the young people involved grew due to so nurturing an environment. Recognizing Genuine Dialogue as a process itself took many years and serendipitous events to bring about an awareness and understanding that enabled the teaching and facilitating of Genuine Dialogue to others.

Would I have benefitted and prospered in an environment of this nature when I was a child? Absolutely! How does one not grow in an environment that is safe, secure, loving, understanding, accepting, respectful and nurturing? What human does not have potential to be more of who and what they are? And, does this potential come out by itself or through and because of relationships with others, in particular those others with power and influence over us? Breathing and aging is self-regulating; but true inner growth requires, even demands, help from others. It can happen in no other way and as I am doing, needs to be restated time and time again.

None of what I have done as an entrepreneur and leader, as I reflect, was a conscious, intentional and well thought out approach to the issues and people I faced. I know I always tried to do the best with what I had and felt and clearly did what I believed was the correct course of action. It was simply and forthrightly the reasonable way to be with others. How I want to be treated is how I related to others and it was my life experiences that most informed me. Yes, formal education and the acquiring of tools are important, but this pales when compared to what is learned from our life experiences.

What I had somehow learned from life was that as leader I had the power and ability to create an environment. And that this environment would be, as I envisioned, the best, respectful and nurturing environment as possible. Where did my belief in the power of the leader to do serious good and to be an important and meaningful influence come from? It had to be my life experiences as a child and my relationship to people of power and influence I met along the way.

Each of us has life experiences, many of which influence us far beyond the experience itself. Each experience might have something in it that is more than just a happening to be unrecognized or forgotten. We need to look back at what has taken place and what lessons are there for us to grasp and to use to our benefit and possibly to the benefit of others. All experiences are a potential "bag of gifts" loaded with lessons that just might have a useful life. Why do so many people pass up what they have paid a price for?

WHAT MIGHT OUR BAG OF EXPERIENCES CONTAIN?

- Ways to do better the next time?
- Do I want to repeat this experience?
- What might I change the next time?
- Is self-protection an issue, and what steps do I take if this ever happens again?
- What about power and leadership? Was I a pawn to others or my own person?
- What more could I have said or done?
- Was my relationship with the other an honest one?
- Did I communicate my true thoughts and feelings? If not, why not?
- What did I fear?

So much, and more, is possible to draw out of our bag of experiences.

An epilogue to the sixth-grade experience: Many years later I received a letter from an old acquaintance and boss, the former principal of the elementary school where the classroom experience in the above story took place. She had been retired for many years but apparently still had to get something off her chest.

In her letter she said that her teaching and principal experiences were very rich and rewarding to her; but that if she could do it all over again, she would do what she witnessed: and that is to build a sense of community using respect for each child as foundational. She wrote that she was initially frightened at the liberties I took but knew deep down that this was education as it is meant to be. In retrospect, what a brave and good leader she was. She had the courage to support the program even as she attempted to keep it hidden from others and the system. In certain respects, she made what we did in the classroom possible. Without her approval and silent support, none of this could or would have happened. I was the leader in the classroom, but the principal held certain powers that made her the leader over me.

BACK TO GENUINE DIALOGUE

One might think that face-to-face dialogue in small groups numbering as few as two to a dozen ought to be a cakewalk when it comes to communicating with each other. But even here, the power of safety, trust, and respect play an influential hand as to whether or not Genuine Dialogue will result between just two. Enlarge the group; and the hope of open, spontaneous dialogue becomes more problematic and challenging. Large numbers of people make dialogue extremely difficult and Genuine Dialogue impossible. Lecturing becomes the communication method of choice, and communication between people seriously deteriorates. There is no comparison between dialogue (minimal give and take) and monologue (lecturing). The more we stretch face-to-face communication and eliminate dialogue, the more we can be sure that problems between us will spread like a cold, with the additional probability that power will be used inappropriately.

Troubled communication leads to more trouble. Eventually, the communications breakdown between people contributes to entropy. Entropy, as used here, is a phenomenon that takes place in business and bureaucratic settings in that as they grow larger and more hierarchical communication becomes more dysfunctional, there is more disorder throughout the organization. It is as if a cancer were spreading to every level, and at some point the organism is not able to help itself and it fails.

Another way to express this is to visualize an organization developing too many levels of hierarchy, making effective communication between people at the different levels improbable and often impossible. In fact, too many people on the same level make communication between (ostensible) equals difficult and, in short order, dysfunctional. This brings power at the top out of balance, out of touch and dysfunctional towards those below and which are the most important to them. The base of an organization is not able to support what is above because communication, at best, is too stretched; substance and understanding do not exist, either vertically or horizontally. Also, as power becomes exclusive and restricted to a few in comparison to the numbers of people below, so does the organization begin to have serious communication issues. The real problem is at the top and difficult, if not impossible, to get to.

I was asked to evaluate an employee communication program a major corporation was about to get involved in. After spending a full day going over the program with three of the corporate people, and based on my questions and comments, they invited me to join them in order to assist in making the program more effective. I asked to meet with the head honcho of the corporation in order to discuss my approach which must begin at the very top of the hierarchy. They said that was impossible and that even my speaking to him was out of the question, and, incidentally, that his Inner Circle included people who sought their own power position in the corporation and competition between them is fierce. I left it at that, but continued to hear from them until they understood my message. Without access to the power and changes at the top any changes below will be cosmetic, at best.

WE HAVE MANY INNER CIRCLES

Consider the different groups we have some involvement with. We are participants in the basic relationship of two or family, friends, community, church, people at work and school. In any of these how often do we experience problems having to do with communication between us? How often do we withhold our opinions and feelings, and how often are they withheld from us in order to avoid arguments and possible harm? This is sure to exist when monologue or top down-bottom up communication is what takes place between us. Compare this to open dialogue and the opportunity to clarify, question, express our opinions and to agree or disagree. What a difference in relationships when mutual respect is felt by each.

It is also true; in particular when our past enters into the present, self-preservation may take over and instead of being present and open we close down. We may simply comply, become defensive or argumentative and aggressive, all of which, makes things worse. So much of our present behavior has to do with our past that when we do not feel safe and secure, and that is, perhaps the key, the only alternative is to protect ourselves. People do not generally jeopardize themselves, their jobs, paychecks and security. The power person owns the problem. This is true in each of our many ICs.

THE DIFFICULTY OF GROWING AS ONE'S OWN TRUE SELF

Changing people's learned behavior is difficult but not impossible, but if this is to happen it is the individual that must make this decision. It is why I state and restate that the leader we are in relationship with must be the first and most willing example. All leaders are role models and teachers, and what they teach is of immense importance because of their influence. If leaders are sensitive, caring, good listeners, exude a sense of safety and trust, and invite dialogue, they teach this through words and behavior. When this is the case, the more secure accept the invitation to join in with the leader. In time and when witnessed as safe enough by the more timid, they, too, will risk participation and growth or will, in time, withdraw themselves.

Growth brings with it behavioral changes and as the leaders' behavior changes, even slightly but is consistent, so does the perception of those who follow the leader. When a follower's feelings towards the leader are well established it is not easy for them to trust any changes in behavior they are witness to. It is why, when a leader chooses to grow they are making a choice for themselves and not with expectations of what rewards from others they will receive.

I repeat: Safety is not assured by words but through behavior and here is where constancy and reliability come into play. Subordinates need to trust that what they are witness to is real and not an act. They need to feel respect, secure that their truth is welcome, heard and understood—but with a clear understanding that agreement is not necessarily part of the deal. If growth is real, and most followers will know and feel this from their leader, they will risk honest dialogue. It is this giant step that facilitates others to choose to grow, to open themselves up to others and their own potential.

If chosen wisely Inner Circle members do exercise their potential and why selected in the first place. These people do not depend on the growth of the leader to lead them to their own growth decision processes. The following story is about a strong, capable, high achieving person who is a member of an Inner Circle, but the leader of this particular IC is extremely dominant and loaded with expectations towards those he has in his Inner Circle. It is also an example of how Genuine Dialogue can take place anywhere and at any time accidentally.

"FY" MONEY

I was sitting naked in a very hot steam room after a workout when in stepped one of the most successful entertainment directors in the country. We were somewhat acquainted, but only through the numerous meetings we had both attended. Until this moment we had no cause for conversation because our reasons for participating in the meetings were worlds apart. He dealt directly with the likes of Elvis Presley and Barbra Streisand and their management people, and I with the recreational and educational needs of children and young adults. Other than working in the same organization I'm confident in suggesting that we had nothing else in common.

Our conversation was easy and relaxed as we talked about the latest world news, sports and weather. Soon the conversation shifted to what we had in common: having the same boss to deal with and participating in executive meetings. It did not take long before we began to talk about our dominant and dynamite leader, who controlled our executive meetings as well as most of the executives in attendance.

Eventually, I asked him about a specific moment and issue that took place between him and the leader in a recent meeting. I told him it appeared to me that he stood his ground in the face of a cynical and challenging attack by the leader, which I believed must have been difficult to do. I added, "In similar situations I have witnessed, people have wilted, backpedaled and acquiesced to the leader's will. You, on the other hand, were cool and candid with him." Without hesitation he responded, "I'm there to do a specific job as entertainment director. I know so much more than he does about the entertainers and their agents, and why I am in the room. When it comes to securing the best entertainment available I'm in charge, not him."

When supposed experts in their field don't speak out candidly for reasons ranging from outright fear of the boss to believing their jobs might be in jeopardy or that the leader is looking for agreement, too often they wilt and become pawns. The entertainment director, however, did not fear the leader or fear disagreeing with him over issues of entertainment. When I questioned him about "keeping his cool," his response to me was, "I have FY money." Being woefully inexperienced in the world of big-time hotel-casinos and back-east street talk, I naively asked, "So what is FY money?" Without a look of surprise or disdain he said, "I've got all the money I'll ever need, and I still have my agency back in New York. He needs me; I don't need him. He wants and needs my best professional advice, and he gets it."

The entertainment director clearly did not fear the boss and trusted that his response was the best he had to give. He had been in the entertainment business for many years and had an outstanding reputation, which I have to believe were the reasons he was hired in the first place. Also, money had little to do with the work he was hired to do since he had his own considerable resources and knowledge to boot. So, "FY money" must mean something more than money. I have to believe it has much to do with how a person feels about one's self and the work they do.

Interestingly, this was my read of the dynamics of our situation and my personal experiences with the leader. Each of us was in an executive position because of our core competencies. It was obvious that all of the executives had considerable experience in the area for which they were responsible. I also surmised that none had their position to simply be "a gofer" for the leader. This was as competent a group of individuals and leaders in their respective fields as I had experienced to that time. No, their problem was not one of merit, but of communicating what they knew in as candid and genuine a manner as possible.

The source of this complex problem began with the resort leader, his way of being, his awareness level, and his intent and way of communicating in meetings. Mix this with the attitudes and backgrounds the executives brought to their work and their relationship with the boss and his power. In the entertainment director's case, if there was a difference it had to do with a strong belief in his own person. He may have had all the money he'd ever need or want; but it was more, and that "more" was in him and not dependent on a whim of the leader. I came to learn, much later, that he was as good an Inner Circle member as one could hope to have relative to knowledge of his field and absolutely no fear of being candid or taking charge in his field of expertise.

If Genuine Dialogue is to happen with a strong, capable leader, all members of their Circle, beyond trust and safety, needs to have knowledge, proven expertise and achievements in his or her field. In other words, there has to be a realistic FY belief in themselves. It also helps to know that the leader encourages Genuine Dialogue. The leader, regardless of the strength and confidence of others, still must be the one to undertake the leadership in this process of cooperation, mutuality and growth. Once again, leaders are the key to the riches that Genuine Dialogue holds for any relationship, personal or organizational.

It was well after I left the resort that I realized the leader of the resort never directly explained to any of his executives his expectations of them and what he needed from them through dialogue. He certainly wanted their best ideas, opinions and feelings about anything having to do with their particular responsibilities. When he brought anything to the table and expressed his plan or thoughts, as I remember, he sought confirmation, not agreement. I never witnessed his being arbitrary; he was always open to their thoughts and feelings on the subject.

What he did not want and would not accept was a negation of what he or others had placed on the table *without an attempt to suggest a better idea or plan.* What he wanted to hear was building on ideas and opinions without tearing anything down. But he did not express this to the executives, and some may have felt that he wanted agreement, not brainstorming. Thus, group meetings, for the most part, ended up with little dialogue and too much monologue.

Because the leader and I got to know each other through our private Saturday sessions, I never doubted his receptivity to give and take ideas and challenges. In fact, I surmised that he enjoyed the exchange of ideas those with an FY attitude brought him. He knew they were on top of their game. In a strange way, maybe this was his way of forcing "go or grow" behavior.

In order to achieve the benefits of give-and-take dialogue, the chief executive should have presented a verbal example of what he wanted in response from the executives. This was never done; so when he received a "thumbs down" from the marketing director without any attempt to build beyond what the president presented, he exploded at the marketing director. I witnessed what eventually led to the demise of the marketing director. It was not a pleasant experience; but there were lessons aplenty to draw from, and I did.

Regardless of the above, my relationship with the leader was such that I viewed him as an excellent leader. Years later I understood the importance of the respect he had for my knowledge and commitment to creating the best possible youth program. He also felt, as I must have conveyed, that I had FY experiences and abilities even if I never possessed FY money. The lessons I learned (not at the time, but much later as a consultant) was his inability to open up and become vulnerable with his executives. It was what he did each Saturday morning with me. Strange that he never became vulnerable with the executives at our meetings. And at that time I could do nothing, nor did I have the knowledge, to help him to become more open and to express what he sought from the other executives at our meetings. This caused fear and constraints instead of questions and candor from many of the executives at the table who did not "feel" that FY component. As a result of his not understanding "communication is the problem to the answer," he caused and perpetuated problems that were usually handled by his exercising more power and control and at greater cost than necessary. What became the "MO" of our meetings? He spoke and others mostly listened and agreed, whether they actually did or did not.

I eventually came to understand that this problem of expectations without exposure and discussion was and is common to most leaders throughout history. In fact, I believe the problems of assumption and expectation without exposure to what these assumptions and expectations are may well be one of the most important communication breakdowns between people significant to each other. Without question, the benefits of Genuine Dialogue are many and make all of the above errors and omissions non-issues. Secrets and lies also disappear, or the person who depends on them does. So, what ingredients are essential to the environment in order for Genuine Dialogue to make its appearance?

WHAT ARE THE INGREDIENTS THAT ARE ESSENTIAL TO GENUINE DIALOGUE? OR, HOW DO WE MAKE CHICKEN SOUP?

Being in the Present

What does being "present" mean in this context? I intend it to mean "Being there *now*, for self and the other" without an agenda occupying one's mind. It means not being in the past or future, but just naturally and effortlessly being here and now—and not anticipating what is about to take place or thinking about what just occurred. Being present is what the goal of meditation is, that is, our being in the center of only this moment.

Relative to Genuine Dialogue, being in the present means hearing the other person and the words he or she is speaking and for that instant, not one's own voice. It is a singular focus on the other; and because there is no inner voice speaking to us at the same time, either agreeing or disagreeing, and forming one's own thoughts, we are vulnerable in this moment to what the other says and does.

At the beginning of teaching Genuine Dialogue to leaders and their Inner Circle, the behavior of the leaders is of central importance. Leaders are the best and most effective example of what being present is to their significant others. What others perceive of the leader's presentness has much to do with influencing them to risk becoming present. Leaders, therefore, are the role model for what is essential when people are together: to be there for each other and themselves without, for this moment, past and future ruling their thoughts and behavior.

In the healthier and better-functioning Inner Circles being in the present occurs when two or more people are fully engaged with each other. Time does not exist, but full awareness of each other does. Ideal communication takes place when we are present with each other and communication is as good and pure as it can get. Before this degree of presentness is possible, any hierarchy or power must be set aside. Mutuality, then, takes its place and people important to each other become as one.

As leaders move to the present so do they leave behind any vestige of what they were and thought a moment ago. When leaders are present without the vestiges of the past they become vulnerable. This makes it possible for others to move to the center, to be in the present and to also become vulnerable. Being present is a free zone with nothing to hide behind and the need for self-protection disappears. Consequences result that potentially feed growth and with appropriate guidance consequences are used as valuable learning lessons.

Being present consists of brief moments. Most of us are not trained to remain in the present for extended periods. Yet where else do babies spend their time? Going in and out of being present is caused by multiple occurrences that take place around us and within us that demand our attention, pulling us back to the past or into the future. This happens to all of us as our subconscious mind is rarely quiet or suppressed.

An exercise to demonstrate the above: Sit or lie down, relax and take a slow deep breath; and as you exhale, say to yourself the number "1." Continue this process slowly and say "2" going up to "10" and then back down to "1," and with each a long inhale and exhale. Many people find this surprisingly difficult to do. They lose count and drift into the past or future. If you do, begin at the beginning and stay with it. It may take repeated efforts and concentration to stay present, but it pays off. This is not because being present is restricted to special people but that re-learning to be present is an experience we need to practice, practice and practice. Babies are in the center and present naturally, but as adults we need to work at it if we are to experience the freedom of *now*.

Again, the leader is and must be the example in the room. No one else has the power to influence as does the leader. If the leader is there, present and in the moment with each person they will influence others to be present with them. The leader and others may, and probably do, have agendas in mind; but by being present they have temporarily set all issues aside. As the reader must know, this is not an easy place to get to without letting go; and letting go is, in itself, a difficult mountain to climb and overcome.

Finally, being present in the moment, attaining the "now," has been an important issue for humankind for thousands of years, and a related message is found in every one of the great religions. When one is present the past or the future does not press, pull, and push us, we are in a place where things and thoughts move in and out of us as easily as breathing. How often in the day do we become conscious of our breathing? For most of us inhaling and exhaling takes place automatically, unless, that is, we take a deep breath in anticipation of saying or doing something. Watch super athletes prepare themselves for the pitch or the jump, and you witness a full awareness of breathing, becoming present and focusing on what is.

Too many people are held captive by the past to the degree that they feel and are trapped by the ghosts of their past. Those of us, who live in the past, miss this moment. Even if totally new, *now* is not experienced as new and fresh but as old and heavy. It is like being trapped and held captive by an old message that replays endlessly. This happens regardless of the fact that each moment *is* and has never been experienced until *now*. Perception dictates behavior; and if this moment is perceived as "what has been before" instead of the freedom and freshness of the immediate, it is what it was.

Being in the present is where truly creative and productive people spend much of their time. This is why enlightened leaders want people in the IC who have proven themselves in their respective fields. Leaders show wisdom in the selection of people who demonstrate their presentness. How else does an IC and the organization they lead benefit from past experiences and knowledge gained if not through people being present? And how else are we able to attain being genuine?

In workshops, as mentor I am responsible for being centered and in the moment as an important first step and model of the process. I make it a point to let everyone in the room know that my body of notes is on my right and that a blank sheet of paper is on my left because I happen to be left-handed. I want them to know and witness that any quizzical looks, questions or interruptions are welcome. My being present with them cannot be in doubt. If I want or need to return to where I am as a teacher, I make a quick check of where I am then and immediately go to the person who needs to speak. Acknowledging them brings dialogue, and in time people begin to become present with each other. Frequently, this experience results in a greater willingness of people to join in. However, it's okay (I make this clear) for those who chose to remain silent to do so. Respect, safety and confidence in the mentor facilitate movement into being present.

Speaking of being in the present: I was and felt as a privileged witness to Barbra Streisand and at another time (same place) Elvis Presley rehearsing with their choral group and orchestra in preparation for the evening shows. Both seemed so totally at ease yet with a focus that felt to me as if this moment is all there is for them. In and out of each moment, the sound, their own as well as what was coming from any performer on the stage, was *now* and instantaneous. It was perfection they were seeking from themselves and all the others even though, as they must have known, total perfection is not attainable. Nothing passed either of them that they did not feel or hear as the best in sound and tempo. I witnessed constant stopping and repeating, going back, becoming present again all to find exactly what they wanted to hear and feel. It was for me a lesson by two of the world's better entertainers. What they had both achieved was not accidental or due to only natural talent, but what I believe to be their ability to be intensely focused and centered in the moment.

Respect

An essential ingredient that must take place between the leaders and each IC member if the experience of Genuine Dialogue is to be realized is *respect*. I give respect an uncomplicated definition that has little to do with position, power, money, religion, politics, credentials, size, weight, strength, gender or how one looks. It is simply that we and all others have in common the fact that we are humans and not that much removed from the high probability of being related somewhere down the line. We are identical in our basic needs in order to survive: Air, water, food and at the beginning period of our lives the caregivers without whom we are helpless until we learn to fend for ourselves. What matters from our very beginning is the need to feel respect as the unique being we are—now—and not as others would have us be.

Who among us does not require respect as the unique beings that we each are? To be acknowledged as the person we are is immensely important. How different from our having to pretend in order to be respected? And, then, what are we respected for? Does the lie we are forced to live in order to be shown respect contribute to our emotional well-being? No! The respect I intend is meant as acceptance as we present ourselves and not false based on the hope of realized expectation. It does mean that we exist; we are seen, heard and understood. It is simple and uncomplicated as long as we understand that this need for *respect* is universal.

Respect for *who* we are as compared to *what* we do is as difficult to achieve as our being present and in the moment. The barriers that are presented to us begin at birth, where the environment sets so much in action. Likes and dislikes are presented to us through our caregivers, and their biases are imprinted on us whether or not we choose them. We see, feel and hear words of bigotry, anger and sadness; and we soon learn that it is much wiser to not speak or express our true feelings and thoughts. We learn that we are not respected for being our true selves, but through meeting the expectations of others. Unless, that is, we hear and feel words of love and acceptance as we are and present ourselves and then we know respect. As humans we are born unique, that is, not exactly identical to any other human. To this degree we are, in many ways, similar to each other. But, we are also different from each other and our differences, although subtle, is what needs recognition and acceptance for us to know respect. The alternative means that we do not exist as the real person we are in the eyes of the other. The power of knowing respect is immense. The damage of not knowing respect is also immense. Which is the better for us and those we relate to?

One summer in the 1960s we invited my father, 82 years at the time, to be with us for the summer at our coed summer camp in northern California. I told him that he was needed, and he was. There was so much carpentry work necessary at camp, and he'd work with staff and children teaching proper use of tools and construction. He was a carpenter and cabinet maker since a teenager, beginning his apprenticeship at around the age of ten in his native country, Russia. He continued this through his working life and always took much pride in his work. Being at camp would give him many things to do, but more importantly I wanted him to feel needed and of value to others. And, as stated, we needed his knowledge badly as a teacher to help us build new structures, repair old ones and teach his love and art of carpentry to campers and staff.

I had no idea that he would become so thoroughly involved with the children and staff along with fixing and building things, and teaching carpentry to both campers and staff. He became so much a part of the fabric of camp what with projects and his helpful teaching to kids and staff that we hardly had time to just be together. Most important to my wife and me, he not only nurtured others but was nurtured himself by the activities and by the people at camp. So fully did he enjoy and become part the camp environment he rarely missed any of our staff meetings and special events, including our evening campfires. He learned and sang the songs, listened to the stories, and laughed at the funny and spontaneous skits. For a man in his early eighties, and old when he arrived at camp, we witnessed him finding his "fountain of youth" for the full length of each and every day.

As all good things must come to an end, so did this summer at camp. It was after the summer was over, the kids and staff had left and we were preparing to leave for home when he came to me and said, "You know, I always wondered why you chose to work with children, and I hoped that one day you would be doing a man's type of work. But after witnessing you and Lenette operating camp, I now know that what you both do and have done for many years is the 'best' of what anyone can do. I'm so proud of both of you for what you do, but more importantly the kind of people you both are."

It appears that my father respected us for the work we did, but I know it was more and deeper. I always felt respect and love from my parents, my brothers and sister. Growing up during the Great Depression, I knew the difficulties my parents went through simply putting food on the table in between moving from one third- and fourth-floor apartment to another. I know I was fed, had a bed to share with a brother, hand-me-down clothes were good enough for me, and life was what it was. I also know that I expected little more than the acceptance and love they showed to all of us (five boys and a girl) and our friends. It was here in our family that I first knew respect, and it was a natural transition to my friends and the street. As for the world around me I felt it as a natural thing and easily respected others. It had to come from my first care givers. Whenever I did experience a lack or no respect I stood my ground for myself and, if necessary, for others. If we are lucky enough, respect comes naturally and early in our lives. It, initially, depends on the behavior of others towards us and if it takes root is not easily taken from us.

This brings up another story about my experiences with a group of elementary school teachers. I was invited to speak to them on the subject of building a community in the classroom. After a brief introduction I began by telling the teachers the importance of "respecting" all children as the unique person they each are and doing this without concern that the children respect the teacher as the authority figure. I emphasized that through sincere and consistent behavior of respect for each of the children, the students will come to respect the teacher; and this respect will translate into a greater willingness to participate as individuals and will grow as members of the class community. My words and intentions are that, "You teach best by being what you teach."

From the back of the room came a grunt from a teacher, so I asked him to say what he had on his mind. "I'm the teacher, have taught for five years, been in the military for six years and I know what respect means—and they need to respect me!" he bellowed.

"So, you strongly believe that it is the responsibility of the kids in your class to respect you because you are the teacher, the authority, the power?" I confirmed.

"Exactly" he said.

I wondered to myself how many of the twenty teachers in the room actually believed that the children *must respect* them as the adult and teacher before the teachers begin to respect the children. I did not feel good about the nods of heads that followed his statement.

We filled the hour discussing our different views, but I left feeling sad for the children and also the teachers who felt this way. Teaching to a group of children is always a challenge; but as I know through experience, building a community out of individuals who feel safe, secure and respected brings out their more selfless side and hence membership in a community. Not fantasy but fact for the teachers who understand and implement, and for the students lucky enough to have a teacher who respects each and all.

For any leader/teacher/parent to believe that they deserve respect because of the position they hold, they expect too much. That any in authority dispense their respect only when it is earned is so telling about the state of leadership in our world. All leaders are teachers whether they choose to be or not and respecting each person as the unique being each is, is a powerful lesson. How else does a healthy and vital community come to be?

Confirmation

Confirmation, as I use it throughout the book, means to assure the one who speaks that we hear them and understand what they are saying—or that we do not understand and need further clarification so that we do understand them. When I listen to the ones who speak to me, I need to be there for them and not thinking about anything else or whether I agree or disagree with them. Anything I do that takes me away from being with the other who speaks, listening and understanding them diminishes our relationship in that moment, and which is likely felt by the speaker. If I know that I am not listening to them or do not care for what they say, the speaker must know this, too. Acting out as if a listener and not listening makes things worse. In any case, to confirm another is impossible without being present and respecting them as the person they are, but not necessarily for what they say or what they do. That is, confirmation does not happen because of position or power, but rather because we are people with opinions and feelings that need to be heard and understood. This is enough to warrant confirmation and confirmation does not mean agreement.

Examples of Confirmation: The speaker express their thoughts and feelings about an issue that we are each concerned with. They are not simply occupying space and time with idle talk, but an issue important to them. As the speaker speaks, anyone may interrupt with: "I do not understand, can you give me an example or at least clarify what you mean?" Or, "So what I think you are saying is "… and I have a sense that you feel strongly about your position." If a listener does not understand what the speaker is saying, interrupting and letting the speaker know this confirms that the speaker is being heard but not understood; and that clarity is called for, which is the responsibility of the speaker, not the listener. When the speaker does clarify and explain to the satisfaction of the listener what is being said, it is equally important for the listener to confirm to the speaker what he or she now understands.

Confirmation as I use and teach the process allows for spontaneity and dialogue to happen any time when someone speaks and it does not come as a surprise to the speaker. The rules are laid out, discussed and clarified before the Inner Circle enters into dialogue. The more traditional waiting for an appropriate break and not interrupting the speaker, whether it is the leader or any member of the IC, is eliminated. To wait, as we have been taught by others only exacerbates the problems of communication between us. If waiting for permission to speak, to question, to get clarification and understanding is put off because of cultural rules to abide by, how are we to remain in the present? Where does our mind go, and what are the benefits to the speaker and to the listener?

This process is designed to confirm to speakers that they are heard and understood. And, if not, they are responsible for a better explanation and examples of what they mean to say to the satisfaction of both the listeners and the speakers. The fact that there is an interruption based on the need for clarification rather than silence that allows minds to wander elsewhere compliments the speakers' belief in their position. And the dialogue that takes place between people is not initially about agreement or disagreement but only has to do with the assurance of being heard and understood. After this is achieved candor takes over between speaker and listener(s) and if decisions needs to be made they come easily thanks to the confirmation that has taken place between them.

Expressing one's opinions, feelings and being responsible for clarification, if necessary, is what this is about and agreement or disagreement is not part of this moment. Keeping people centered on the issues, speakers and involvement through the spontaneity of confirmation to a considerable extent eliminates distractions and minds going elsewhere. Because confirmation as a process is so little understood and practiced, "Communication remains the problem to the answer." More often than not, people are at different levels and places on the roadway of communication, too often thinking in opposite directions while still appearing to be present with each other. We know this via parent versus child, parent/parent, boss/employee, employee/employee, teacher/student and even friend/friend. Yes, someone is talking; but who is listening and working to understand, and how do we really know if not through confirmation?

Technological advances constantly speed our ability to connect with each other but may be contributing to a diminishing and probably worsening of meaningful dialogue between us. We are in touch with each other instantly 24/7. We are able to see each other, but do we feel each others' emotions, breathing and intensity beyond the often shorthand words exchanged in the hand-held device? It is easy to depart from listening, therefore understanding, confirming and being effectively present with each other. The result appears to be shallow friendships, relationships and certainly less face-to-face dialogue. This is not an attack on technology but a warning that something very important between humans is being altered in ways we are yet to know and what this will mean to our present and most certainly our future relationships.

The Process of Confirmation is Powerful: The story of confirmation that comes to mind is about a group of professionals facing a serious schism with one partner headed for the courts. It is likely to be very costly and potentially destructive to the organization unless it is confronted, understood and resolved by the partners.

Having been asked to mediate between the partners in the organization, I arranged for an evening meeting that would take place after dinner and told them "no alcohol during and after dinner." There was to be no time-limit on the meeting and that it might well run into the early hours of the next day. The gathering began at approximately 8:30 P.M.

The process and rules we were to play by had been experienced by a few I had worked with. For the benefit of the others, I reviewed the rules of the process about to take place and the reasons behind taking the time to confirm each speaker. I explained that understanding a speaker's comments and feelings is absolutely essential and that it is the speaker who must feel this. When anyone who is not the designated speaker expresses an opinion, agrees or disagrees with the speaker, I will instantly stop the exchange. Confirmation of what is heard and understood had to be the accepted process. This event was not going to become a free-for-all for anyone. Any attempt to express an opinion or feelings while someone else was the speaker would be squelched instantly unless the questions or comments were confirming to the speaker.

We sat in a circle with a chair in the center. I invited a volunteer to sit in the center chair and explain his or her personal understanding of what was taking place in the organization. I invited spontaneous interaction with the speaker at any time from anyone who needed clarification or questioned what the individual was saying. It is important to get everyone as centered on the person in the chair and focused on what they are saying as is possible.

The meeting continued until well after midnight; and, finally, when all had been given their time on the chair except the dissident member of the group, I called a brief break and announced that it was to be his turn on the chair when we reconvened. When we began again he reluctantly took center stage and volunteered that his attorney had instructed him to remain silent and would do the speaking for him. I pointed out that he had witnessed throughout the evening his partners speaking and being given the opportunity for clarifications and the answering of any questions. "Why not take advantage of this opportunity to tell us what the problem and issues are so that your partners understand you, your position and for you to feel confirmed, and, which you have not experienced since making your decision?" I added that he would be given every opportunity to make his needs known without argument from anyone and that this was only about the need for each individual in the room to understand his intentions and why. We waited, and silence in the room became very heavy.

Much to my relief (and that of the others), he spurted out an expletive and began to present his problem, needs and what he thought was a fair and equitable solution. Everyone in the room let out a communal sigh, followed by a flood of support for him and his position. The meeting was just as quickly adjourned.

We had achieved Genuine Dialogue in that everyone in the room was fully present and they all respected each other. It was obvious that confirmation continued throughout the evening, which must have contributed to the distressed partner's opening up even after he stated that his attorney had told him to say nothing. Finally, the manner in which each speaker was confirmed must have weakened his resistance to opening up. Confirmation eliminates having to justify, argue and do battle with others who simply refuse to see and understand the other side's position.

The story ends well: The evening and dialogue led to adoption of a formula to be used by the partners so that any, when they chose, could leave without friction or heartache. The organization continues alive and is growing to this day. Confirmation and Genuine Dialogue saved the day, and the expenditure of considerable money for legal and court costs was avoided.

Confirmation is not agreement, but it assures understanding. And, how often does this occur when people meet or, and much more challenging, are of divergent opinions?

Candor

Candor, when mixed with respect, being present and the use of confirmation, brings the best possible values out of our human relationships. It has nothing to do with power, domination or the forcing of agreement. Candor is merely stating, as clearly as possible, a position and a willingness to stand responsible for what they say. Candor is making one's true feelings and thoughts known without fear of consequences.

This brings to mind a story of candor: I considered it an honor to witness candor between people who had worked together for years volunteering things about themselves that may not have been necessary but did contribute to their being better known and understood. It had to be the result of the work we did together and the safety and trust that grew between them because many of the stories shared had never been told before. Candor is not a journey of leaps and bounds but the taking of one step at a time without expectations.

In this particular case I asked people to think about what they wanted most to be or to do apart from the job they were doing. As with all such questions, any response was purely volitional. If someone chose to talk, they did so; and total attention was given to them.

The office manager, a disciplined and most efficient member of the Inner Circle, spoke first and said, "I've always wanted to be on stage and to be a famous actor." That this came as a surprise from others in the room was obvious as eyes widened.

Without letting a moment pass I confirmed her by saying, "So you have always wanted to be an actor in live theater?"

"Yes" she said, "it's been my dream since I was a child."

I then asked her what plays or acting she had done.

"None!" she responded.

I asked if there was a theater in town.

"Oh, yes!" she said, "and a great little theater it is."

"Have you volunteered at that theater or others to help in any way and to be around what you so love."

"Oh, no," she said.

"Why don't you follow your dream if even just to help out and be around the stage?"

"I have never found the time, and I also love working here." After a moment's pause she said, "I know it's a dream, and I'm okay with that. It's just a fantasy I enjoy having," and she smiled. And, so did the group.

Being candid with one's self and others lifts the veils on the necessity of hiding one's thoughts and feelings or suppressing old wounds, sadness and pain. Candor is not meant to be cathartic but to contribute to our knowing each other better, and yet under certain circumstances may actually be cathartic. As we progress towards the experience of Genuine Dialogue, people who have been unable or unwilling to be candid become so. In safe-enough environments people will risk being honest and open. All relationships need this to prosper.

GENUINE DIALOGUE CAN BE MADE TO HAPPEN

I believe it is impossible to be both witness and participant in the same moment. For participants to witness the beauty and brilliance of ongoing Genuine Dialogue, they need to move outside of it. This is because when Genuine Dialogue between people takes place, the environment and moment are totally enveloping for them. The event is dynamic: participants are present, they respect each other, confirm and are being confirmed; and candor is as natural as breathing. It is an environment of people interacting as one and yet unique in a most creative way.

When was the last time you met with others at a meeting, over dinner or in a gathering of friends and the hours seemed to "fly by"? Where did the time go, and what made hours seem like minutes? When fully in the moment, time does not exist for us although time continues outside of our awareness; and what consumes us and time is our truly being with others and them with us. Being present with others is a gift that wants to be repeated; yet when we attempt to repeat this enervating and remarkable experience with the same people, it invariably fails. Why? Is it that Genuine Dialogue cannot be planned for—that it is simply an accident?

As stated often throughout the book Genuine Dialogue does occur accidentally for most people. The problem, and a serious one, is that trying to make it happen again without understanding the essential ingredients and the process makes its occurrence unlikely. The path that gets us to Genuine Dialogue is through learning its ingredients and practice, practice and more practice. The foundation for all must be safe, inviting, and cooperative without a hierarchy while it exists. Also, power is shared and the feeling of mutuality towards each other fills the space. All of the people involved become like owners and/or followers. Only events dictate which.

In order to experience Genuine Dialogue through deliberate planning, it essential to understand the process that leads to it: the vulnerable leader, a mentor to facilitate, respect, being here and now, and the art of confirmation and candor when it happens. In time the IC members are required to commit themselves to also be vulnerable to the leader and to each other. The leader must be believed and trusted by their significant others if being vulnerable is to spread. As trust in the leader grows, slowly, one step at a time, trust in one's self happens; and as trust becomes the environment, most are compelled from within to let their guard down and to become vulnerable. When this begins to take place we are close to entering into Genuine Dialogue with each other, and it is not accidental.

Consider the story about the evening gathering of professionals to resolve a partnership problem. During our evening together Genuine Dialogue existed and at times it did not. There were periods where time moved slowly and minds, including mine, wandered—but this is not uncommon. It's something like coming up for air. But in the end, candor due to the conditions of Genuine Dialogue brought about a remarkable and positive conclusion to a most serious problem. I also believe that when the office manager shared her fantasy about being an actor with her Inner Circle, it helped make her more human to those she worked with than perhaps she had been in all her previous years with them. And, would not this alone contribute to better communication between them?

The rules and factors that make Genuine Dialogue possible are also necessary in a relationship of two. Trust and assurance of safety must be the experience of both persons, but it is the person who holds power who brings Genuine Dialogue about. Behavior, not words, does so. It has so little to do with an organization's structure and everything to do with the vulnerable and eventual candid behavior of the one in power. As the leader's changes are perceived and believed, the more secure people test the waters; and soon enough others join in. Those who experience an open and safe environment become fully immersed and grow, and those unable or unwilling go.

Behavior of the leader and not words spoken by a teacher impacts the environment. It is not easy for traditional leaders to become vulnerable to those closest to them. The mentor emphasizes to the leaders that they need to eliminate "expectations" that others will become more open because the leader is open. Scar tissue is overcome by the individual from within, not from without. This does not happen outside of relationships by one's self. Relationships create the environment that envelops people. If relationships are perceived as safe and inviting it attracts being a part. If controlled and held hostage to a fixed hierarchy this means "be careful" or "outright danger exists." Due to what each perceives people make their own decisions about whether to open up or to protect themselves.

Giving up power, if even briefly and for the best reasons, may not be possible for some leaders. In the minds of most traditional leaders, if it works, even if not well—"I don't want what we have and do to be messed with." The problem for too many leaders is that they do not see themselves as the responsible creator of their environments and therefore the major influence on those closest to them. Solutions, as they see them, must have to do with and be found with the people they lead.

WITHOUT GENUINE DIALOGUE, IMPORTANT ISSUES ARE NOT ADDRESSED

The following story is briefly touched elsewhere, but here I extract specific Genuine Dialogue lessons that contributed to my further understanding of the value and even necessity of an effective Inner Circle and why Genuine Dialogue is vitally important to an organization's survival and success. This pertains to a community project built in Las Vegas, NV. The people who were financially involved and I never became an Inner Circle, and we never experienced Genuine Dialogue. It proved to be a serious mistake and none could have anticipated what was to come without our having frequent meetings where we just might have been able to understand each other. It never happened.

It all began when my wife woke up one morning in the mid-1960s and shared a dream that we had built and were operating a "Youth Hotel." We wondered at how foolish a fantasy the dream was, and yet for her it was as real as our looking at each other. It was all so clear to her that she described the facility and the variety of activities taking place there. We continued to talk about her dream for a number of days, including where such a program should take place. What kept coming to mind was Las Vegas, Nevada because whenever we went on vacation (usually right after closing the camp in mid-September) we choose Las Vegas because it was so different, adult and cheap. We found inexpensive rooms in swanky hotels, great buffets and entertainment all for relatively little money. And when recreating at the pool we would often comment on the number of families and children there. We also observed that there was nothing for kids to do, which must have been a problem for parents, their children and the hotel.

We decided to investigate my wife's dream and see what we might be able to do with what was becoming a firm picture to us. We had no money, so finding investors to build and support our entrepreneurial dream was essential. I decided to speak to some parents who sent their children to our camp, reasoning that because they trusted us with their children they might also trust us enough to support an investment in a wild idea about a youth hotel in Las Vegas. I spoke to one of the parents from camp about the idea and its possible location, and he brought other parents and friends together to hear more. Eventually a group of ten was formed to support our moving to Las Vegas in order to search for land ideal for the recreation center we proposed building.

After considerable research, my wife and I found the land, five acres at an excellent price in what we believed to be an ideal location. It was right across the street from the biggest church in the vicinity, less than a block from the intersection of two main streets and surrounded by a stable, middle-class community no more than four miles from the Las Vegas Strip. My wife designed how the physical environment would be laid out, and our financial partners arranged a construction loan with one of the local banks. My wife and I did all the necessary legwork, including obtaining permits, finding an architect and a builder. Long story short: because of due diligence and hard legwork on our part, everything fell nicely into place, and the complex was completed for much under the initial estimated cost.

My wife's design of the facility was beautiful and remarkably functional. What came out of her creative mind was due to years of our living and working with children. It was a utilitarian dream for children and our staff of well-trained professionals and college students. The facility had multiple uses, including a dance studio, arts and crafts area, kitchen, dining room, overnight accommodations for children, classrooms, space for tutorial and guidance services, pre-school and after-school recreation programs (including serving all meals), weekend programs, summer camp, a large swimming pool, basketball courts, ball fields and more. We believe that for its time, 1968, it may have been one of the most complete and unusual private children's facilities and programs in the country.

As with all new businesses; we needed continuing financial support as it grew in importance to the community and to the church across the street. At the same time, I was developing inroads and connections with the hotels on the strip. Then the financial backers began to notice that the value of the land and facility had substantially increased. Where my wife and I only saw the children, staff and programs, the investors saw the potential for a quick profit if the land and facility were sold.

The only barriers to a quick profitable sale were my wife and I. We were not the least bit interested in selling, regardless of profit, what we had worked so hard to build and operate successfully. We had given birth to the idea, found the location, designed the building and supervised its construction, and developed and administered the programs. We loved the growing influence it was having in the community at large and looked forward to other programs coming from our original dream. From the governor of the state down, it was one of the most inclusive relationships we had ever experienced, as was the support we were given by so many.

We ran special programs for church family members, and during this time I began a relationship with one of the priests. He was so supportive of what we were doing that our relationship soon became a friendship. We would meet often, and share ideas and (always) laughs. He understood what we were doing and often expressed how immensely important what we provided was to the church and the community.

When I realized the intentions of the investors, I approached them and emphasized our goals and "good" they were supporting. What became very clear, however, was that they intended for us to be, legally, taken out of the picture. The spokesman for the group stressed that "they had other ideas in mind, none of which had to do with a children's program." I made it just as clear that if they did not support the program, it was not going to be easy for them to sell the property from under us. I promised them I would find a way to pay back every penny they had invested—and with a profit, I hoped. I told them the bank loan, too, would be paid off in full and that the program would continue. However, they did not believe that I had the ability to raise enough money to clean up every penny of indebtedness to them and the bank. And as it turned out, they were right. No one with the resources came to our aid.

Had we been an effective Inner Circle and had we understood Genuine Dialogue, I have to believe that we would have found a way out of our problems. We tried several times to resolve our divergent views, but to no avail. Having no other option, I crossed the street, sat down with my friend the priest, and offered the whole package to the church for the exact and total amount I needed. I knew that under the church's stewardship the program would continue without a missing a beat. He called me in a few hours to tell me the purchase had been approved. We shook hands on the sale, and it was all over. Fifty-plus years later, it remains a church and community center for children and numerous church activities.

The original investors received every penny they had invested and did not pursue any other action. I believe it had to do with our relationships established with their children. As for my wife and I, we learned an important lesson about how the business world too often operates. I had no argument that profit is essential to a business; and we were a business, but so should the good an organization does for its costumers and the community be an important consideration.

This is why I state that an IC made up of knowledgeable, talented people of different disciplines that experience Genuine Dialogue with each other is essential to any organization. I believe my wife's dream and our commitment to the program and its quality were, apparently, never "heard" and understood by the investors. And my wife and I did not understand the intentions of the investors. We thought they supported our dream for an extraordinary children's program. A controlling few of them saw it as a way to a quick profit. Communication between us left much to be desired. But, it was a powerful learning experience.

Did confirmation of our goals and purpose ever take place? Did my wife and I understand the reasons why they invested in our dream? We each assumed we were on the same page. Had we understood the essentials of Genuine Dialogue and actually experienced same, and by each of us; our issues might have been worked out much before we actually become involved with each other. Maybe the result of Genuine Dialogue would have meant no financial commitment to invest. And as true entrepreneurs, my wife and I would have gone on our way seeking other means to give life to the dream. Finally, there is always the possibility that had we all understood each other we might well have arrived at a consensus to fully support the program until it fully supported itself. This never took place. Live and learn.

Not all was lost or wasted. Our program in Las Vegas brought us to the attention of the builders of a new resort-casino being built off the strip next to the new convention center. Thanks to our reputation, we were invited to present a program in competition with two major universities for a children's program for hotel guests—and our program was selected. It was chosen over the other submittals because it emphasized the importance of relationships between people, not activities. Genuine Dialogue, in this particular case, may well have been the magic that won us the contract. Again, much before we began to recognize it as a process and teachable. Portions of the story of our Hotel/Resort experience and education are to be found in the beginning chapters.

Finally, it must be apparent now that Genuine Dialogue is not going to take place, intentionally, unless the leader is Genuine and is proven so in the minds and hearts of those who are close to the leader. Without this assurance wrapped in consistency it may happen between people, and does, but is accidental and accidental is not good enough.

CHAPTER 7

EVENTS DICTATE THE EXERCISE OF POWER

As events happen
Someone needs to grab the reins
A leader rises.

When in my teens, I worked as a dishwasher at a summer camp for boys. It was just prior to World War II, and we were beginning to work our way out of the Great Depression. I guess, as with most fourteen-year-old boys, I believed I was an indestructible *man* and felt capable of taking care of myself under any circumstances. One of my closest friends worked with me in breaking speed records washing dishes. It was crucially important that the dishes we cleaned be as spotless as possible, and we did our best to make this our number one priority; but it was also our desire to finish our job each evening as quickly as possible. This resulted in sparkling clean dishes but also a few chipped and broken ones.

This particular night we planned to finish extra fast so we could hitch a ride to a local town that we heard had the best barbeque ribs around. We remember being told that the town was off-limits to all staff members but didn't ask or felt a need to know why. Until, that is, we heard about the ribs and then it did not matter. We figured that we would not be missed since after handling our dishwashing responsibilities we had plenty of free time. In any case, the picture of succulent ribs and fries overwhelmed any concern we might have had about breaking a rule for which we had little concern. As luck would have it just prior to leaving camp we ran into one of our friends and invited him to join us on our rib quest, but he chose to remain at camp. So we took off down the road looking to hitch-hike a ride to the town.

We were soon picked up by a car heading in the direction of the town. About a quarter of a mile before the town we saw a county road sign that gave the name of the town and, in bold letters, "**No Jews or Dogs Allowed**." As two Jewish kids growing up on the west side of Chicago, the sign did not frighten us. We were familiar with anti-Semitic sentiments, but the sign answered why the town was off-limits to the camp's staff. Growing up in a Jewish ghetto/community, one learns to fight back, to back off and avoid confrontations or to hide being a Jew. In our particular case, it was always choosing to fight. We could hardly wait to get into town and enjoy the rib reward it promised. Frightened? Who, us? Not that I can remember.

It's probably important to mention that we were both wearing t-shirts with the camp's name blazoned across the front. To quote Forest Gump's mother, "Stupid is as stupid does." We were the dumbest! It also happened to be a Saturday night, and the town was enjoying a street party. We hardly stepped out of the car before some people took note of two strangers in their community of locals, and soon we were being followed by a pack of citizens with expressions of anger and hate on their faces.

We fled into a nearby drugstore that looked like a safe place to us; but the people in the store, including those behind the counters, hurried outside. My buddy and I moved to a corner behind a counter and grabbed bottles of whiskey with which to defend ourselves. We were fools, and our surging adrenalin prepared both of us for what we both thought was our impending doom. Neither of us felt fear, but a total readiness and presentness I was to learn more about in events yet to happen in my life.

Fortunately for us, the friend we'd left behind mentioned to one of the adult staff members that we had gone to the forbidden town for ribs. The staff member immediately informed the camp director, who, without a moment's hesitation, leaped into a camp truck and shouted to the staff member, "You and the rest stay put no matter what!" and drove off to the town.

In the meantime, the crowd gathering outside the drugstore began to shape itself from a chaotic mass into some semblance of order; and at the head stood the mayor of the town. As he and others began to enter the store it, looked and felt to us as if the crowd had become one united body. That we were in serious trouble was clear, and that we had become the focal point was equally certain. With a leader at the front spearheading them, people spread out so that they could get to us from different directions behind the counter.

It is said that in certain situations time appears to stand still or moves in slow motion. That's how I remember the following events. Much to our surprise and relief, the director of the camp appeared at the front of the crowd in the store; picked out the mayor, whom he apparently knew; and without uttering a word slapped the mayor across the face, sending him to the floor. The camp director immediately turned towards us, told us to get behind him, and the crowd parted like the Red Sea must have when the Israelites escaped the Egyptian Army. The three of us headed to the truck, with the motor still running, and took off down the road for camp. Not a word was exchanged between us. Even as I write this story, seventy-plus years later, I am able to see, smell and feel this experience. Amazingly, the camp director said nothing during our ride back to camp and nothing after the event. Apparently he knew that we had learned an invaluable lesson—and we most assuredly had.

This story sheds light on mob behavior and the loss of individual responsibility. It also shows how one capable person could and did insert himself into a strong leadership role when *events dictated* immediate decision-making and action. This person became the spear point and we, correctly, his obedient followers. Being an intimate participant in this drama taught me lessons I have used and live with to this day.

I learned that when a moment or event happens that requires the instant intrusion of another to take control of a situation, it needs to be done forthrightly and with courage. I know that I witnessed the director's courage in the face of true danger. I also learned about a leader's behavior in the face of irresponsible and inexcusable behavior by others (my friend and me). In addition, I learned more about myself and how I respond to events beyond my power to control. And most important, I learned about quality leadership and the appropriate exercise of power.

WHY EVENTS SHOULD DICTATE THE USE OF POWER

The preceding story is a classic example of what I mean when I write that "events dictate the exercise of power." It is an essential part of a well-functioning IC that when an event demands immediate leadership the best-qualified member within the circle responds. The response does not necessarily come from the person fixed in power because all IC members are empowered to be what they have experienced being.

The story is also about behavior of a crowd that becomes one body with a head. We saw that identifying the leader of the mob, in this case, the mayor, was key to effectively disrupting or stopping mob action, if even temporarily. I learned that we have no choice but to act assertively, even aggressively, in the face of situations dangerous to one's self and those for whom we are responsible. There are events in our life that call for immediate action and leadership—from whom shall leadership come?

I am reminded of an event that dictated this response earlier than the event in the forbidden town. I was in elementary school when this took place, and it happened during a recess break. A well-known and feared bully, whom most kids tried to avoid, was picking on a smaller kid. The bully was a big guy and used his size and strength to push others around. I apparently had had enough of his behavior and went at him as if he were beating up on my sister. I had to be a head shorter than he was and probably thirty pounds lighter, but I bloodied his nose and knocked him down. He pulled himself up off the ground—with me standing over him ready and eager for more—and turned and slunk away. The kids around me cheered and clapped me on the back and shoulders. I admit that my victory over an evil predator felt good.

When class resumed, the teacher received a message that the principal wanted to see me in his office immediately. I knew, or at least certainly felt, that I was in deep trouble. I thought, "Maybe I'm going to be thrown out of school" and/or, "They are going to send me to juvenile prison," or, worst of all, "The principal will write a note to my mother and father saying that I was a 'bad' kid." My mother would often say to us, "Never do things that will bring the police here to take you away." The way I read it was that, "I can do what I want to do as long as I don't get caught."

The principle was a tall and very stern-looking man. He was not someone I ever wanted to be standing in front of. He closed the door behind me and walked back to his desk but did not sit down. He stood about ten feet over me and glowered for just an instant. I remember that at this very moment I thought, "The worst he could do is to kill me or have me killed. After that, nothing would matter anyway."

"What did you hit the bully with?" was his first question to me. "My fist," I said and showed him my right hand. He reached out and placed his hands on my shoulders and smiled a warm, admiring smile. "Don't tell anyone that I said this, but you did a good job on him and a wonderful thing for the other children to see. I don't want to have anyone fight and be hurt; but in this case he deserved what he got, and I hope he learned a lesson about being a bully." He shook my hand and told me to go back to class, and to not say one word to anyone about what we talked about. Of course, my wife knows the story (she knows them all) and now you do, too. In closing this story, I pose the question: Do I understand and live by "events dictate the exercise of power?" I believe I do, and hopefully have both led and followed accordingly.

This chapter opens with the story about an event that could well have been disastrous for two stupid teenagers, a small town, and the people who lived in it. Fortunately, because of the actions of one person it became a valuable learning experience for the two of us. I will never know what it meant to the others involved. What matters is that an event happened that demanded a certain response. The "right" person was informed and instantly made a number of correct decisions, took action and saved the day.

This is the point that needs to be emphasized, recognized and understood by true leaders: It will not happen if the leader does not empower capable others to take a leadership role when events call out for the right person to take charge. All people build multiple Inner Circles of one sort or another; in most cases it is their gang, family members, friends and coworkers. They are each made up of different people with different abilities. Wisdom dictates the needle of leadership ought to go to the most able to handle the call and not to a fixed leader.

The noise I make in Chapter 5 is that Inner Circles, particularly in organizations, need to be made up of exceptionally talented and experienced people who have different backgrounds. This is done so that as issues and problems arise to which IC members can respond, the more different their life experiences the more likely it is that someone within the group is better able to handle the situation than the leader. But this will not happen unless all members of an IC know they are empowered to take charge, and are capable of leading.

This seems so rational an action to take: surrounding one's self with people of different backgrounds and experience, and empowering each to take a leadership role as events dictate. This requires constant affirmation that power is shared and supported.

So how does anyone stand up to power leaders who yield nothing to their Inner Circle members regardless of the talent that is available? This is the more likely scenario since too many leaders are blind to their power, and events simply give them the vehicle in which to wield their power. Standing up to power when not empowered to do so is dangerous territory to place one's self in and is likely the easiest path to being demeaned or punished—and for others to witness and know this is not what they will allow themselves to be put through. This makes for wasted talent and experience due to inadequate leadership and misuse of power.

Which brings me to the question: Why does anyone want to be a leader of others? If relationships are everything, in fact essential to life itself, why is it important to some people that they dominate those they need? What drives some people to have to be in charge of or have power over others, even those they supposedly love? We understand that events happen in life that may force leadership upon an individual who has no intention of leading anyone. This may happen during an emergency. We also know that leadership often takes place on the basis of talent or ability, experience, intellect, charisma and appearance. But what I consider to be the most common is that individuals want to lead and work hard at becoming a leader.

Some people are so driven to be at the top and to possess power over others that they will do whatever they see as necessary to attain this goal. But these people are unaware that power is a tool that has potential to do a great deal of good or evil, and if evil, may even destroy them and those they hold power over. There is also the reality that leaders' who seek to control all events are bound to fail because one cannot be all things at all times. Unless a leader is surrounded by the totally inept, and what does this say about the leader? There is going to be someone more capable and in this case, events must dictate, not the leader.

Leaders want "expected" outcomes, not outcomes that surprise or cause additional problems. When events and outcomes are helter-skelter, leaders cannot be secure nor are their followers. Leaders who do experience frequent hit-or-miss outcomes generally have little faith in their key people. Inadequate leaders are not likely to be aware that their followers have little faith in and are also insecure in their relationship with the leader. In contrast, if leaders use their power thoughtfully; empower others to lead; and nurtures mutual dialogue, followers will feel and know inclusion and community. All involved—benefit from being empowered and respected for what each brings to the table.

My consulting experiences are, at first glance, with mostly dysfunctional organizations. This should not come as a surprise when we consider the reasons why most consultants are employed: In my case what I most frequently heard was that, "Communication between my people is a big problem and troubled relationships exist amongst them." When people are together in a living or work environment, authentic dialogue between them is relatively rare and precisely why I was employed. At the beginning I approached the problem as if it were staff and personnel issues, but I soon discovered that most interpersonal and communications issues begin with the leader. Since I had been a leader of many for at least twenty five years the thought that I might have been the main problem and cause of the issues of communication, this shook me up.

When I had the epiphany that the leader is "the primary problem to the answers" they sought in order to resolve their relationship and communication issues, this shed a whole new light on the problems I would have to deal with. What had to be confronted and eliminated was the blindness on the part of the leader that they either controlled all the power in the organization, or were too weak in the way they misused their power. It was a problem of getting to the "middle way" and that meant the sharing of power through empowering others. In this case, events needed to be taken charge of by those most capable of dealing with the event.

Strong, controlling, even capable leaders who seemed to always take charge of events dictated the actions of others as if pawns and yet were dissatisfied with the inability of individuals to take charge and exert leadership. These leaders did not see themselves as keeping others from stepping into the breach and taking responsible and leadership roles.

With weak or indecisive leaders, events were opportunities for a subgroup leader to take control and subtle leadership. In such situations, respect for the actual leader is minimal, and communication between everyone is as troubled and dysfunctional as with strong and all-controlling leaders. The cause is the leader and the affect travles throughout the organization. Treatment has to begin at the top, with the leaders being the most willing to be vulnerable and be the student. Leaders must know how those closest to them perceive them. Not an easy task to achieve and impossible without the courageous and volitional commitment of the leader.

Care must be taken because when dominating leaders let up and allow others to take control, IC members need to be prepared and even eager to step into a leadership role if the event points to them. It is why having people with the widest possible variety of experiences as members of the Inner Circle is vitally important. But until and unless they are empowered, no one will step into the role the event calls for. Trust in others to lead is the essential words and feelings here.

Initially, leaders do not easily look to themselves as the cause to why their best people do not take control of events. Instead, they blame their people for not stepping into the leadership breach or for errors and omissions. Leaders, too frequently, heroically charge in and attempt to make things right, feeling justified in their power role. By the not so simple act of stepping back and supporting key people to do what they are able to do better than the leader is wisdom at work and an excellent way to improve and grow relationships. Sharing power is a gift returned many times over; but if misused or abused by a subordinate the leader may still grab the reigns and take what actions are necessary. Failure, in most cases, may be our best learning opportunity. Still, the differences between a mutual relationship and one that is frozen in place are many, and taking the risks to have a mutually beneficial relationship far outweigh anything created by fixed power. How else do events dictate and the "right" leaders take charge?

None of the preceding is an issue with quality leaders. *Events do dictate* who shall be the leaders, without conflict between the true leaders and the ones who take control of the situation. Now it is only about the tasks at hand and the ones best qualified with experience and knowledge. This concept fits perfectly with the reason why IC membership must be about merit, rich experiences, and the courage and willingness to express one's self. Quality leaders surround themselves with people of quality. Those with a variety of life experiences are preferable, but the young without experience who are passionate students willing to risk unknowns are also desirable. In fact, in the present time of exploding technologies, not including young "techies" can cause the IC to be under informed about the current culture and technological events.

LEADERS NEED TO UNDERSTAND THEIR POWER

After years of working with a wide variety of organizations assisting in their interpersonal journey it became clear that subordinates are not the problem in most organizations. It is also true that leaders need, desperately, to understand the power and influence they have over others." This "flash" of enlightenment had to be made known to the leaders I worked with and this was difficult because they employed me to solve "other people's" communication issues. This was a simple matter to explain when talking to a new client.

When new and or potential clients called me, I would explain that if they wanted to change the behavior and attitude within their organization, it must begin with them, the true leaders. I added that the way to do this is to learn how their key people perceive and feel about them and their leadership style. An effect way for this to occur is to ask Inner Circle individuals "what are your expectations of the leader?" With the help of a mentor this process opens up dialogue not justification and excuse making. Leadership had to accept that their behavior is what keeps them locked into their power positions and that they control events too much or, interestingly, too little. When expectations are shared and with sensitivity kept under some control the value of dialogue become apparent to one and all.

So either through the words of others who have recommended me, or a first conversation over the phone, leaders understood that I believed that quality leadership is hardly about interpersonal tools but instead about behavior and perception. I would explain that the perception I refer to is that of the people who know them best—their IC members. I further explained that if and when their key people trusted the leader's receptivity and the environment felt safe enough, individuals would begin to share feelings and thoughts about the leader and the organization. I emphasized that this, then, translates into others taking charge of events and freeing the real leader to be a major resource and supporter of others to lead—the true purpose and meaning of leadership.

To realize this goal demands proof-positive in the eyes, hearts, and minds of those involved in the Inner Circle. Words change nothing, but vulnerable behavior on the part of the leader, empowering others and allowing events to dictate leadership from others at the table, are the only concrete experiences that will make this happen. When individuals believe the leaders have empowered them to take ownership, as events dictate, then and only then will talent and experience come forth from those who have them to give.

BEING WHAT OTHERS WANT US TO BE NEED NOT KEEP US FROM BECOMING

We are conditioned from early on in our lives to be what others knowingly or unknowingly want us to be. This is learned behavior as compared to what is truly unique in each of us. However, what is learned whether by intention or accident can be unlearned. It may be the luck of the draw, but through the efforts of quality leaders who choose to grow as a person, the leader also offer this opportunity of growth to those they live and work with. In safe and nurturing environments people are able, if they choose, to undo what has been done to them and to become more themselves. Relationships, when mutual, cooperative and safe offer each of us the opportunity to be more our true selves. As a result, when we grow we become much more than we have been taught and are. *Being does not keep us from becoming.*

I remember many of the exceptional leaders I had when I was a young. I knew they were special but I was unaware of their impact on me. Yet, I clearly remember people, events and what they said and did. They were my parents, brothers and sister, playground instructors, teachers, initial employers and bosses, and leaders I met in the military. Many, not all by a long shot, are indentified in stories throughout the book. All have contributed significantly to what I am and perhaps still becoming.

When I was a teacher, counseled troubled social/emotional children, created and directed summer camps, and became a consultant to powerful and successful people, I owed much of what I brought to my work and personal relationships the many prior events and the people I had known. I am not what who and what I am through lectures, books and reading about the leaders of the past and present. The strongest influence came and come through face-to-face encounters with real people and real events that I have personally experienced. I know that had I not met certain people in my life or experienced certain events that there is no question my life and my life's work would have been very different.

For this to happen to its fullest I believe it is imperative that we each be present in this moment in order for an event and the people involved to have their full impact on us. If not, we miss the lesson or portions being delivered by the event and the people. The event is a happening, and the people involved may have no knowledge of what is to be delivered, and to whom. Our part is to be a full and present participant in the event. It is then that we receive the gifts wrapped up as lessons. How interesting are the words "present" and "gift."

We recognize good leaders when we witness them in action, not by listening to what they say or write, but through their behavior, what they do. People who seek personal growth are true students, are unafraid of being open to significant others and want this openness from those they are close to. Inadequate leaders, on the other hand, are not interested in their own growth or the growth of their key people. What they seek is winning and achieving certain ends.

If inadequate leaders are students, they are too selective in what they seek to learn. Instead of a search for whom and what they are, they seek to gather relationship tools to further their aims. What are these tools they seek to master? They have to do with appearance and effectiveness as compared to greater awareness of themselves and nothing substantial is changed.

Personal growth is a totally different experience and requires a vulnerability that has no pretence. It is the "truth" of a person for people they are close to, to see and know, and events have a way of forcing this inner being out. Being and appearing to be are, at first, difficult to separate; but in time growing awareness of the differences between authentic behavior and appearance behavior made me more selective in the leaders I chose to work with. Many leaders may have thought they were interviewing me to do a specific job they wanted done; but, in truth, I was interviewing them to discover their degree of openness to the complicit and significant role they played in their organization. Some sought sophisticated tools and others true personal growth. It was imperative that I know the difference and select those to work with whom I believed sought personal growth.

Through many experiences with a wide variety of leadership styles, I became more proficient in identifying leaders who were unafraid to personally grow and eager to assist their significant others to grow. They were mentally and emotionally healthier; and although unsure of what might result, they still wanted to become the best person they could be for themselves and those they were close to. The true students of growth were quick to understand and eager to employ "events dictate leadership." These leaders empowered others to take full leadership roles, including that the true leader become a resource and also a follower of the one who does step into the breach of leadership.

Healthy leaders come to accept, albeit reluctantly, that certain individuals are unwilling to risk growth and/or being vulnerable. They learn that external pressures may force some behavioral changes, but not within the person. The discovery of each person's true intentions happens sooner or later and people will opt out of any program that threatens their veneer. This is because in an intentionally open environment one either participates or leaves the scene volitionally. Rarely must leadership force them to go, but the environment does.

Dialogue, safely and cautiously approached, is the process we use in order to uncover, facilitate and nurture potential in each person. Also, individuals in the Inner Circle need to at some point accept and demonstrate their willingness to participate and take ownership/leadership positions. Those who remain reluctant to participate in open dialogue and take responsibility as a leader force themselves to choose between "growing or going." Hiding behind agreeable faces and words does not protect those who have self-centered agendas. Events, when allowed to dictate which person needs to take charge, strip away masks people might wear. I know and stress that when a key person chooses to remain silent or attempts but fails to undermine what is being done, they will choose to volitionally withdraw. When this takes place it is usually a good indication that a healthier environment is replacing the old one.

It is not difficult to discover leaders who are too controlling because it becomes clear to the mentor when others are not taking leadership positions in response to a particular event. In such a case, the members of the Inner Circle are well aware of their controlling leaders and do not attempt to compete with them. They acquiesce instead because they have no power to do otherwise. As dialogue between them improves and the controlling leader becomes more a participant, events are taken charge of by those best suited to lead. The environment nurtures this.

People learn what to expect from their leader; and if constantly witnessing heavy-handed control, whether obvious or subtle, they learn to wait for instructions from above. At times, waiting on more information or things to develop further makes good sense; but events have a way of letting us know when and what actions to take and by whom.

In the summer of 1960, I was a back seat passenger in a small bus with a group of eight campers, counselor and junior counselor. We were heading towards the Warner Mountains for a backpack trip into a wilderness area. We had never been to this area before, so I decided to join them on this hike. During the drive the kids began to talk about their respective religions. I listened attentively to see in what direction this was heading, and soon it became clear that six of the kids were of one religion and the other two of a different religion. There was no problem with the discussion until the majority began to gang up on the two who believed differently. I waited to see if the counselor might use this as a "teachable moment." I know he heard them, but he did nothing to intervene or to take advantage of the event occurring right behind him. I listened carefully to their dialogue, but where they were heading with it became too assertive, defensive and potentially harmful. I waited for the counselor to make what I was hearing into a "teachable moment" about acceptance and respect for differences, but he did nothing.

The discussion was too inviting not to try to turn it into what I felt was a learning opportunity for each camper, so I jumped in. "Stop the bus," I said to the counselor. "Let's find a nice spot to stretch and enjoy a snack." The counselor nodded his approval and parked the bus in a quiet pull-out along the road.

We all got out and did the "nature" thing, and I found a great clearing where we could sit together in a circle. I began by going back to the conversation they were having in the bus and asked, "Why is it important to talk about your religion?" The responses were varied. One camper said that being of a minority religion; it felt good being in the majority for once. Then I asked, "But why did it seem to me that the six of you were ganging up on the other two who are of a different religion?" They all had a puzzled look on their face that said "Who, me?" One spoke out that he did not do this on purpose. "They are my best friends," he said. Each person had a say, and it was clear that no harm was intended by any of them and yet harm was being done.

We spoke in depth about the importance of differences, and acceptance and respect for our differences. The counselor and junior counselor had done a fine job of bringing them together as caring and supportive of each other. They had become one congruent body. But for this event I would have preferred that the counselor take control of the moment and lead a discussion about respect and differences. It was a "teachable moment" and ought not to be missed.

His mind, however, was where it should have been, and that was on the road and his driving. Events, once again, dictate a person's actions. I led where I would have preferred that the counselor lead, and the teachable moment was utilized. Events dictated that something needed to be taken advantage of, and it was.

The following stories are about young adults who take charge and lead in remarkably appropriate ways when *events dictate.*

This event took place in a beautiful and dramatic setting. A small band of campers and their counselor and junior counselor were enjoying a day trip to Lassen National Park. The kids were learning about nature and volcanic action at a place called Bumpass Hell, located in the heart of Lassen National Park. This is an area of bubbling volcanic mud pots, steam-spitting vents and the wonder of a living volcano. The group leader was identifiable on this hike because he was taller than any of those he was responsible for although he did not have any obvious sign of control or behave in a controlling manner.

Each camper had to be on his own walking the narrow path that meandered through the bubbling mud pots in order to avoid getting burned. The instant one of the campers stepped off the path and his foot sank into a boiling mud pot, leadership happened. In that instant the group's leader pulled the camper out of the mud and immediately cut off his boot. The rest of the group heard the "stop and freeze" call and immediately froze where they were.

The group followed their leader, who was carrying the injured camper, to their vehicle. Within minutes of the event they were all heading for the closest village and medical care. The damage to the camper's foot was minimal, but the doctor did say that had the boy's foot been in the hot water or boot just a minute or two longer, the burns would have been severe and permanent scaring would have taken place. The accident dictated immediate action, and the leader wasted no time in taking control. Events dictate!

It is important to note that all counselors and junior counselors were trained in dealing with the usual emergencies; but not all emergencies are alike, and training hardly assures correct action. In fact, it is impossible to predict the behavior of anyone in the event something unexpected takes place, and it usually does. This is a great argument supporting why leadership needs to be shared by any and all in a group and why environments need to nurture individual growth.

In this story we had just finished telling the same group of campers to be especially aware of rattlesnakes when hiking in a forest to identify edible and medicinal plants. We taught them to never step blindly over a log without searching the ground around it for any sign of a snake. And if anyone spotted a snake, they were told to immediately call out "snake!" as loudly as possible and move away from it. Soon everyone on the hike was busy looking for plants, nuts or fruits that resembled the pictures and descriptions in the survival books we carried with us.

Suddenly one of the boys saw a large rattler curled up next to a log. He immediately cried out "snake!" and everyone but one youngster froze as instructed and moved away from the snake. This camper bolted towards the snake, and in that instant I grabbed him by the back of his shirt. I wasn't close to him by accident because I knew this boy and his behavior well. I was fully aware that anything unusual would trigger his passion to get close and personal with exciting things. In fact, he was the same boy who stepped into the scalding mud pit in the previous story. Need I say more?

In one movement I grabbed him and threw him about five feet behind me. He might have been injured by his flight and fall, but I thought a possible broken bone and lacerations would be better than a poisonous bite from a diamondback. Events dictate, and I responded based on knowledge of the boy I was with. Walking right behind him was no accident. Is this also good leadership?

The final story also involves our wilderness camp in Northern California but with a slightly older group of campers on a backpacking trip in the Thousand Lake Wilderness area of Northern California.

In the high country the campers were enjoying a large snowfield they discovered by testing the variety of ways they could slide down this wonderful summertime find. Relaxed and happy, they slid down and climbed back up until one of the boys lost control and went head-first into a pile of boulders. The counselor was over the boy immediately and saw that he was unconscious and bleeding. It flashed across his mind that the boy might be dead the counselor said later, but when he checked the boy he saw that he was breathing and so began to stop the bleeding from the lacerations.

He called to his junior counselor, a youth of sixteen (the leader was all of eighteen years old), and told him to run down the mountain to the ranger station they had passed while driving to the trailhead. Not incidentally, the path downhill to the trailhead was about nine miles. "Alert the rangers to a possible emergency, give them our location and call camp."

The counselor began to revive and treat the injured boy and also brought his group together. The junior counselor, running the nine miles, made it to a ranger station and called camp. Since there was no road to drive on, only a narrow foot-path to where the campers were, I demanded that the Park Service Rangers get a helicopter as soon as possible to airlift the boy to the closest hospital. By the time the camper arrived at the hospital, he was all smiles, having enjoyed the whole new and exciting experience. The counselor led the group down and out of the mountains, and everyone returned to camp safe, sound and happy.

In each of the stories above, it is clear that there was always a leader with considerable responsibilities; but it is also clear that leadership was a non-issue most of the time. Leadership was neither evident nor necessary once the boundaries were established, and no one was controlled or restricted beyond a few important rules of behavior. Events simply unfolded one moment at a time, and the campers were each doing their own thing. So why impose anyone to lead? Events decide more than an individual whether a leader is necessary. We know when and if to lead and, as we discovered, leadership is rarely needed. It's events that say when and whom.

Thoughts to consider: Why do we need a fixed leader if and when leadership is allowed to shift from person to person depending on events, merit and talent? Why not gather talented individuals in one room and let events dictate the formation of a hierarchy around the one best able to handle given issues, or to set the issue of leadership aside when not needed? In this way, hierarchies are dynamic, shifting and mixing to allow each participant to exercise his or her potential and likely grow in the process. Under these circumstances is any fixed leadership necessary? No, not if individual IC members are chosen for their knowledge and given the opportunity to take charge of events that matches their talent.

In nature we see this when a flock of birds follow one bird, but the lead bird changes many times during the flight. Here again, if events are allowed to shape the spear point it does not become dull and blunted as in human organizations. This is exactly what takes place in a well-functioning IC. We lead or we follow, but it is the event that decides which we will do. As told in the three brief stories from camp, we were, more often than not, each our own leader until an event dictated otherwise. At that moment we, ideally and willingly, supported the one who has the knowledge and ability to take charge.

Most of us need to and want to be responsible for our self, but life does not make it easy for us to do so in select situations. In fact, as the preceding stories show, depending on events in our daily lives there are times that we need leaders to take control of what we do. They lead us as babies, children, students, workers, soldiers and citizens as events dictate. Ideally, leadership is not cast in bronze, unyielding and permanently fixed in positions of power, but transfers easily to the one best suited to lead and only then.

Generally, mature adults are capable of leading themselves; but when people join with others for some common good, leadership whether by choice or accident appears to be necessary. When events arise in a group that exists without a leader, the group members may become an aimless and confused mass. At a minimum, leadership gives form and direction to a group of two or more, but it is not a leader that dictates or should lead unless an event calls and no one responds. And then, where is the leader and why does this happen?

Although I was not involved in this brief story I did work with the leader and hero of the events that took place: It was during the Coral Sea battle of WW2. He was a JR officer on a destroyer assisting the Captain of the ship when in the heat of battle the Captain fell apart and was unable to lead. Without hesitation the JR officer took control of the situation and led the ship to complete its mission. Events dictated that someone takes charge and the leader of the firm I worked with did. Events did not allow for the traditional hierarchy to work, leadership had to happen—instantly and it did.

Rare is it that we are born to be. More likely, we are made to be. Humans are not, through blood alone, programmed to be what each becomes. Our first care-givers have much to say about what we are and become as do the many influential people and environments we will meet and know. At first there is no choice given us, but as we age some of us become selective in whom our mentors are to be. They could be family members, friends, acquaintances, teachers and others who have influence over us. Also, there are the mentors who share their wisdom with us because we seek them out and are receptive to them as students. Teachers and the students need each other, but it is usually the student's responsibility to knock first. Rare is the door that opens of its own volition.

It may be during our beginning events (experiences) as babies that nurture our being students, followers or leaders. We know that others have power and control over us and for a time we have no choice but to comply. Many people are so well taught and conditioned by the time they are adults that they remain compliant for life; still others never give up their desire and passion to be themselves, whatever this may mean. Interesting that the power to be one's self is natural, but to want and have power over others is learned.

My concern, then, is how to mentor those who are leaders and aspire to be the best and most effective in leadership roles. Quality leaders of people do not become so in a classroom. If that were the case, all societies and cultures would have had and presently have quality leaders. History makes it clear that experience and participation in life's events are necessary to growth and becoming what we are, and not what we read or hear. That is why after a period of enlightened leadership things change when leadership is changed. It may get better or things may get worse, little more than change can be assured. "The Queen is dead, long live the Queen."

When a vacuum of power takes place, a person or group will attempt to fill the vacuum; and conflict is likely to arise. How is it possible to predict the quality of new and unproven leadership if intentions and words guarantee nothing beyond hope and expectations, and expectations invariably lead to what? At some point events will dictate that a person or persons take a leadership role. It may be one or a committee, but the vacuum of leadership will be filled. The fact remains that any band or group of people will follow someone in particular when events dictate. Without leadership, people become as grains of sand being pushed in every which way that the current and waves dictate. Human potential is put to better use with leadership than without. And even then, how often is effort dissipated on the rocks of chaos, infighting and futility? The greater despair is that bad leadership or no leadership is invariably at the heart of dysfunction of any group of people when leadership is called for.

SIMILARITIES BETWEEN QUALITY LEADERS
APPEAR TO BE MUCH GREATER THAN THEIR DIFFERENCES

Excellent leaders surround themselves with talented, experienced people who are unafraid to express their opinions and feelings. They also allow events to dictate from whence leadership comes. Good leaders share power and, more importantly, empower members of their IC to take and use power. Experience is what impresses this knowledge on them.

Experiences, failures as well as successes, result in quality leaders if the leader is a student to the lessons in each event. As events happen and key players enter our lives, from this mostly accidental mix comes what we learn to be and become. The "academic" way introduces leadership theory and the stories of others. I believe this schooling is at best an introduction to the art of leadership, but hardly the most effective way to become a quality leader. Experiencing and learning from our own stories is the true path to knowing, being and becoming.

If quality leaders accept responsibility and learn from events, then poor leaders would become better leaders if only they did the same. Inadequate leaders are leaders in name only, constantly abdicating their responsibilities and accountability to others or refuse to do so. In such an environment, leadership comes from a subgroup leader whose existence is a by-product of the inadequate leader. Subgroup leaders in this situation happily take the leadership role without the title of leader; they remain the power behind the throne and thrive in the position they are in. Significantly, subgroup leaders are usually excellent at what they do, but what they intend has little of the "common good" as part of their goals. Subgroup leaders are primarily committed to self-aggrandizement that is primarily emotional and self-satisfying and will do their utmost to control events that protect and endear them to others.

Where quality leadership exists or grows, people and their systems function in a seamless manner and events, as they occur, bring focus. When leadership needs to happen in response to an event, it does. But the "first responders" may be different people for different events, which is both timely and appropriate. The important difference between good and bad leadership is that the good leader allows events to dictate who is to lead, and the bad leader does not.

In the more traditional Inner Circles when an event calls for leadership, the true leader leads or selects another to lead, in contrast to the spontaneity of a healthy IC. Since, as I argue, experience, proven talent and knowledge make the right leader, it is essential that IC members be empowered to be what and who they are, not what the true leader has decided for them to be. In any case, how can one leader be every place at the same time or lead in every event? No human leader, past or present, has been capable of such omnipotence and omnipresence.

LEADERSHIP PROGRAMS ARE ESSENTIAL

A leadership search and training program must be built in all human organizations in order to establish continuation of an existing healthy philosophy and environment. An IC is the ideal place to identify and prepare leadership. It is here, at the top of the hierarchy, where we are supposed to find people of experience and merit, who, as events dictate, take on leadership roles.

If we could be invisible observers of any Inner Circle of people living or working together, we would witness leadership attributes in certain people. Even in situations where the leader is frozen in place, there will be indications of leadership in others. The healthy IC and organization are particularly sensitive to those who demonstrate leadership qualities at any level and when discovered are nurtured to lead. Opportunities are made available for those neophyte leaders to grow into more meaningful and influential leaders within the organization. It is important to remember that all core IC members carry the search for leadership to their own ICs. What better way is there for an organization to discover leadership potential? If understood and used correctly, all Inner Circles are a breeding ground for growing quality leaders.

The true leader still holds the key to whether events are to dictate selection of the most qualified IC member to respond to a particular event. The appropriate person to do the job does not necessarily rise up out of a chair and take charge. The leader, in this case, may order another to take charge—but how different is this than that the most able person volitionally takes charge?

Why not identify and acknowledge upfront those who have qualities of leadership and nurture them at every possible level? Why not have each leader looking for and enrolling those who show leadership possibilities? By increasing challenges and opportunities to demonstrate one's desire to grow and to take on more responsibilities, true character will come out. This is exactly what happens in quality environments: people have every opportunity to open up, to be and give the best they have. This is due to, and through, the efforts of excellent true leaders who recognize and accept that they are role models, teachers, students and members of their own IC. Events, expected and unexpected, are an excellent filtering device for the separation of possible gold from fool's gold and the wise leader makes use of this to know their people better.

Most people do not see or understand the considerable part they personally play in the way they are, and blame events and people for their lot. They believe themselves to be what others have made them and are unwilling to accept that they are also significant contributors to their own being and becoming. The dilemma of whether we are our self or made by others may represent an endless conflict until and unless we accept both the other and ourselves as co-makers of whom and what we are and will become.

Many relationships and events take place accidentally but are also intended and deliberate. For example, a student intentionally seeks a particular teacher because of his or her desire to learn something specific. It may be as simple as deciding to learn how to play the piano and then seeking out a piano teacher or the graduate student seeking to learn from the best in their field of study. It is our desire to learn that makes us students, and as students we are motivated to find appropriate teachers; which is "deliberate and intentional."

The following story is about a minor incident that turned into a life-changing event and how a stranger, in a brief span of time, had a major impact on my future direction. But note: I must have been a willing participant.

It was a dark, quiet evening in 1946 on the island of Okinawa, and I was standing guard on the perimeter of our base camp. It was uneventful until I heard the sound of a Beethoven quartet not far from my post. I moved closer to the tent where the record was being played in order to enjoy the music I loved.

Apparently my shadow hit the side of the tent; and with sidearm drawn, the captain of our company charged out of his tent to check out what was happening. "Soldier!" he yelled, "what are you doing here? Are you on guard duty?"

"Yes, sir," I answered. "I heard the Beethoven quartet being played and wanted to hear it better."

"You know this piece of music?" he asked, looking surprised.

"Yes, I'm familiar with most of Beethoven's work," I replied.

"What's your name?" he demanded. He wrote it down and then ordered me to get back to my post.

It all happened over a period of a few minutes. As I moved back to my post, I thought that I was in serious trouble and would suffer some consequences for my action. Consequences happened, but none I could have possibly anticipated.

The next day the captain called me to his office, where he had my file in front of him. "Ogulnick, you never finished high school!"

"No, sir," I replied. "With two of my brothers in the service, I did not want to miss being in the war. And I didn't think school was as important."

"What are your plans after you get home?" he asked.

"I have no idea other than possibly joining the merchant marine and traveling the world," I responded.

"We're going to take the GED test for your high-school diploma. I'm going to send for the exams," he stated, not asking for my feelings or thoughts about taking the tests.

"Yes, sir" was all I could say.

"I'll be in touch with you."

"Yes, sir."

And our meeting was over. It was a much better turn of events than I expected, but I thought taking the test and acquiring a GED was unnecessary. College was never a consideration for my future, but world travel and adventure were.

A few weeks later I was called to the captain's tent, where I was informed, "We take the test tomorrow. See you here at 8 a.m." The next day I began the series of exams.

After grading the tests the captain called me to his tent and told me that I scored in the upper percentiles of each exam and that I was "excellent college material and you are going to college!" It did not come out as a statement, but as an order. I heard him loud and clear. He was telling me *what* to do, not what I *ought* to do, and extracted confirmation from me. It was not long after I returned home that I enrolled in college.

Although it was brief, chance encounter, the captain must have sparked something dormant in me because his voice woke me up. Obviously, the insignificant event beginning with the music, the brief encounter and the tests changed my life significantly. The influence of the officer was so much greater than either of us could have known.

How different a leader was the U.S. Army Captain as compared to the camp director who may have saved my life during the mob scene in the small town? Or Yamamoto, the POW who took off into the hills to bring back the escapee over the matter of *honor*, and to save my ass? Each of them, and others, had immense influence on what I was to become. The captain on Okinawa did not act to save my physical being from harm but my*self* as a potential to grow and contribute to society. His brief, accidental appearance into my life was of profound importance to the direction I was to take. And what influence did the camp director in that small town have on my sense of personal responsibility as a leader of others? And what seed was planted by the POW and his sense of honor? As I reflect, I see clearly that events and people strongly influenced my life and the direction I was to take. Relationships have this power to influence our lives. How can we know at the time the event occurs?

These stories of people and the influence of their actions are similar in that they, without knowing, changed another's life due to an event that called for them to take charge. They were each strong leaders, perceptive, caring, nurturing and responsible people who stepped into my life because events dictated they do so. None hesitated to take control of a situation they personally felt they could do something about and, in fact, were best prepared to lead. None asked for my permission or input, but each and others to come, made a significant impression on what was to be my own leadership philosophy and style. Also, it is important to note that in each case they were the appropriate people to take the action they took. In ways we may never understand, Events *do* dictate, and we are all pieces on a chess board waiting to be moved by the hand of fate.

Our behavior during events we are caught up in tells much about whom and what we are. Our actions let us know whether we are conscious seekers of learning or specks of dust simply thrown from one spot to another. I have always believed that I was a student of the events taking place around me. I certainly remember that I wanted to experience life first-hand, which was why I quit high school to go into the army and why I looked forward to being a merchant marine.

A brief example might explain this better: I was a buck private on a troop ship heading west towards Hawaii for additional training. I was standing in a long line of a few thousand troops waiting to get into the mess hall to have my stand-up dinner. I passed a porthole and looked in and saw young men (two or three years older than me) dressed, seated at a table covered by linen and being served their food by people wearing white cloves. I asked out loud to no one in particular, "who are they?" the answer came from one of the troops "officers!" I knew at that moment that the next time, if there is a next time, I wanted to be one of those officers seated at the table and being served. What did I know? Obviously, not much, but, hey! I'm learning.

I write that what identifies the wisest of leaders/teachers is not what they say or repeat from books they have read, but their behavior over a period of time. This is how they share their own stories, even if not spoken. Our best leaders are the accumulated lessons they draw from their own stories as followers and as leaders and why they are and become. This is essentially true of most people. When we personally experience events and people, we build our own book of stories, from which we are truly shaped.

In the story about standing guard and wanting to hear the music in the background, I moved towards the sound; but I was also aware of my responsibilities as a soldier on guard duty. I didn't choose one or the other because I accepted my responsibility of standing guard while at the same time sneaking a better listen to the music. The captain understood this and wanted to know more about this young soldier who had a similar relationship with the classical music he loved and prodded him to go further.

As leaders we need to accept and understand that we either facilitate or impede people's potential. Good leaders/teachers know this and are acutely aware of indicators. In a case such as mine, and often without approval, quality leaders sought to nurture what, apparently, cries out to be nurtured. They take action because it is necessary and squeeze potential to come out of people and events. Many of the leaders I worked with as a mentor did not, at first, see or accept this as their responsibility. Nor did they accept that as leaders they played a major role in much of their staff's behavior. It's a hard and complex message to swallow that they, as leaders, may be the key to their followers' behavior.

Another of my brief stories: The leader and his IC were achieving much in our workshops, and because of this I was asked by a member of the core IC to help him with Genuine Dialogue in his own IC. I eagerly accepted the invitation since I knew that, given time, Genuine Dialogue travels well in an organization that attains it in their core IC. My working with this person and his group would help them get to this level of communication much sooner, and why not? Their level of education or experiences did not matter. I felt that this was an excellent opportunity to move the good that was being done in the core IC more rapidly throughout the organization.

The business had 170 employees, and all were affected by what took place in the core IC because what we do in the core group workshops is not intended to be exclusive. I saw his request as a volitional opportunity to spread the benefits of dialogue around. As in the story above, my move to hear the music, although unintended, opened the door enough to have changed my life. What this IC member asked me to do, and with the blessing of the leader, I saw as an important door opening and challenge to reach people from the top of the hierarchy to bottom of the organization.

I don't usually ask that people take notes of what's occurring in a workshop because I much prefer that we get to some kind of dialogue through questions to me or to each other, spontaneously if possible. I know that getting people to express themselves, in particular those who have never experienced authentic dialogue from a person of authority, is rare. I do not concern myself with whether people understand what I say or teach. It is, after all, my responsibility as teacher to be understood; and if it's street talk that will achieve this, that's what we do. Why engage in teaching if there is little understanding? And, I believe the teacher/leader is at least 80 percent responsible for understanding to happen.

In this work group, a man in his early twenties made it a point to sit in a chair next to me. He always brought a notebook in which he took notes of what was being said throughout our workshop, even after I mentioned that taking notes was unnecessary because dialogue was our goal. Much to my surprise and pleasure, he asked lots of questions, always seeking clarity and also keeping his notes. He was clearly a determined student who, as I soon discovered, aspired to being a leader and the most effective a leader he was capable of being.

He was soon given opportunities to be the leader of a "quality control" group. As soon as this occurred, he asked me to meet with his own IC. He so clearly understood the value of open dialogue and wanted this to take place with him and his co-workers. Soon after we began our work together, his department's work performance and productivity improved to the highest level in the company's history. He clearly understood and conveyed that events dictate from whom leadership takes place that his own IC members began to take on leadership responsibilities. As for understanding the pragmatic philosophy of mutual dialogue, his team was made up of immigrants whose primary language was not English.

The story ended for us when he left the firm to become a manager of a similar-type company. Not long afterward I was informed that he was elevated to second-in-command to the owner/leader of the firm. I was also told that he immediately began to spread the philosophy of Genuine Dialogue throughout the whole organization. He is a student, now leader, teacher and superb role model.

Clearly, he was determined to grow as a person and pushed his envelope to meet his vision of himself. When he joined us in his the first workshop with me as mentor, he decided to understand and get more of this "music." And, as with me and the captain 60-plus years earlier on Okinawa, we both got more than expected. He is an excellent example of what being a student and a quality leader is and does.

Something had to happen for this positive journey to begin. It takes a leader to make this possible, in this case the owner/leader of the company I worked with. It was this person's willingness and passion to grow himself and his organization that initiated the process that feeds growth. And he was the one who paid for this experiment in mutuality through dialogue and the sharing of power to be brought to everyone in the organization. Not all grew, and it is not likely that many were able to carry the experience of Genuine Dialogue beyond the original workplace. On the other hand, what might have been my life had I not heard and moved towards the music?

People need to push themselves to be students of what it takes to be a quality leader. Accidents may temporarily bring out our best, but the role people play as leader and teacher with the power that is at their disposal is too important to be taken lightly. And, of necessity, I believe it essential that a person seeking leadership responsibilities needs to be both in the moment and able to squeeze lessons of quality leadership from each and every event in his or her life. To achieve this level of growth and awareness, wise leaders seek and find the best possible mentor to aid them in their quest. In contrast, many potential good leaders do not achieve their quest because they are busy doing what needs to be done. They are good at what they do but have not set aside the time necessary to being a student. They are "being" but not "becoming."

When any event dictates taking action, leaders have a vested interest in avoiding trouble and in the heat of the moment may take charge. An experienced mentor may ask, "Are you the one who needs to be the leader, or is there someone more qualified at the table?" It may be the leader who is the best qualified, but they know and understand the people in their IC through Genuine Dialogue that someone else may actually be the one that leads and easily support them to do so. Mutuality, cooperation and candor make this possible.

I have one final story for this chapter. It is about two related events. Both support, as well as any story I could share, that events do dictate the exercise of power and by whom. The "who" in this case happens to be a dog, but the lesson is clear about events dictating behavior.

Heidi was a remarkable (to those who knew her) German shepherd that took full charge of specific events, but only when she felt it was appropriate to do so. Events dictated her reaction in one moment and minutes later dictated a completely different reaction. Humans sometimes demonstrate this capacity in emergencies, when out of the crowd steps a true leader, a hero for the moment— and when the event passes, he or she fades back into the crowd. Given the healthy and inviting environment, and due to quality leadership, this is what ought to take place between humans.

Heidi was a very special animal. Her attributes included unconditional love for her family of two adults, a teenage boy, a smallish beagle named Brutus, and Cleo, a white and very prolific cat. Responsibility oozed out of the shepherd's very being. When she was "on guard," her ears were fully up and forward, her eyes wide open and radar-like, scanning her immediate world. When she was relaxed, so were her ears at half-mast and her eyes showing contentment with where she was. She was a large shepherd, about 100 pounds but never overweight. She was muscular and carried her well-toned body with elegance and grace. When "off" duty, which seemed to only take place in our home, she wore a gentle face and eyes that spoke volumes of love, kindness and sensitivity.

Heidi was a gift to us as a six-week-old puppy from two of our campers and their parents. She had all of the protective characteristics of the definitive, pure-bred German shepherd dog running through her veins—there was no misinterpreting her intentions when she was "on-guard." She was the alpha dog at camp, acknowledged as such by everyone and the other animals, too. But Heidi was able to switch from being on-guard to off-guard so effectively and reliably that we never had cause to fear her being around children and adults.

On a quiet day in early June, my wife, Heidi, Brutus and I were exploring the wilderness surrounding our children's camp in northern California, investigating the impact of winter storms and snow on the forest and stream that flowed through the northern portion of camp. As I described in the story about our long search for the ideal site, the camp was located in a setting of thick virgin deciduous and pine forest, streams, lakes and beautiful meadows, with access to thousands of wilderness acres for hiking and riding trails.

Prior to building our own lake I had arranged to use the lake on the neighbor's property, about a mile's hike away, so we could teach swimming, canoeing, even sailing. But there was one problem: the neighbor's dog, a Siberian Husky he had trained and used to hunt bears and cougars that lived in the wilderness around camp. His dog, at well over 100 pounds, hadn't been a problem for us in the past because the hunting season took place in the fall, well after camp was closed; and the owner kept the dog chained and otherwise controlled during the summer.

The neighbor's dog appearance as we walked in our own forest was totally unexpected. Heidi was walking next to us, and Brutus, the beagle, was following every scent he could find. It was a moment of total serenity in a beautiful setting when we saw the big Husky heading for Brutus. I immediately ran to Brutus, scooped him up in my arms and challenged the Husky to retreat. Instead, the Husky leaped at Brutus in my arms, and to defend both of us I instinctively swung with all my might at him with the machete I was carrying. I intended to hit him with the flat side of the machete, and because of this it flew out of my hand. My whole being was focused on protecting Brutus and fending off the Husky; but the Husky was equally determined to take Brutus from my arms.

During this briefest of moments I completely forgot about Heidi. The instant the Husky grabbed Brutus from me, Heidi hit him like a linebacker not only knocking the runner down but jarring the ball loose. Heidi's charge forced the Husky to drop Brutus, and I immediately grabbed him back in my arms. Brutus was limp as a rag, and I did not know whether he was dead or alive.

The Husky turned his full attention towards Heidi, and the two of them began to circle each other like gladiators about to fight to the death. My wife and I were transfixed by what was now taking place in front of us— two large animals clearly in a fight where the intent of each was death to the other.

I flashed, momentarily, on the battle between Buck and the leader of the pack of wolves in *The Call of the Wild*. This wasn't fiction, however, but a real-life drama unfolding eight feet away. I needed to find a club or something else substantial enough to chase this animal away from us.

They were both on their hind legs reaching as far up as they could stretch and viciously pawing at each other when Heidi feigned an attack. The big Husky went for it; and in that split second Heidi lunged at his throat, gripped it between her jaws, lifted him in the air and twisted him onto on his back. The big dog froze, and Heidi was about to end his life. In a flash I grabbed Heidi's tail and screamed "NO! Heidi! NO!" She hesitated enough for her eyes to catch mine, and she let go of her death grip but remained frozen over his prostrate body. The Husky lay still on his back with his feet pointing to the sky in a surrender position. Heidi slowly backed off. The dog remained in the full surrender position for what seemed minutes, but in a few seconds he rolled over and slowly crawled back into the forest on his stomach.

Brutus, unharmed, burst from my arms and leaped at Heidi with such love and elation, kissing and licking her face. The little dog, as if human, expressed everything any of us could express had we been saved by another. It was a remarkable event and an example that expressed, for me at least, that "events clearly do dictate the exercise of power, and by whom." But the story continues.

At the first campfire of the summer I told the campers and the staff the whole story of how Heidi saved Brutus. I also warned them to be aware of the Husky when they went down to the neighbor's lake. Although the Husky was supposed to be chained and under his owner's control, they needed to be alert to the possibility that the dog might break loose. I told them that people were not in danger but other animals were. Campers and staff were allowed to bring their pets to camp. We had ours, so why not others theirs?

In the late 1950s and early 1960s restrictions on what a summer camp could and could not do were loose. In any case, our camp was also the campers' and staff's camp. The rules of behavior and degrees of freedom were assiduously and fairly followed by all of us.

Everyone loved Heidi; but at camp she was always alert and aware of her responsibilities to camp and rarely acknowledged or, it seemed, sought attention and affection. She, if she could have said as much, "Was just doing her job of protecting camp and its people." Events dictated her actions at all times.

The first time the campers went down to our neighbor's lake, I joined everyone to be sure that all went well. Words may be enough; but with young people, don't bet on it! The event definitely called for my being present to make sure that everyone followed the necessary precautions at the lake and our responsibilities to the land owner. It was a beautiful day, just perfect for our first use of the lake. Everyone was having a wonderful time when out of the tranquil moment one of the campers screamed that the Husky was loose. The Husky immediately headed for a camper's dog. I stepped between the two dogs, grabbing and carrying the camp dog to the end of a diving board to make it a bit more difficult for the Husky to reach us.

The instant the camper cried out that the Husky was loose the campers began to shout for Heidi. We could tell that the sound carried across the meadow and up the hill because the next thing we all saw was Heidi running full out towards us at the lake. "She's coming! Heidi's coming!" the kids yelled; and sure enough with huge leaps she came rushing towards us and then toward the Husky as soon as she saw him. When the Husky saw her coming, he turned to head back to his barn. It was too late. Heidi crashed into him head-long and rolled him over and over. He froze as before, and Heidi stood over him taller than she was and waited a second or two. The Husky rolled over on his stomach and as he had done before slunk back to his home. Heidi turned slowly and regally walked back to the cheering mob of campers and staff.

It was over, really over for the Husky. Apparently the owner soon decided that his dog could not be trusted around other dogs, and the Husky was never seen in the area again.

A hero often comes out of emergency situations, and that is what Heidi was to us. She acted instinctively. I had nothing to do with her behavior and defense of Brutus and of camp. With humans, where are those who are capable of taking charge when the moment is under the control of a fixed-in-place leader? The leaders who nurture people to be all they are capable of being is going to get this response from those with whom they live and work. The quality leader knows when to take charge, when to observe as a silent witness, when to suggest and when to support others to lead. This is truly the rarified air of wisdom and the wise. I witnessed it all in a dog.

Is there any question that events do dictate whether to act now or wait, and in what manner, and by whom? This is exemplified in each of the stories told in this chapter, and it may well be the way of nature for all living things. Time and again I have witnessed situations that demanded immediate action on the part of someone, and that someone was not necessarily the leader. But, leadership is the answer to whether the most able person steps forward.

CHAPTER 8

THE ANATOMY
OF A WORKSHOP

To have dialogue
We rediscover what we know
We do not forget.

I am a teacher, a practitioner of what I teach and a storyteller eager to share a worthy and very pragmatic philosophy and processes having to do with leadership and the use of power. Relative to this is the critical importance of bringing together experienced, emotionally healthy people, somewhat different from each other, who make up the leader's Inner Circle. It is in this Inner Circle that Genuine Dialogue needs to take place, and if certain essential conditions essential to a relationship of mutuality exist it can, deliberately, be brought about.

None of the book is based on theory, speculation or expectation but is a result of hard-earned, hands on experiences. It has been an adventure throughout beginning with my own entrepreneurial and leadership experience and culminating over the last thirty five years as a mentor to other leaders and their key people.

In the summer of 1975 I was invited to speak to a group of professionals. My subject had to do with troubled relationships and communication between staff and how these problems can harm an office, even spreading to clients they all serve. Apparently, I struck a nerve because what was supposed to be an hour lecture turned into an extended question and answer session.

Immediately following the questions and answers I was approached by a number of people asking "would you consider coming to my office to hold a workshop with my employees?" This was the beginning of my career as a consultant with the specific task of correcting staff attitudes and behavior towards each other. The need must have been immense because in a short time I was traveling to every part of the US holding workshops with different professionals and their office personnel.

My consulting work continued to grow to the point that new request would often have to wait for a date to hold a workshop for as long as six months out. Also, offices I met with wanted to continue with what we were accomplishing so I arranged for follow-up workshops to take place three to four months apart. It was during this period of approximately five years that I began to feel that the problems I dealt with in organizations of every type were symptomatic of a deeper and more complex problem.

What precipitated this was a group taking three steps forward during and immediately following a workshop, but soon after falling back two steps that bothered me. I discovered this when on subsequent visits I would have to review much of the work we did during the previous workshop. So, yes, people communicated, somewhat, better with each other, but much of the dialogue we experienced together seemed to not have "staying power." It was like I had to re-visit portions of the same steep sand dune each time I returned to an office.

It was following these experiences repeated too often over a considerable period that left me questioning the problem of why slippage occurred so frequently. It was July 1980 on a flight heading back home after a week's work on the east coast that an epiphany hit me between the eyes: The problems of staff relationships and cooperation or lack thereof had little to do with the employees; I began to sense that they were only a symptom of the problem. That as long as

I treated the symptoms and personal relations between employees, slippage was going to continue and the games people play to protect themselves will become more sophisticated and nuanced.

DISCOVERY THAT THE LEADER IS THE CAUSE

At that very moment I thought back to the youngsters at camp living an experience that emphasized personal responsibility for them and others. For the most part, weeks or months following the camp experience, campers who were held fully responsible for the making of their bed, cleanliness of the cabin, personal hygiene and communicating well with each other became, at home, dependent children once again. Where does this power to erase camp's influence on a child's behavior come from? Where did the power to influence come from when the kids were at camp? At home, it had to come from their parents, and at camp it had to be their counselor, junior counselors and as directors, the influence my wife and I had on each counselor? I concluded from that moment that if I was going to help an office including the leader to resolve their issues and communication difficulties it was the leader that needed to change if they seriously desired change in the office and relationships. What did this mean to me, my work and preparation at that moment?

1. Leaders must accept responsibility for the environments they create. The primary fault is not with others. Others will add seasoning to the environment, but they are not the master chef who makes it what it is.

2. As the teacher, it is essential that I be given power by the leader to assist them in being and remaining a true and equal participant with others during a workshop. Also, to "model" for them and those in the room what enlightened leadership looks and acts like. In other words, I needed to create an integrity-based believable environment where each participant felt safe enough to risk being open with their thoughts and feelings. Eventually it is this path that leads to the experience of Genuine Dialogue.

3. Most difficult to achieve, leaders needed to become vulnerable in the eyes, mind and heart of their key people. If this does not take place key people will not express their thoughts and feelings openly. As I learned, without a personal sense of safety and security people will not disclose their true

perceptions to a powerful leader. This has nothing to do with assurances by the mentor, but has everything to do with one's perceptions. In line with this, leaders need to let go of their power if others are to feel empowered. In this case, the more people believed they are empowered the more secure both the leader and the led become and growth is more likely to take place. What a leader discovers is that the more they empower others to take ownership, the more power the leader actually has. Power, when shared, goes from limited and exclusive use to inclusive and unlimited possibilities. This required considerable work with leaders I worked with because they employed me to help with the problems of communication between their employees. The leader was not, necessarily, involved in my initial reason for leading a workshop. Now, it became a completely different reason for working with them and I had to inform each leader of my discovery that "the leader is the problem to the answer they seek." Who amongst them would be open to accepting themselves as the primary cause of the "people" problems they hired me to resolve? Making this known to potential clients up front, I reasoned, had to be the best way to approach this.

It turned out that a few leaders disagreed with my placing them at the center and primary cause of their personnel issues and they opted out of the program. The majority, on the other hand, accepted, not easily, that they "might" be the problem and had the courage to continue on this track.

Another problem we encountered, initially unanticipated, was that as the office environment became safer, more supportive and nurturing of people being themselves and mutual in ways not normally experienced or expected they wanted this in their personal lives. As office issues were more easily brought out, discussed and resolved and dialogue grew between them the problems people began to bring to workshops was increasingly about personal relationships at home and with family. This subject is more fully discussed later in the body of this chapter.

FURTHER REFLECTIONS

Before entering into the workshop experience I need to return to the epiphany on my flight home. I felt I had discovered something extremely important relative to my "Sisyphus" like problems I experienced whenever I returned to an office and its leadership and personnel issues. If leadership is the prime cause of relationship and communications issues in the body of an organization, then growing the *true* leader into a healthy role model, teacher and student to their key people is the key and appropriate answer and task to resolving most relationship problems.

It took time for me to grasp that the leader, through their Inner Circle, influences the whole body of an organization. It followed that as leaders grow so must those within their Inner Circle grow or go. I began to understand that without a leader's full and courageous commitment to sharing power with their key people and to be vulnerable with them there is no possibility of growth, only the "appearance" of growth and this makes matters worse. The following is how this was initially handled.

ESTABLISHING THE GROUND RULES FOR A WORKSHOP

My teaching begins when a leader first contacts me in order to establish, immediately, the considerable part they play in the state of their organization. If the leaders accept that they are the main creators of their work environment, including many of the communication and personnel issues, then I conclude that successful resolution of problems, and growth of individuals and the organization is likely and the seed to our relationship is established.

Another condition of our working together is that the leader understands and accepts that during the initial workshop, I as the mentor will be in charge, not the leader. In fact, the leader is to be the "exemplary" student ready and willing to "sit at the feet" of the mentor. This is more than the sharing of power by the leader with the mentor: it requires temporarily giving up power to another. And, as noted, this is something that can be very difficult for many leaders.

From the beginning, it is essential that I, as the mentor, build trust with each of the members of the IC. Also, in order for them to feel totally safe no one is required to express their true thoughts and feelings until they believe in the openness and receptivity of the leader. It is why IC members need to experience that the workshop is controlled by the mentor and that the mentor is neither puppet nor subordinate to the leader during the workshop. It is a lesson that becomes a reality for each of the IC members in that they too are given real power to fully express themselves and to take a leadership role.

I do not attempt to convince anyone that all are "safe and can trust" what it is we are to do. All participants must feel this from within themselves, and personal perceptions, not words, make this a reality. The leader is well informed that I am not responsible for any "changes" that might take place. I do state that if and when key people believe the leader is vulnerable and a serious student to them they will, individually, begin to express themselves. Change does follow what one perceives.

Before any of this takes place it is likely that the leaders who seek me out worked with other consultants and tried a variety of "techniques" to at least treat relationship problems in their organization. Also, since most leaders heard of me by way of their friends, associates, and the professional "grapevine" I had a strong suspicion that they knew what I do and where I place responsibility. Thus, those that did reach out to me set themselves apart from most leaders in that they, apparently, were open enough to consider the possibility that they might actually be their own worst enemy.

The story and events that follow are typical of what takes place prior to and during my work with organizations. The dialogue and experiences captured on the following pages are as close to actuality as memory allows. In this chapter, I present dialogue and problems that I found to be reasonably common to every type of firm, whether a professional office or a manufacturing firm. People are people and the more educated are simply more educated, but not necessarily brighter or smarter. Everyone understands what it means to "not be" because they have learned the consequences of attempting "to be" and losing. What needs to be understood by the leader is that those who choose compliance and passive obedience close off or deny a part of themselves and in the process give less to their job and the leader. All suffer in the bargain.

What is certain is that leaders have more influence to affect change on those they lead than the led have on the leader. But, none in a relationship are without influence, it simply being a matter of degree and whether direct or indirect. Regardless of influence and whether positive or negative people need people and when we are two or more someone will assume a leaders role. I believe this to be a biological need relative to survival, and with humans it often becomes more a matter of "events dictating" that someone take charge. It may be the fleetest, the sharpest eyes or smell or the strongest? It may have started this way, but we have evolved to the extent that leaders and followers are less about survival and more about personal relationships and the making of a living.

I say all this to leaders during our first conversation so they hear and understand that I have no ability to change anything. That the changes are going to take place as they, themselves, change. That I intend to help them become aware of whom they are and what they do and mean to their significant others. I also tell the leaders that it is those they work closest with who know them best, and that if they would know themselves better and more deeply key people need to share what they perceive of them. It is only through the leaders' courage and willingness to be perceived as being vulnerable does this happen. In the process of working as a facilitator between leader and follower I, also, assist individuals participating in the workshop to volitionally become more transparent with each other. But, if this is to happen the leader exemplifies, first and clearly, every condition we seek of others.

An immediate concern is to make sure that the leader does not expect magic bullets and tools that will solve their communication and interpersonal issues. Once workshops begin this subject needs to be discussed with the IC members because, they too, have expectations. Here, once again, each person in the workshop needs to understand that growth (change) takes place from deep within each of them. It is not as simple as merely changing the way we look or dress—we, as individuals, must change and this is often a painful and heavily resisted process. Growth, if it is to take place at all, is due to the courage to risk being vulnerable to another's voice and letting it in. It is an invaluable gift of learning about oneself in the only way this can be done through being genuine with each other. It may well be our most valuable gift we have to give to each other.

THE MENTOR'S ROLE IN THE WORKSHOP

The mentor needs time and the proper environment in which to use power that previously belongs to the leader to intervene at any moment and, if necessary, in the middle of a sentence. At the same time the leader becomes the "example" student that IC members will, in time, have to become. The mentor, from the beginning, builds trust with the people in the workshop; the need to feel and know that one is safe to risk being open is paramount. The leader is still the key to this through being perceived as fully open and the committed student both to the mentor and any of the key people who do risk candor.

Nothing relative to the organization and relationships therein is avoided. Rules of the workshop, the responsibilities of the mentor, and expectations and intentions of the leader are all exposed, and opened to discussion and clarification. The mentor makes it clear that it is the leader through words and behavior who must confirm, not through agreement, but by behavior, what is taught. Changes in the leader, as perceived by IC members, facilitate each one's personal openness. As has been stated again and again in the book, change in the leader's behavior, when believed, has the power to force others to make decisions as to whether they, too, grow or go. No question as to the power of the leader to influence.

Getting maximum participation from everyone is an important goal. Whether individuals do or do not join in has much to do with their level of trust in leaders, period. History, our past conditioning, plays a huge role in whether to accept what we are witness to. As each person deals with the experience of the leader being vulnerable, and that power is actually shared many go inside themselves searching for their own answers to being or not. The mentor supports this self-searching process and if people choose to not say anything, nothing is expected from them. It helps all participants to know and have confirmed constantly that the mentor plays a protective role when necessary. The mentor is there to facilitate dialogue, but to also protect and support if reluctance is indicated.

These are issues that show themselves as the workshops progress. Until that time the primary concern is the person/leader that holds the power to hire, fire, and create the environment. Still, and regardless of dialogue between us and preparing them for what the workshop will attempt to achieve, some leaders remain stubbornly blind and deaf to their considerable complicity in the state of their organization. They "act" as if they heard and understood my words, but actually what they seek are tools and change in the behavior of others. They believe themselves to be smart enough to fool any and all, but what is true is that they only fool themselves. In those cases, our relationship did not go beyond discovery that their intentions have only to do with others changing. The leader believes they are fine and trouble is found with their key people. This is the leader that seeks tools. Inner growth and change is demanded of others. It will not happen.

WHO WE ARE AS PERCEIVED BY THOSE CLOSE TO US

Considering the many environments in which people function, most of us live multiple lives and have multiple personalities, or are at least viewed differently by different people. As employees, what are we to those who hold authority over us? What are we when we hold power/authority over others? Are we seen and known as an individual? How many of us ever attempt to find out? And if we try, how candid will the others' answers be?

The picture we think we are and the picture that others have of us are rarely the same. In fact, they are often two totally different pictures. It is difficult for each person to know how they are seen by others, in particular those close to them. The problem is in our intentions and then our behavior. We may believe that who we intend to be is who we are and being one with one's self and others. Others, in particular, those close to us may experience us in a different way. Unless we do know from and through others their true perception of us, how do we know? This is problematic at the very least and potentially destructive to significant relationships at its worst.

Duality is about who and what we believe we are and others, important to us, who see us differently. This is the common condition of most relationships. Unless we create the safest possible environment in which to communicate to each other, how does our relationship become more what we believe or want it to be? Since "truth is in the eyes of the beholder," would it not be enlightening to know how our significant others see us? After all, it is how others read and see us that dictate their behavior towards us. It may not be what we want to hear or know, but it is what others experience of us that determine how they respond to us. That is why the differences in perception must be made known, dealt with openly and made congruent if we are to maximize receiving the potential benefits of our significant relationships.

The Mentor's Job: Raise Awareness Levels Beginning with the Leader and Moving to Each Member of the Inner Circle. Dealing with the differences and problems of perception is what the mentor attempts to bring out if the group is to move towards Genuine Dialogue. But, it is the leaders' words and behavior that are the fuel that feeds the fire. As the leader awakens to this reality, and their fears of losing power fades, they become more open and receptive. As others witness this they too open up to the leader. Mutuality and cooperative seeds are being planted and nurtured to grow in this, a changing environment.

At all times, the mentor's job is to raise awareness levels and to bring troubling issues and fractured communication between people in to the open, to facilitate trust, safety and eventually bring mutually beneficial dialogue to fruition. Hearing each other, understanding what is said, to confirm each other and to respond, not necessarily in agreement, but candidly nurtures the healthier relationships and through this a better, more productive organization.

PREPARING THE GROUND

During beginning workshops, building blocks are presented and discussed as thoroughly as is possible with the group, which probably knows nothing of quality dialogue. There is no rush to understanding, and time is not important. Each step on the ladder of understanding is secured before going to the next step, which takes place when confirmation begins to happen from the students in the room. Each question and doubt is approached with an openness and acceptance of where each person is. No one in the room is forced to feel pressure to "get it." It is the mentor's task to use as many examples and processes as necessary to bring an "aha" to each person in the room. Considering the wide range of education and personal life experiences, making the environment "safe enough" for people to open up is often one of the more demanding challenges.

For most people, the workshop, and the information shared and discussed, is a "rush of fresh air" and may have no resemblance to anything like this occurring in their lives. As I have written, Genuine Dialogue is not a new experience; it will have taken place during the first few months after birth. Or, for the lucky, well into their youth because of enlightened parents. Due to our initial caregivers, some people are very familiar with Genuine Dialogue and know the experience as a common occurrence in their lives. These are the people who will risk, sooner rather than later, asking questions, going into deeper and more personal issues. They are the secure and self-confident students every organization needs to bring on board. They are the people who first accept the leader's behavior and stated willingness for mutuality and Genuine Dialogue. It is the leader who opens the door to healthier relationships, but it is the true student that accepts the invitation and walks assuredly through the opening.

People who have experienced being led, being subordinate to a rigid, insensitive, uncaring leader also know the truth of what is written. They also know what it means and feel like not having the power or freedom in which to affect change whether by what they do or say. Not having the good fortune of a leader that understands this problem of prior conditioning only adds layers to the problems people carry with them. To have a leader who undertakes this challenge of personal growth may mean a life line, inadvertently, thrown to others open to growth.

Being a leader and having power and influence are not problems, but a condition of living and our relationships with each other. If a leader uses power badly, all involved suffer. If power is used for "good" and is why a person ought to seek power to begin with, people associated with the power person will benefit. The beauty of this is that the benefits accrue to those immediately involved and continue in an every widening circle. Unfortunately, this is also true of bad leadership, only what is accrued is negative and always potentially cancerous to individuals, relationships and those they lead as well as themselves.

Leaders are not responsible for the history of those they lead, but are responsible for the immediate environments in which people live and work together. The more enlightened leaders in the process of becoming conscious of the power to nurture and grow themselves actually help heal the past wounds of those significant to them. This takes place through an individual's belief that it is safe to open one's self through dialogue. But being open is a big risk and people generally hold fast to the lessons and consequences they have previously experienced. Regardless, to be what one feels and thinks is "being" and given a solid sense of safety most people will make themselves known.

THE WORKSHOP

The following is a somewhat fictionalized look into a mix of my experiences with leaders, Inner Circles, and organizations I have worked with over the years. The beginning, the middle, and the ending all happened, and happened frequently. It is a kind of "anything-goes soup" based on what actually takes place from the initial phone conversation with the leader/owner of the business through the intro and work with an IC to achieving our goal of Genuine Dialogue.

I describe, often in detail, certain issues and events that come up as the level of safety is established in the workshop. The safer people feel the more open they become with their feelings and thoughts. They need to know, and to know is to experience, that they are respected, safe and invited to express opinions, feelings and that they are listened to and understood and invited to be candid. Based on what is my experience this must be considered a remarkable event by many people.

It all begins with a phone call: I was sitting at my desk trying to make meaning out of the many notes I had from the previous week's work when the phone broke into my "recall" moment.

"Hello! Is this Sy?"

"Hi!" I responded. "What can I do for you?"

"My name is Pete, and I'm a dentist with a practice in Maine. You work with Bob, a close friend of mine. He often speaks about the good things you are doing for his office. I know that he's had lots of issues with staff stuff, I guess as most of us do. He's thrilled with the changes taking place in his office. He holds you accountable for the improvement in the practice and I'd like to know more, and what this entails."

"What else has Bob told you?" I asked.

"Well, he told me that you hold him responsible for the environment within the office and the people he's got on his team. Now, Sy, I've been in therapy for almost fifteen years, and I don't want more of that. I think I know my issues and just don't want to revisit any of that. I don't want to go there."

"Look," I said, "I have no intention or desire to play therapist with you or anyone else. What I would help you understand and hopefully achieve is that you need to be as open with your staff as possible. In fact, how do you want and need your people to be with you? This is what you need to be with them. They have to feel that you respect them, and it is imperative that you accept this as a prior condition to their respecting you. In other words, their respect for you will come as they feel and know you respect them. It is not about respecting you because you are their boss.

"And equally important," I said, "they need to experience you really paying attention to them when they speak to you. They need to know they are being heard and understood when they talk to you. They need to experience this either by your telling them what you heard them say or by a response that tells them you heard and understood. In other words, you need to acknowledge them. And by the way—this has nothing to do with agreement or implying agreement.

"What we work towards is candid talk between you and your individual key people as if there is no leader or authority figure in the room. It has to eventually become a mutual and equal exchange between two or more people. If this is to happen you *must* be willing and active in sharing and empowering others. Ideally, a sense of ownership is felt by all."

After some silence he asked, "How does all this take place? Not with you and I alone," I responded. "I am not your coach or therapist, working one-on-one with you. All this is going to take place with you and your key people, or all of your people if it's a small organization. Of course, the more comfortable and confident the individuals in your group are, the easier it should be to bring them to share their picture of you as leader. It really depends on the type of people you've surrounded yourself with, but we'll find this out quickly."

"First things first," I explained. "You have to give me the power to run the show, to teach, to interrupt when necessary in order to take advantage of learning opportunities. When we close the door behind us figuratively, and actually, the people in the room, including you, temporarily become equals, with the organization as benefactor. There is no authority or power person in that room other than me, because I teach and act as a role model to what it means to be *present*, to have *respect*, to *confirm* an understanding, and to use *candor* at every opportunity presented. At the beginning I will use my power often due to "teachable moments," but in time less and less; and as Genuine Dialogue begins to take place between you and them and they to each other, I become essentially a witness. As individuals indicate an ease in opening up what I do is to shape and sharpen their awareness of what's happening to them and their relationships with you and each other. The people need to know and experience what true mutuality and cooperation feels like with someone in power. This is what empowers them, not words.

"Pete, you're the one who has to be the most vulnerable with your feelings and thoughts. It is essential that everyone in the room experiences this. You have to listen and work to understand what they say and share with you. I'm going to get them to talk directly to you about how they see and hear you, and what it makes them feel like. You've got to hear and understand their picture of you, and it is probably not the picture you have of yourself as their leader. This is never easy, and I use every tool I possess to make all that takes place as palatable as possible to everyone in the room. It does little good and potential harm to allow anyone to have a cathartic experience attempting to get even with you or the ghosts of their past dictating what they say to you. I stop this as quickly as it begins by placing what they say in proper perspective.

"If growth and change are to happen, it begins when we, individually, accept the picture others have of us. This is where listening and working hard to understand the other person from his or her perspective is essential. Few of us are aware of how quickly and adroitly we become defensive and protective of ourselves. This is why you must be the most receptive and inviting to others as this openness takes place. In its most positive and healing sense this is what being vulnerable means. Being vulnerable does not mean *weakness*, it means being *courageous.*

"Most of your people will remain silent initially, but a few will dive headlong into what has to be seen as an opportunity. Of these, some thrive on openness and candor and simply do what they do in their private lives and express easily their true thoughts and feelings. They will offer what they sincerely believe is best for you and the organization. Others, as mentioned previously, seek to harm you, to get even for past insult to their "being" by more powerful people than they. They may also see this as an opportunity to demonstrate their own overblown sense of power and talent that they feel is not being acknowledged.

"Don't doubt for a moment that I am the person who both assists you in being vulnerable and the others opening up and, also, the one who teaches at the same time. I have this mental picture of myself as a hungry tiger about to pounce on a deer the instant it enters that dangerous space—or to react as quickly and sensitively when people with their own agenda or pent-up anger seek to take advantage of what they see as an opportunity to bring you down a notch or two. And, actually, by this effort to elevate themselves, and these are wonderful teachable moments.

"Together we create a feeling of trust and openness between you and the group. It's your show, and I simply facilitate it taking place. Also, you share power with each of your key people. Mutuality rules and they are each empowered to be all that they can be, including exploring a true sense of ownership. By the way, after the workshop or meetings you hold with or without me, when you all leave the room traditional hierarchy and authority resumes. To a lesser degree, or different, but it exists because people that have not shared in the workshop know only their own work and living experiences. The people, including customers and anybody else that do not participate in the workshops, expect what they are accustomed to, and that's what they want to see. Nevertheless, when it works behind closed doors a different feeling towards power and authority is generated when the door is open and throughout the organization. This may be subtle, but everybody feels the change."

"Well," Pete exclaimed, "I admit to having some anxiety about hearing how my key people see and feel towards me. But I have immense regard for Bob; and, well, he's sold on what's taking place in his office thanks to you. I may have trepidations, but I'm willing to go ahead. When can we begin, and what are the details?"

I quickly checked my schedule: "How would the 10th of November work? I'd arrive early evening on the 9th so we could have dinner and spend some time getting to know each other better. Please put me up in some hotel or motel near your office so I have little to contend with other than showing up at your office about 7:30 the next morning. Our first workshop will occupy a full day; and depending on how things go, we should be able to cut this down to about four hours once every three or four months. We'll both know when the workshops have run their course."

"The date works for me, but Sy, I understand that you stay at Bob's home when you work with his office," Pete ventured. "We'd be so happy if you stayed with us. My wife would love to meet you, and you'd meet our kids. We'd all like that."

It's what I do with many of the people I work with, and it does give me insights I'd never be able to get by only working with and at the office. This goes back to my younger days when I met parents at their homes to show slides of camp and talk about the program. I always learned lots about the kids and their environments through spending an evening with their parents. Similarly, but more directly and definitively, spending an evening with the leader where they live and witnessing relationships with spouse and kids is invaluable information. Knowing how leaders work their authority with their employees is essential, but knowing how they live with their family may be equally so. There are considerable differences between leadership at the office and leadership and power at home and it is invaluable to be witness to those differences. "Sure, I'd be happy to spend the night at your home. It'll work just fine."

It's important to emphasize that personal relationships are different from relationships at work. Spouse and children are not employees. They cannot be fired or dealt with as an employee, although I have witnessed a close proximity to this, and the relationship between members of a family are far more complex. The spouse may have more influence on the household than the leader of their own business. There may be competition for power and influence over the children. The leader of the office may be a compliant member of the family deferring to the spouse as the leader of the home and the family. Or, the leader of the office is also the leader of the family.

What takes place under the roof of a home adds to what I know about the leader at work. To be sure, I am not employed to work with the family and its issues, but being a witness to the family dynamics contributes significantly to my understanding of the work dynamics. As will be dealt with later in this chapter the work we do at the office is directly related to the relationships within the office, but will have degrees of impact on their personal lives. That this occurred, initially in unexpected way, became an important issue that had to be dealt with at most offices including Pete's. As I discovered, it is impossible for a leader and IC to not go from work relationship issues to personal ones. In particular, the more issues of leadership, relationships and communication problems were resolved, the safer and more secure people felt with each other. As work changed from monologue and top down communication to mutual dialogue and then Genuine Dialogue people began to feel a safety and comfort at work that they wanted in their personal relationships.

I arrange to arrive at the every work location early enough in the evening to enjoy dinner with the leader and, if I stay in his or her home, with family. In this particular case, when I arrived at Pete's home the first time, he wanted just the two of us to go out to dinner. I understood why in seconds after we greeted each other—he was very nervous and, obviously, insecure about what was going to happen the next day.

During our dinner conversation I felt that he believed he held the reigns of his organization tightly, and this through his office manager. He came across as very dependent on her. He seemed most concerned about how she would react to my entrance into her area of responsibility. I tried to reassure him that we will walk slowly and carefully so that none need feel, immediately, threatened by what we do. During the evening he asked many questions, and I did my best to answer each of them. He was concerned and nervous over what people might say about him. He did not want to hear that he was insensitive to them, that he was too busy to listen and understand them, that he did not devote proper time to them, or that they saw him as impatient and, often, wired. Pete wanted a good working and pleasant environment. He liked the people he worked with and thought he treated them well; but he was unsure and insecure about how this would play out. "Would they take advantage of the opportunity to beat me up, to get even with me?" he asked.

I did my best to assure Pete that before people expose their perceptions and feelings about him and his leadership style I would be very careful in preparing them for what I label "a growth experience." I told him "I believe I am capable of discerning a person who might see this as an opportunity to "get even" with you or for venting their anger at power in general." I could feel Pete's need to be assured that what we were about to experience was appropriately structured and controlled so that a "free for all moment" will not happen. He needed to hear, more than once, that the whole reason behind what we do is to move towards cooperation and a sense of shared ownership. I also made clear that "there is a great amount of information that needs to be placed on the table and openly discussed by me before moving into dialogue. Understanding and confirmation must take place before I venture into any of their issues with you, work relationships and any other problems."

"Most importantly," I said, "your people need to witness that any dialogue you and I have must demonstrate respect and mutuality between us. We need to be the clearest example of what is to eventually take place between you and each of them, and they with each other. You will introduce me as the teacher who will help *you* become a better partner with them and a better listener so that you will more fully understand their opinions and feelings. You must demonstrate, verbally, an understanding of what takes place between us as I must do for you. We will be confirming each other and also be seen as candid through our questions and responses to each other."

"This is not staged by either of us and must be witnessed and understood by your key people. They see you involved with me, and I, face to face, involved with you. They see us listening to and working to understand each other. They see that we are not expecting or asking for agreement, but for understanding and any questions to clarify what we say. We are there for each other, fully present, respectful and spontaneously candid with each other. I will go to them at any moment to seek their understanding of what they are witness to and if any clarifying is necessary— it's what I do. No one is forced to understand, but until I receive confirmation I do what I can to find each one's light switch. As the teacher it is my responsibility to make what I do and say understandable to them. I'm not seeking anyone's agreement. We do not move forward simply because the clock is ticking."

When I meet the participants for the first time I tell them about me, my background, about the pragmatic philosophy that I intend to present and to teach. I let them know that they are invited to ask any questions at any time and that spontaneous interaction is a good thing. I show them a blank sheet of paper on my left and my notes on the right. If someone asked a question—or interjects something they think is pertinent, which, again, I emphasize I want them to do—I might jot a note as to where I am at and immediately turn my full attention to them. They need to hear and witness I am there for *each* of them and not only for the leader. I need to physically, intellectually and emotionally show them that they *are* the center of my attention. My response to their questions or comments needs to corroborate my words "I am here for each of you."

I inform everyone: "At the beginning, it is Pete who has made the choice to grow, to be a student, and to accept each of you as a teacher. Yet, Pete remains your leader, there is no change in this, but what does change is his empowering of each of you to be leaders when events dictate that you are best suited to take a leadership role. You know best when this needs to take place and Pete becomes one of your troops. As Pete empowers each of you to be leaders and to take ownership of problems and issues that are your strength, and you do, each of you will begin to grow in this more nurturing environment. As Pete's behavior is received and believed by each of you, the pyramid that exists today becomes more a circle and mutuality and full cooperation become the norm at work."

Within the first hour of our initial workshop I was defining my use of the word "Power" when Ellen blurted out, "I hate that word 'power!' Can't you find a better word that is not as loaded for some of us?" I was thrilled at the candid words and feelings from Ellen. First words out of my mouth were "thanks for expressing your dislike with the word." My next response to her was meant as a "teachable moment" for all in the room. "Ellen, why don't you say 'I don't like the word power, and just speak for yourself? It may be true that others feel this way, but I'd like us all to speak only for ourselves. If others choose to do so, they can say I agree, or yes, it's a word that brings up bad memories for me. Say what you have to say, but speak for yourself in every case."

A discussion ensued between Ellen and me, and others began to join in expressing their own opinions and suggesting other words. After throwing a number of words on the table, most agreed, without my interference, that the word "power" is acceptable. They simply agreed to use the word only when necessary. What I felt as most valuable was the dialogue it generated and not my monologue. That's a good thing.

I was not finished even as many in the room accepted the label power. I thought that finding out what each person in Pete's office felt about, and perhaps would share, an event having to do with power—good or bad—that most influenced them. As intended—and it is important that they recognized this—I turned to Pete as the first one to speak his thoughts on the subject. Pete did not hesitate to tell a story about his treatment in dental school by a professor who belittled him in front of his classmates. He remembered this so well that the embarrassment of the moment and the hurt he felt returned to this time and our workshop as he spoke. He looked at each person in the room and emotionally said, "I never want to intentionally do that to any of you. If I have, I sincerely apologize. It is not me and I won't accept this kind of treatment from anyone, nor do this knowingly to anyone." The silence in the room was palpable, and I let it be. After a minute or two I looked to the next person and said, "Only if you feel you want to share a story about power do so, but if you'd like to pass, that's fine." Teachable moments are like raindrops on a window pain. If closed the rain is seen and heard, but too much is lost. If one opens the window they not only see and hear the rain, but feel and smell it. Opening the window is not just looking outside anymore and you're likely to get wet.

Most people, initially, are reluctant to participate beyond being "good" students and asking safe questions. People need, substantially, more evidence that the environment is safe and that the leader is sincere in his or her commitment to being one of the group rather than a fixed in place leader. To level the field is essential, but to get people to trust that this is the case is not easy to accomplish. It takes time and a leader who is willing and able to simply be one with the others. History weighs heavily on everyone, but honesty, sincerity and candor—particularly when it comes from the leader— opens minds and hearts. And when this takes place the window is open to the rain and full involvement.

Back to the workshop: We spoke more fully about power in general and thoughts having to do with both abusive use of power and good uses of power and its consequences. "Is it simply that someone experiences abuse by the person in power and that's all? Or, do people who are abused feel anger against the perpetrator and, perhaps, anger at themselves for complying passively? Do we find ways to get even?" I asked. These questions brought forth a flood of responses, and by containing the subject and confirming what each was saying the initial experience was enough to build some confidence and safety between us.

As indicated, at the beginning of our working together it is best to establish boundaries/guide line and direction. Initially I do not push for issues, office problems or about Pete and his use of power. My immediate goal is to be a good teacher, to be clear and to invite any and all questions. Individuals need to feel safe enough to ask the question or to suggest they do not understand. The goal is always dialogue and thanks to Ellen's discomfort with the word "power" we were able to get to dialogue quickly. Each and every moment we are together needs to have this possibility. In the process, people, slowly but surely, build trust and feel safer. Feeling safe, as so often stated, is the best and most solid foundation to launch growth from.

At this early period in our workshop meetings, I keep conversation centered on the ideas of mutuality through dialogue and to avoid dealing with specific office issues. Learning how to communicate in a way that keeps minds and different opinions from closing is essential. Once rules are established and a reasonable degree of comfort and security built, we get to work on the more personal and relationship issues taking place within the organization.

In the process of moving to more open dialogue we do many processes that are safe and often fun to do. In preparation for these unusual events I call process I would ask that they dress down (in jeans, etc) for the workshop. I want them to be as comfortable as possible. Example of processes I would make use of is intended to facilitate the experience of being "present." While sitting I would instruct them to close their eyes and slowly breathe in and when they exhale to say the number one and with each subsequent breath to the number ten and then back to one. For many this is a difficult exercise. They would lose count and their minds would stray to places, including past and future. With patience and our talking through what they experience during this process they begin to let go of both past and future and be more fully present. When this happened so did anxiety disappear over their possible loss of control.

Often, with the same purpose in mind of experiencing the present I would ask that they find a place on the floor and make themselves as comfortable as possible. I would bring a tape or CD and player and with eyes closed we listened to about three minutes of baroque music. I would ask for their feelings and thoughts about what they experienced. After this first exchange I would replay the exact same three minute section and again would ask for their thoughts and feelings. For the third listening I ask that they pick one instrument and as effortlessly as they are able to only listen to the instrument selected. The results of this experience were often phenomenal based on the comments and emotions so many shared. Talk about people being genuine with each other? It is an amazing, and teachable moment, when people, maybe for the first time, are aware of only this moment and no interference from the past or future.

These, and more, are centering processes I used to aid people in experiencing and understanding what it means to be *present*. As stated above the results of those special moments were often remarkable and often emotional enough to them to bring tears, not of pain, but a sense of being and freedom they had not experienced before. At these times I would explain that letting go of both past and future is essential if we are to experience this moment. Some might call this "a natural high" and it probably is, but I also saw people being vulnerable. This can only happen when people accept themselves as they are, not as how they or others want them to appear.

It never failed that following exercises of this nature people became more open and, yes, vulnerable with each other. They listened, they understood, they expressed themselves in a positive and genuine way. They felt connected to each other and dialogue flowed. Any resistance to each other, apparently, disappeared. It may have been temporary for some, but, nevertheless was experienced by all. And, of course, it was the leader I always sought out as the first to volunteer their thoughts and feelings about the experience.

As we moved forward I ask about their jobs, relationships to the leader, the people they worked with, and whether they feel resourced to do the best possible job. When someone ventures forth to speak, I look to the leader to respond to what he hears, understands, and thinks. It is the interaction of the leader that has the greater impact than I as teacher, and why I assist in shaping how both the IC members and the leader interact with each other.

From the beginning any attack, or attempt to take advantage of the perceived openness of the leader, is cut off at the pass. I might offer different and less confrontational words without changing their intent of, perhaps, anger at some past event. I do not speak for them but work to raise their level of awareness and sensitivity of the other person as a person, and the" respect" issue. Ideally, each IC member needs to experience, feel, and hear a sincere desire and witness effort at mutuality from the leader. Also, that hierarchy and power are not "fixed" in the room, but for this workshop fully shared or found to be totally unnecessary and any thought of power is set aside.

Relative to the above, it is vitally important for all to feel that sooner rather than later the leader is open to being one with others in the room. Simply put, the leader is not the leader during the meeting, but a full and equal participant. As teacher, my task is to facilitate the leader being perceived as an equal among equals. Bringing the leader to the role of member, not as leader of the Inner Circle, is ongoing and needs to be believed and confirmed by each individual. It all has to be real, others have to experience it and playing "nice" never cuts it.

The journey I take Pete and his group on has a definite goal, and that is Genuine Dialogue between all of the IC members. This is not because leadership is not required during a gathering of the IC, but that it needs to come from any of the good and talented people in the room. This would never take place as long as leadership is frozen and fixed in place. Or, and dealt with in chapter five, Inner Circle membership is made up of weak pawns who do what they do only as a result of what the leader wants and expects of them. Interestingly, Pete had some strong and talented people as well as "go-fers" in his Inner Circle. As Pete grew so did the Inner Circle change and became healthier.

The subjects we discuss and the problems we take on are fuel that takes us to a more open and nurturing environment where cooperation, mutuality and willingness to take ownership increases. At the beginning, my notes to what I intend to cover are important, but each hour and time we are together my notes become less important. In fact, the more time we spend together the more the subjects to discuss, often in great detail, come from anyone in the room. The more secure people feel, the more individuals jump in to the dialogic mix. So does their ability to think creatively, to problem-solve, and to use their new-found power for the good of the organization.

A classic observation I make sure we deal with is thought to be the tenth-century aphorism, author unknown: "Communication is the Problem to the Answer," which I discuss in earlier chapters. I pose the question to the workshop group: "What does: 'Communication is the Problem to the Answer' mean to you?" Blank looks and confusion are the common response, rare is the person who answers: "We communicate so badly that it's the way we communicate is our first barrier to arriving at any reasonable answers to a specific problem."

What I've learned—and it has taken years and a boatload of experiences to appreciate—is that the "how and what" we communicate to each other are not simple issues. Words and intentions attached are major barriers to overcome before we start attempting to answer our problems. How do I know this? Let's look at the numerous problematic ways people communicate with each other: Top-down, monologue, no respect felt or given, not being present as a listener, pushing a hidden agenda and unexpressed expectation. Added to this is our prior conditioning history, culture, power experiences, and learned communication styles. Also, never to be forgotten, and one of the more common barriers, is when the speaker wants only agreement and compliance, not other opinions. These and a slew of other barriers can and do cause communication between us to break down and to make difficult any semblance of mutuality. To assume that people agree on problems and answers without honest dialogue is to guarantee errors, omissions and negative feelings.

In Pete's office we go directly to this problem of communication as our first problem to overcome. It is fully discussed and demonstrated that if we knew how to better communicate we would not just have an answer to our problems but also many quality answers to choose from. When time is taken to hear, understand, and confirm what the problem *is*, and if necessary from every possible angle, people will choose to participate. And, which requires receptive listeners, freely given and authentic dialogue takes place and creative and innovative answers do pour forth.

B1, B2 AND B3

At some point I will feel that some members are ready to share how they see and feel towards Pete as their leader and as a person. Playing leader and being a person is not, necessarily, the same thing. At this time I introduced a process I label B1, B2 and B3. B1 is a spontaneous outburst, usually genuine and expressed in the moment about that moment and event. It is how babies and the young communicate until they are taught to not react to the present. It is a very "now" contribution. It's what I seek when I teach because I view this as a flash of light that potentially illuminates what is being discussed.

B2 has to do with what has passed but needs to be shared. An example: Shirley says to Pete," I have a B2 to share with you." Pete turns his attention directly to Shirley and makes it clear that he is there for her. "When I come to work you rarely acknowledge me even when I say good morning to you." I feel hurt and even question what I may have done wrong. I sometimes even feel I might lose my job. It troubles me." Pete waits for Shirley to finish and looking right at her tells her he is glad that she shared this with him. "I am so totally unaware of anything but getting to work or my own issues that I literally close myself from anyone. I am sorry that I have caused you pain and concern for your job. You do a wonderful job and I do admire and respect you. Please, whenever I do this let me know." And looking around the room makes this clear to everyone. "Don't let me stay in the past or future, help me be present with each of you. This is stupid of me."

Following this exchange Judy tentatively raised her hand to speak. "I can't believe what I'm about to say to you, Doctor, but often when you are concentrating on a difficult operation you pick your nose." This embarrasses me for you, and I am sure that it has to be a problem for the patient." Pete looked incredulously at Judy. "You mean I pick my nose when concentrating on a patient?" Yes!" Answered Judy, "and, I have never, up until now, been able to share this with you although I kept telling myself that you would want to know this. It has bothered me for a long time." Pete leaped across the room, put his arms around Judy and thanked her profusely for sharing this with him, and expressed regret that she felt unable to come to him immediately upon witnessing this. Speaking to Judy he also spoke to everyone in the room. "Please don't assume and protect anything about my behavior. Stop me in my tracks to help me become more aware, more conscious of where I'm at, what I'm doing and even what I'm saying when it seems to you I'm off track. I promise I will do this for you and want and need each of you to do this for me." B2 may come a bit late, but it comes when an environment is perceived as safe and secure and will, eventually, lead to more B1 behavior.

B3 is stuffing important experiences and feelings into a huge bag that, for all anyone knows, may be loaded with "stuff" from early childhood. Those that live in B3, regardless of reasons, carry this weighty and increasing mass with them throughout their lives. The problem, and it is a serious one, is that what is stuffed and not allowed to see the light of day influences our present behavior. Those that do this are ruled by the ghosts of their past. They are the losers, but so are those with whom they live and work.

PROBLEM-SOLVING IS MORE THAN JUST THE PROBLEM

The problem with problem solving is that a given problem is not necessarily what all agree upon is the problem or even of its importance. Nailing a problem's importance is often as essential as agreeing on what the exact problem is. Unless a problem is an emergency that demands immediate action a quality IC sets aside time to examine and evaluate a problem before agreeing on what action, if any, to take. Time is also given to placing a priority on the problem. If highest on the list it moves to the forefront and we use Genuine Dialogue to get to a "best" possible answer. Leadership arises from the ranks as do the troops and resources and the problem is confronted and resolved. This assumes a safe environment where mutuality and cooperation is at its highest level.

If this is not yet the case and the environment is perceived as unsafe we might use a silent, but powerful tool. First, the problem must be agreed on and even its wording may be important. When this is done members write on a slip of paper what they would do to resolve or deal with the problem. No names or identifying marks and all slips of paper are placed in a hat, pulled and read one at a time and fully discussed. This process is repeated three times and surprise of surprises agreement usually takes place. No one knows from whom the original solution comes from. This is an effective tool until and unless the group attains the freedom and power of Genuine Dialogue and which is the best of all ways to communicate.

With Pete and his Inner Circle, we used real office and organizational problems as our teaching examples. We remain with a stated problem until everyone had input on the problem." Is this how you see it? Do you agree on its importance, or are there more important problems to deal with? Let's create a priority list from the most important to the least." We place the list on paper for all to consider and based on discussion move problems around until the majority agree on what's first to deal with. The dialogue moves to: "Would you describe the top problem differently?" We stay with the shaping of the problem until consensus that we've nailed it. Then I ask: "When a problem arises in the organization that offers time for dialogue, does everyone involved feel clarity and agreement with the problem? Do you (the individual) feel comfortable with the details, and have you expressed your thoughts? Are there other ways to look at and handle the problem that have not been mentioned?" A sense of "ownership" is sought throughout the group.

Time is not always available with problems and the need to solve them. But here, too, in a well-functioning IC, where power is widely shared, anyone—in particular people with experience—take full control of an emergency situation. It is not left in the hands of the true leader to be the one in charge in every single situation. As I have experienced it, as individual's progress in being able to express their opinions and feelings, they also assume a leadership role. When power is shared through Genuine Dialogue, an attitude of "ownership" develops with those who are committed participants. Problems are more quickly uncovered and taken charge of by those best prepared to do so.

As the reality of authentic dialogue sank in, individuals in Pete's office began to speak out about issues as if they were the owners and leaders of the business. Growth, when witnessed by people who work closely together, is contagious. At some point in our relationship instead of my opening subsequent workshops with my notes and intentions we have IC members calling me or writing that "We need to discuss and work on this particular problem before you go on with your plans for the workshop." They are ready and willing to express themselves and to open up any issue. Many are eager to get to Genuine Dialogue about any issue as soon as possible.

It is clear that the initial reason for workshops is to help the leader grow and to accept and understand that as leader, others, who know them best, are the key to the leader's growth. As this takes place, the experience becomes a powerful influence on the growth of others in the IC. As the leader begins the journey towards being more fully awake and aware of their self and with this the selves of significant others, the process of change has huge impact on all involved. People are pressured by their own feelings and thoughts demanding behavioral change. It is why, as mentor, I visually and verbally support people's need to feel secure before they volitionally become vulnerable to the leader and each other.

As changes in perceptions take place, so do our workshops become more of the IC's making. They will often dictate the direction and issues they feel need to be opened for discussion, and not my agenda or that of the leader. We remain with their issues, some of which are not easily solvable; but at least there is more clarity as to what the issue is that needs more time, thought, and work. What happens is the unfurling of complicated issues that see the light of day for the first time. Genuine Dialogue may not answer every problem, but, assuredly, will bring a "best possible" understanding of the problem. It is said that correct diagnosis is 95 per cent of getting to the answer.

It is important to note that workshops are not intended to be for the purpose of solving specific problems. They are held in order to bring interpersonal growth and communication to as high a level as possible and which will facilitate problem solving. Pete and his people will be capable of dealing with most issues and their resolution without a mentor once they reach the level of mutuality we seek from the beginning of our working together. The workshops are the vehicle that takes most or all of the people to a more complete participation and to Genuine Dialogue. It must become very apparent that everyone in the room has a responsibility to everyone else, and to their own integrity. It is teaching when necessary, and being only a witness as each dynamic unfolds between them. This experience is remarkably rewarding.

To get to this point of the IC contributing to the direction of the workshop real office issues are the "logs that heat the room up" and are the problems they want to be resolved. Not surprisingly, people see most issues from a subjective viewpoint and until they feel safety is assured say little or worse, comply as if pawns on a chess board. The fact that most thoughts are subjective is not my concern. Hearing people express themselves is a giant step forward. The more assertive or secure speak out, and which is a good thing to take advantage of. I appreciate this and thank them for letting their thoughts and feelings out. My task is not to pull anything out of anyone, but to facilitate enough safety between them so that who and what they are comes out of their own free will.

I repeat: getting to dialogue and eventually Genuine Dialogue, beginning with the leader and then everyone in the IC, is the primary reason for the workshop. Given this vitally important experience and understanding, the participants will handle their issues on their own very well.

THE IMPACT OF GENUINE DIALOGUE

When Genuine Dialogue enters people's lives, an awakening takes place and what is natural begins to make itself known once again. People begin to make their feelings and thoughts available to others important to them. Even disagreements are openly aired during Genuine Dialogue. When involved, we want to be heard and understood; agreement, unless felt as absolutely necessary, is not the issue, but expressing one's self, is.

Ideally, when Genuine Dialogue occurs, decisions are made and responsibilities to assume leadership are taken by those who have the experience to lead. This action is volunteered and supported by the group and which now includes the true leader as a participant. This is a result of the work that leads us to the actual experience of Genuine Dialogue.

Prior to this breakthrough, in particular with weak leadership or leaders who are too rigid, it is the subgroup leader and those who are members of the subgroup that seek and take control of the organization. And, although it was not indicated during our initial telephone conversation, during our first face to face dinner conversation I had a feeling that a subgroup leader did exist in Pete's office. Problematic communication within an organization is the nurturing grounds for the building of a subgroup, which is almost assured to take place.

The subgroup leader in Pete's office did what is typical of anyone who has a love of power, a personal agenda and followers they protect. Subgroup leaders will do their best to undermine, and even sabotage, the cooperation and mutuality sought by the true though inadequate leader. Therefore, the likelihood of losing control or being unmasked forces the subgroup leader to take action, in this case, against the mentor unless the mentor unknowingly (or knowingly) becomes a foil for the subgroup leader. As a key member of the IC subgroup leaders are close to the leader and play, obviously, to the leader's weaknesses. This fact is easily indentified, and if the true leader has trust in the mentor, that is, serious about their own growth, this leads, inexorably, to the full disclosure of the subgroup leader.

It must be kept in mind that subgroup leaders are usually outstanding at what they do. They are successful at their job, and, of course, the true leader feels they cannot be without the talent of the subgroup leader. If and when the true leader seriously commits to growth, the environment also begins to change, dialogue as compared to monologue happens and they cease to nurture and support dysfunction in themselves and anyone key to them.

In Pete's case the subgroup leader was the manager of the office and held tight reigns on both the front and the back (those that handle scheduling, billing and the business end and those that directly assist the Dr). Any thought of anyone going up against her tight control was out of the question. Pete's comfort was in that things got done, but the tension created is probably the top reason he followed Bob's advice and reached out to me.

Whenever a vacuum is created by a leader's inadequacy as a leader, it will be filled by someone who sees this as an opportunity to take power. What a subgroup leader wants is to maintain the status quo of being the power behind the throne. They do not want to sit on the throne, but to control it. This action is played out as an obedient servant to the leader, but a ruthless control freak to others.

Given an inadequate leader and assured dysfunctional Inner Circle, subgroup leaders thrive, as does their circle of influence. They build a domain within a larger domain where, although they do not own the business, believe they are key to its success. In effect, it is as if they own and operate the business, but without any of the true responsibilities of ownership. The subgroup leaders wisely build their own Inner Circle that is designed to assure their continued influence and success. Each of their IC is strategically placed so that no one in the organization feels safe enough to make this illness known.

When Pete hired a mentor to help him to grow as a person and leader, he was ready and willing to tackle personnel problem in his office, which came as a serious threat to his subgroup leader. An interesting and important characteristic of subgroup leaders is that they are not immediately threatened by a new consultant on the scene. They have dealt with other "strangers" many times and are confident that this, too, will pass. This feeling of confidence continued in Pete's office until the subgroup leader became aware that "this" mentor represented something they had never come across before. Suddenly, it was the leader that was the acknowledged problem as a person and as a leader— that it is the leader who must change, grow, become vulnerable with those most meaningful to them, not as a leader but as one of them. It is the leader's growth and new awareness that exposes the subgroup leader and subgroups cannot long exist in a healthy environment.

When I first met Pete's IC, they were fully informed of the work that he had agreed to begin and to stay with. They heard, loud and clear, that I hold the leader primarily responsible for problems in the environment in which they work together. They had been told up front that Pete, their boss, had agreed to join with them in making "our office as good a place for each of us to work in as possible."

I clarified what is monologue and what is dialogue, and said that our intention was to help everyone climb to this level of safe dialogue, even Genuine Dialogue. Probably, the most important words they hear is that as the leader grows so will the environment change. They know this means that they, too, will have to grow or if they choose, to go. The challenge, for the subgroup leader, was one they had not likely faced before.

Clearly, the openness of our workshops and the work set for the leader and, in time, for each of the IC members tend to strip away the masks people hide behind. When duality begins to depart from the leader and "what you see is what you get" becomes more apparent, this creates an environment that does not allow for hiding and alternative agendas by others.

The concern a leader has with the subgroup leader being uncovered is not fear of "civil war" within the organization. The concern is that the job the subgroup leader does, and which is usually highly efficient and productive, is necessary to the success of the organization. "Who will be able to handle what they do if they leave?" The answer becomes obvious almost as quickly as the subgroup leader's acceptance that their game is over.

Upon the subgroup leaders' departure, and many do leave for greener pastures, their former position is filled with highly motivated employees, and the operation actually improves. People are free to be more themselves, creative, innovative and cooperative with each other as never before. Also, the empowerment of key people spreads responsibility and accountability throughout the organization. A feeling of ownership takes root and more importantly, is nurtured.

REACHING GENUINE DIALOGUE

The IC is ready to develop a dynamic of Genuine Dialogue when conversation between the IC members is easy and flowing. IC members have to trust by now that the leader is committed to the program and they also accept the mentor as a fair and non-judgmental part of the circle.

As I explained in Chapter 6, Genuine Dialogue is a "happening or an accident" for most people, most of the time. It feels good after the fact and we want to recapture those moments or hours again, but how? Not without intent and an understanding of the essentials of Genuine Dialogue. In order for Genuine Dialogue to take place with some degree of assurance people must be *present*, in the moment, with each other. It also demands a *respect* for each other not due to position or talent, but in simple mutuality person-to-person. It is eyes-to-eyes, face-to-face, and hearing and understanding the other's words and position. *It does not imply or mean agreement*, but it does require *being confirmed*. Being *confirmed* means we feel understood. This happens through feedback from others. Either we are understood or we are not, and if not it is the speaker that *must* be responsible for making themselves clear and understood. The leader that *expects* to be understood is wrong and responsible for turning dialogue into monologue and this is true of all of us that would communicate with another.

Each of the preceding ingredients is important to Genuine Dialogue, but the "golden thread" that ties it all together is *candor!* Candor without listening and confirmation is like "spitting in the wind." Only the speaker is going to get the message. What is candor without the other being present and having respect for the speaker as a "person?" Add candor to any dialogue that contains the other three conditions—*being present in the moment, respect,* and *confirmation*—it completes the genuineness and value of our being together. It brings us to the level of mutuality and where our energies are exponential relative to creativity and problem solving. Why would any healthy leader not need, want and highly value this?

In Pete's IC, we approached Genuine Dialogue by spontaneously selecting different people to confirm what a speaker was saying. I did it at first. No one spoke that I did not respond by asking them "so you're saying or mean ———." If they felt understood we move on to others to speak out about any subject they wished, and this process would be repeated until I turned it over to Pete, and he to others as we moved around the room. Everyone listened to the one speaking since none knew if they would be called upon to confirm the speaker. The speakers were held accountable for what they said and if what they said was not understood they had to clarify their thoughts and words.

Candor began to happen as subjects being discussed began to include office issues. It becomes more meaningful when confirmation is sought even when candor is taking place. Pete was speaking when someone interrupted and asked if he could give an example. "Sure," said Pete and gave an example of why he felt as he did. The other person said "So what you mean is ——."

"Exactly!" said Pete."I need to acknowledge each of you for how you have contributed to my professional and even my personal life." "I've been blind and silent for much too long."

Was everyone present, was respect felt, did confirmation take place and was Pete candid? This is Genuine Dialogue when for a brief period people experience and feel a "oneness" with the other and others. Yes, this is positive, volitional and Pete and others were vulnerable at that moment. If the subject is negative, a problem that has to be exposed, is there a difference? No, because the safety and security during Genuine Dialogue is an immersion into an environment that has no up or down, top or bottom, good and bad and no leader. Our agendas are set aside and temporarily we become one.

Every speaking moment between two or more people has to have dialogue as part of the process. If it is monologue how do we know we are heard and understood, and if we do seek agreement how do we know that what we get is compliance, not agreement? Ideally, I believe that by inviting a spontaneous response we often also receive confirmation and candor is able to flow. On the other hand, some people prefer to be fully heard and assume they are understood. How much better that as we speak we also receive confirmation from the other? For most people the experience of sharing one's opinion and feelings is never easy. Communication is truly the problem to the answer.

Pete, not the mentor, after all, is the key to how the members of the IC will eventually communicate to him and to each other. For good or bad Pete is the role model and as such is truly the teacher. As a witness to Genuine Dialogue I am a silent observer, but as teacher my responsibility is to react to every possible learning opportunity that "knocks" in ways that bring insights to others. My teaching will not make it so, but Pete's behavior and vulnerability will. Since we are all subject to errors and omissions, every teachable moment, whether directed at Pete or other IC members is the teacher's responsibility.

Moving into actual Genuine Dialogue is a beautiful experience to behold; but by beholding, I am not part of the scene that unfolds in front of me, but rather a witness. This is ideal. My task is to bring individuals into this experience through whatever means I have available to me. Witnessing the movement from silence, non-trust, non-belief to Genuine Dialogue is an exhilarating experience.

Trying to find a story that demonstrates Genuine Dialogue I believe is unnecessary. Genuine Dialogue is simply conversation between two or more people. The difference is the full presentness of each, degree of understanding and feedback that takes place and the candor that goes between them and it is timeless to them. Those involved are unaware of any of this taking place, only the observer. If the participants did become aware they would, in that instant not be in Genuine Dialogue.

Suffice to say that in Pete's office trust was everywhere and cooperation between one and the other was as good as it gets. As we advanced into the territory of Genuine Dialogue I was able to go anywhere I felt we needed to go. At the same time individuals began to contribute significantly to the direction of the meetings. They would identify issues that needed a facilitator, not a teacher. They wanted to talk to each other and until Genuine Dialogue was owned by them they felt I was needed to bridge the gap. Odd as it may seem, people went in and out of Genuine Dialogue with each other and they only knew they "had" engaged only after they disengaged.

It was not many workshops before Pete and Pete's Inner Circle began to function as one healthy body with each willing and able to take ownership of what they do and the over-all operation. Some became better leaders to the benefit of the whole organization, and others better team players. Pete not only set his power aside, but empowered others to step into the breach of leadership in their respective areas. As I have experienced time and time again, the more power Pete shared the more empowered he became. And, not surprisingly, he needed to use his power less than ever before.

SAFETY AT THE OFFICE LEADS TO A DESIRE FOR SAFETY AT HOME

It is easy to understand that as the workplace becomes safer, more secure so does awareness that communication in their personal lives may not be as safe. It became obvious that a few of Pete's IC want to know how they can transfer this atmosphere/feeling to their homes. This shift from organization and communication issues to other and more personal "stuff" is one of the better indicators that work issues are being resolved. It is then that participants in the workshop begin to share communication issues taking place in their personal lives. Their musings, questions, and comments are not thwarted, but they are aware that the workshop is not about personal issues. On the other hand, if I am able to turn personal issues into non-specific and possible learning experiences that apply to the organization in general, we do so.

At Pete's office we discussed steps that might be considered to try to bring this new found feeling and being at work to their homes. Professional counseling is always the first option suggested. I also suggest that by being their true self, that is honest, open, respectful, confirming, and in particular being fully present when at home with family or friends, change is possible. But, I also add the caveat that "expectations" of making points or breaking through barriers MUST be eliminated. I often use the example of asking your spouse or child how their day went at the same time, back turned to them, preparing dinner. Is this being present or in two places at the same time? What message is sent?

I compare this to asking the same question, but turning to the person without anything or task between you and them. Give your full attention to the other, hear what they have to say and confirm them either through more questions or seeking clarity. In other words, get to real dialogue by using "real dialogue." You need to show those you live with and love that they are the center of your attention, now, and that you sincerely care, and want to hear what their day was about. It is so dramatically different than what we know happens too often at home. And how does our modern technology contribute to authentic relating? In most families technology is the newest serious barrier to what is already a battle field of non-communication. Once again, "communication is our problem to the answer," only, exponentially, more complex.

"If," I say to the IC "you are the leader or share leadership at home (the ideal) and exemplify openness, presentness, receptivity, empower others, respect them as the unique individuals they are, then, real change is probable." Real mutuality cannot be a promise, but needs to exist and through every sincere effort in "face to face" dialogue, Genuine Dialogue will, likely, take place. It is so much more difficult a trail to climb at home because, as I have previously said, "Parents cannot fire each other without considerable pain and despair, and certainly they cannot fire their children. "

I came to fully appreciate the need and desire for quality communication to be part and parcel to each person's life. But, when I first discovered the power and influence of leaders on those they lead I also appreciated the necessity and ease in indentifying who holds real power in an organization. If the ones in power refuse to accept this major responsibility for what they create around them, and that *they must be the one to change*, which in turn includes their Inner Circle, nothing, regardless of demand and expenditure, will change. What takes place is an atrophying from the top down and the bottom up and continues to decay and eventual death. This is organization everywhere and anywhere there is a true power person that loves their power and is unmovable.

As true as this is in organizations of people it is also true in our families. Whenever leadership is fixed in place as against being dynamic and moving from one person to another depending on the event and true capabilities, everything and growth depends on the leader. If, as with Pete and so many others I have worked with, they are willing to be accessible, vulnerable to those that know them best. As this is experienced and deeply felt by those close to the leader (I label the Inner Circle) change takes place deep within the leader and inexorably move out to change others. And, what part of the organization remains unaffected? And, what part of the family remains as it was?

TYING IT ALL TOGETHER

All of the good growth took place with Pete and his people. As Pete grew, each employee, albeit with caution, began to grow, and those who feared and resisted their being volitionally uncovered left. The sense and reality of safety resulted in greater trust—and for some, trust for the first time—in the desire for mutuality, cooperation, and even taking ownership as events dictate. Each participant experienced what it feels like to be empowered, to be open, to take a leadership role, and to feel worthy. Communication between people in the organization beyond the core IC also changes due to them carrying Genuine Dialogue into their own ICs.

I emphasize in workshops that understanding what we talk about is vital if we are to proceed. To this end, getting confirmation is essential regardless of level of education, culture or experience. I also emphasize that I am responsible to teach, but that they, as students, must want to learn. Not an equal responsibility, but close. And, yes, the leader must be the most vulnerable and the behavioral example. In time, and different in different organizations, it is the IC and each one's personal willingness to step forward and to open up that brings a general wakening. We talk about organizational "expectations" and the need to eliminate them as silent thoughts while at the same time to make them into discussion items. I suggest taking the long road, experience the experience and talk out loud about thoughts and feelings and always listening and understanding what others say so that no one speaks without being confirmed by someone.

I tell them to avoid lecturing but to be open to spontaneous interruptions as long as these outbursts confirm that they are being heard and understood. I facilitate people to share experiences and feelings the workshop produces. I tell them to be conscious and accountable for what they say and feel at all times. I stress that people will understand the changes in relationship and dialogue offered them and that time is not an issue. The goal is for each person to become more themselves and to express their thoughts and feelings without fear of retribution. At some point "communication will not be the problem to the answers they seek" and cooperation and mutuality will replace conflict and tension.

Change/growth/learning are slow processes, but when they occur it happens to the whole of us, not as a part. Those closest to us will know that something positive is taking place. It may take time, considerable time, but it will happen. If we are in a position of power (influence), as are parents, teacher and bosses of every ilk, as we change and grow so will those we directly influence. If subordinates and followers, they will either grow or go. If our children it is almost assured that they will grow.

Speaking of time: How long does it take to witness Genuine Dialogue actually happening and the growth of individuals within an IC? It depends on the true leaders and their personal willingness to be vulnerable to their key people behind closed doors. As the leaders prove their openness and adopt the other attributes of Genuine Dialogue, members of the IC will, individually, begin to either join in or begin the process of withdrawal. Feelings of safety and security will, in time, bring forth the best of people, and is worth waiting for.

Giving up power temporarily or setting it aside must be difficult for truly powerful leaders. When a leader speaks as an equal, as part of the team, to their

IC and is confirmed and in turn does this when an IC member speaks this is setting power aside. If this is consistently experienced it becomes an empowering experience to those significant to the leader. This change has nothing to do with using "tools" having to do with being a more effective leader. It has everything to do with the leader's inner being, their emotions as well as conscious commitment to change. It happens when leaders become the role model they seek in others. Now they are teachers to their key people and now are a student to those they lead. It is all about the process that began when we are born and that is "being and becoming our uniqueness, and facilitating this occurring in others.

It is a condition of the believability and trust placed on the leader and his or her behavior. It may take only hours to plant seeds, but months, possibly longer, to begin to be felt and believed by those closest to the leader. Changes in a leader's tools and tactics are never enough to engender trust and faith in key people. Leaders must be experienced consistently and often as one who is fully committed to sharing power and wanting Genuine Dialogue with key people. It takes many dialogic events and experiences to trust a leader's behavioral growth and change. When a leader's openness and receptivity is believed by individual member of the inner circle, a healthier and more inclusive environment permeates organization. There is no assured time when this will happen. Leaders influence those significant to them, and those significant others in turn influence those significant to them. And so it goes.

Enlightened leaders create a nurturing environment in which the people they are responsible for are given the opportunity to become more themselves. This in turn benefits the organization they all work for. More importantly through their personal growth they each bring what they are and are becoming into their personal lives and relationships. Like a stone thrown into a still pond the waves created when the stone hits the water move out touching and influencing well beyond the first wave. Each receding wave is smaller, but never the less influences that which is beyond it. And so it is with enlightenment and personal growth.

Our inner growth becomes what we bring of ourselves to others. Our significant others experience this in us and are influenced in kind. This all begins somewhere and I strongly believe that the "somewhere" in not "Over the Rainbow." It is real, here and now, and initiated by those in our lives who, through accident of birth— our parents, the special teacher or teachers in school, or the boss we work for. Each person that has been or is our leader either nurtures our becoming, or inhibits and even attempts to destroy our being.

Without question we all need each other. In truth, we exist because of others and we need to be nurtured by others. Are we not the other to the other?

EPILOGUE

Without getting into the tragic details a dear and long time friend lost his wife in an accident caused by a drunk in a head-on collision. It took place early morning the 3rd of April, 2014.

The epilogue is about what took place soon after his wife's death and the people that gathered around him and his daughter. This group that hardly left his side are people who had gone to camp with him as early as the mid-fifties through the 60s. My wife and I were there with them all and offered what solace is possible at a time when nothing coming from others can soften their tragic loss.

What we participated in and witnessed was a "love in" that incorporated the full ingredients of Genuine Dialogue. What I mean is that at times we, about twenty four people who had experienced camp together became one with the husband and daughter, but also the two of us became observers of what was taking place between them. What we witnessed were people that were children together as much as sixty years ago relating to each other as if time had not passed and, in fact, for the moment did not exist. It had to be because they were each totally present with each other. Their regard and respect for each other was as obvious as the hand in front of your face. Eyes were looking directly into the other's eyes, heart and soul. They listened and confirmed each other. Laughter and tears, candor and spontaneity came forth as naturally as breathing. As observers it was particularly moving for my wife and me, at times, to be on the outside looking in at what was so genuine a moment for the others.

They are of a different generation than my wife and I and the dialogue taking place between them was of their generation and not ours. And this has always been the case. In the fifties and sixties it was our task to build a bridge from us to them so that they we could meet somewhere in the middle and learn from each other. We believed early on that building an environment from our perspective alone would never be good enough and that with the input of kids and staff it would be. Different generations bring different views to the table. We needed to hear and understand their view. How to bring this about came out of a philosophy that honors both the individual and the group and the need for both to prosper. Dialogue rather than monologue became our way to do this. It is, after all, how growth becomes possible. Recreation and stuff aside, it was what camp was about.

So, here we are in Ashland Oregon, April 2014 attempting so inadequately to be there for another in a time of their terrible loss. But, for this moment, my wife and I were looking on as observers to what was taking place between the others. Suddenly, one of the group walked up to us and said: "you both caused this you know." And, clearly we did. We were the leaders, role models and primary teachers. Hopefully, we were also students.

When we did what we did back then we were unaware of the full and deep responsibility of having that much power to create and manipulate an environment. But, we did, and in having this power we influenced the lives of those involved with us. With certainty we believed totally that our responsibility was to provide children with an exciting and safe learning experience. We had no thoughts about our having influence that would stay with them for a life time.

It took working with other leaders and their key people, years later, for me to realize that the primary problem in the world of human relationships is about power. I was "that" power and am grateful that even out of child-like ignorance we apparently did a pretty good job. Of course, the book is all about become aware of the power leaders do possess and using it to benefit not just one's self, but that of others, too.

—Sy

ABOUT THE AUTHOR

I'm a teacher, I know that for sure. I also believe I'm a good student, or at least I've tried to be during the more mature part of my life. I do remember as a child loving music and sports of all kinds, and being a student just got in the way. Eventually, I did begin to grow into my responsibilities. I love to read history and lean towards existential philosophy. One thing for sure, I always used dialogue as my style of relating. Being the sole speaker and long-winded has never been my way. Seeking feedback began early on and got more intense and meaningful as I grew. When I became an entrepreneur, leader and educator (in that order) the people I most enjoyed being with and working with talked, argued and showed feelings, but also listened to each other. Is there any other way? I certainly hope my book gets this across to those who are responsible for inhibiting most of the people with whom they live and work.

GLOSSARY

The author is a speaker who values dialogue as his way to teach and learn. Certain key words, below, are used throughout the book and are easily explained to a small group. Words in italics indicate the term is defined elsewhere in the glossary.

Attributes: Characteristics that humans learn. And because these attributes are learned, they can be unlearned and new or better attributes can be learned. Eliminating undesirable attributes and replacing them with better and more effective attributes is common to the student.

Candor: An openness during dialogue that is honest, sincere and direct.

Confirmation: The speaker is confirmed when the listener indicates that he or she hears and understands the speaker. This in no way implies agreement.

Empowerment: The giving of freedom to others to express their ideas and feelings honestly and candidly as possible. This is taken to the point that individuals have a sense of ownership towards the organization and what they do.

Genuine Dialogue (GD): Being in communication with each other and no barriers to obstruct. Requires four conditions to exist simultaneously: Being *Present*, having *Respect* for the other, *Confirmation* and *Candor*.

Inner Circle (IC): At its very best is made up of a leader and a limited number of people who represent different expertise and life experiences. IC members each

315

know success and failure, and have a history that demonstrates quality, courage and honesty through dialogue. They do not fear taking a leadership role. In well-functioning Inner Circles it is difficult to isolate the leader from the follower; they are all leaders and followers. Events will dictate which.

Leadership: Those who hold true power and influence over others. This could be a parent, teacher or any authority figure who exercise their power unilaterally. No others hold power over this leader: "the buck stops here." Leadership exists in every relationship at some time, whether a relationship of two or many.

Mentor: A teacher who has considerable experience, much beyond the academic, in what he or she teaches. Example: Mentors who teach leadership have been a leader. Mentors to an entrepreneur have also been an entrepreneur. Mentors are considerably less about theory than they are as a result of their own life experiences.

Mutuality: A feeling of oneness and reciprocity between those involved in a space where time becomes irrelevant. During this period there are no feelings of hierarchy, power and authority.

Power: The power of authority, position and degree of influence a person possesses over others. People in power create the environment in which they and their followers live and work. Change the leader, and the environment changes. Power used properly and with wisdom produces immense good for those involved. Whether family, a classroom of students or at the workplace, leaders who use their power for the common good grow; and their growth facilitates the growth of those they lead.

Present: Being present with other people is intended to mean here and now. The event is taking place in real time. Neither the past nor the future exist during this moment.

Respect: Accepting the other in a relationship as they present themselves and not as others would have them be.

Students: People who are unafraid and open to learning about themselves, others and a specific field of endeavor. The true student is aware and alert to finding the appropriate mentor and to do for what they must do in order to be accepted by the mentor. These students have a passion to understand and to be their best in how they live and what they do.

CPSIA information can be obtained at www.ICGtesting.com
Printed in the USA
BVOW01s1634210814

363669BV00001B/1/P